ANCESTRAL MEDICINE

"Ancestor reverence is one of the pillars of Yoruba traditional religion, and it is my pleasure to recommend this book on ancestral healing by my student (ọmọ awo), Daniel Foor (Ifábọ̀wálé). Through numerous visits to our home in Nigeria, I have overseen his initiations to Ifá, Òrìṣà, and the ancestral medium society (Egúngún), and I know him to be a person of good character. I urge everyone to benefit from his guidance on ancestral reconnection. Remain blessed."

OLÚWO FÁLOLÚ ADÉSÀNYÀ AWOYADÉ, ÒDÉ RÉMỌ,
OGUN STATE, NIGERIA

"Daniel Foor invites us on a journey to meet our ancestors, those we know about, those we have never imagined, and those who might like to talk with us. He draws not only on personal experience but also on the shared and tested relational practices of indigenous communities in Africa, North America, and elsewhere. This powerful book arises from years of work with groups and individuals so that as we read it we can benefit not only from the teaching but also from practical exercises. *Ancestral Medicine* offers a host of possibilities for our further reflection and practice."

GRAHAM HARVEY, PROFESSOR OF RELIGIOUS STUDIES
AT THE OPEN UNIVERSITY, UK, AND AUTHOR OF *ANIMISM:
RESPECTING THE LIVING WORLD*

"In traditional societies, ancestors are venerated and considered sources of wisdom even after they have left their physical bodies. In contemporary times, few children are conversant with their cultural and ethnic heritage, much less the lives, occupations, and even the names of those family members who passed on only a few decades earlier. In his remarkable book, Daniel Foor provides an antidote for this regrettable situation. Foor's text and exercises provide numerous ways to make one's progenitors a living presence—one that is inspirational, instructive, and, for many readers, transformative for themselves and their families."

STANLEY KRIPPNER, PH.D., PROFESSOR OF PSYCHOLOGY AT SAYBROOK
UNIVERSITY AND COAUTHOR OF *PERSONAL MYTHOLOGY*

"As a priest of the Yorùbá indigenous system known as Òrìṣà (or, at times, Ifá in the form of its sacred oral literature), honoring and remembering one's ancestors is both essential and transformative. Daniel Foor offers a multicultural perspective and practice that helps diverse individuals on their journey of spirit to grasp the liberating and empowering foundations of ancestral work."

NATHAN LUGO (CHIEF ÀÌKÚLỌLÁ IWÍNDÁRÀ), ÒRÌṢÀ PRIEST

"The illusion of isolation and its associated fear, fury, and shame of abandonment is the core wound in the heart of humanity. The cure is in turning our love and attention to the stream we rode here on. We are boats of flesh on a river of blood born to heal the ancestors, to be healed by them, and to know, reveal, and grow our souls . . . thus elevating the stream. This river is the salve of the soul, and Daniel Foor clearly knows this. His book *Ancestral Medicine* is soul medicine for all. The world needs it. Life applauds it. Read, enjoy, heal, and become!"

ORION FOXWOOD,
AUTHOR OF *THE CANDLE AND THE CROSSROADS*

"Daniel Foor illuminates a field that has too long been neglected in mainstream American culture: acknowledgment of the role our ancestors play in the lives of all of us. Blending his many years of study with a variety of spiritual teachers with meaningful practices he has developed for contemporary people, Foor offers a compendium for recognizing, working with, and honoring connections with our human ancestors—and in the process healing relationships with our family and ourselves. This book is profound, important, and deeply engrossing."

TREBBE JOHNSON, AUTHOR OF
THE WORLD IS A WAITING LOVER

"This book is a real treasure and, the gods be praised, is highly practical. Crafted in thoroughness, wisdom, and deep sensitivity, *Ancestral Medicine* gives us keys to appreciating, coming to terms with, and even healing our ancestral wounds. More than all this, Daniel Foor calls us to carry the best of our past into the present and future, and to fully live in place and time in Earth-honoring and heart-open ways."

C. MICHAEL SMITH, PH.D., AUTHOR OF
JUNG AND SHAMANISM IN DIALOGUE

"Daniel combines extensive practical experience with intellectual rigor in his ancestral work, providing one of the best approaches out there today. I recommend his work to anyone interested in truly knowing themselves and gaining solid ground on their own spiritual path."

GRANT H. POTTS, PH.D., LODGE MASTER OF
SCARLET WOMAN LODGE, ORDO TEMPLI ORIENTIS

"The author's culturally inclusive approach adds much to this work, and his passion, clarity, and compassion make *Ancestral Medicine* invaluable to anyone interested in exploring personal healing, ancestor connections, remediation of family relationships, or healing and reclamation of one's culture of origin."

BEKKI SHINING BEARHEART, LMT, COFOUNDER
OF THE CHURCH OF EARTH HEALING

ANCESTRAL MEDICINE

Rituals for Personal and Family Healing

Daniel Foor, Ph.D.

Bear & Company
Rochester, Vermont • Toronto, Canada

Bear & Company
One Park Street
Rochester, Vermont 05767
www.BearandCompanyBooks.com

Text stock is SFI certified

Bear & Company is a division of Inner Traditions International

Library of Congress Cataloging-in-Publication Data
Names: Foor, Daniel, 1977– author.
Title: Ancestral medicine : rituals for personal and family healing /
  Daniel Foor, Ph.D.
Description: Rochester, Vermont : Bear & Company, [2017] | Includes
  bibliographical references and index.
Identifiers: LCCN 2016052290 (print) | LCCN 2017013038 (e-book) |
  ISBN 9781591432692 (pbk.) | ISBN 9781591432708 (e-book)
Subjects: LCSH: Ancestor worship. | Dead—Religious aspects. | Families. |
  Healing—Miscellanea. | Rites and ceremonies. | Spiritualism. |
  Intergenerational relations—Miscellanea.
Classification: LCC BF1999 (e-book) | LCC BF1999 .F65 2017 (print) |
  DDC 299/.93—dc23
LC record available at https://lccn.loc.gov/2016052290

Printed and bound in the United States by Lake Book Manufacturing, Inc. The text stock is SFI certified. The Sustainable Forestry Initiative® program promotes sustainable forest management.

10 9 8 7 6 5 4 3

Text design by Priscilla Baker and layout by Debbie Glogover
This book was typeset in Garamond Premier Pro with Baker Signet Std, ITC Berkeley Oldstyle Std, and Gill Sans MT Pro for display fonts

"When the Rain Begins," poem by Elise Dirlam Ching from *Faces of Your Soul: Rituals in Art, Maskmaking, and Guided Imagery* by Elise Dirlam Ching and Kaleo Ching, published by North Atlantic Books, copyright © 2006 by Elise Dirlam Ching and Kaleo Ching. Reprinted by permission of publisher.

To send correspondence to the author of this book, mail a first-class letter to the author c/o Inner Traditions • Bear & Company, One Park Street, Rochester, VT 05767, and we will forward the communication, or contact the author directly at **ancestralmedicine.org**.

*Dedicated to all those working to
protect and creatively renew ancient ways of life
that respect the Earth and the many beings.
May the ancestors guide us well
through the ordeals that lie ahead.*

CONTENTS

❧

PART ONE
Foundations of Ancestor Work

∞∾

PART TWO
Healing with Lineage and Family Ancestors

∾

PART THREE
Honoring Other Types of Ancestors

☙

List of Figures

ACKNOWLEDGMENTS

From the ancient tribal ways of northern and western Europe, through centuries of intense cultural change, to our recent arrival as colonists to North America in the sixteenth through the nineteenth centuries, I thank my family ancestors for their tenacity, levity, and character. I praise my parents, my siblings and their families, and my extended kin for their support of my genealogy research and my deep dive into the mysteries of the ancestors.

Thanks to the spirits of the land in northern and southeast Ohio, those near to Chicago and the San Francisco Bay Area, and the wild kin of the North Carolina Piedmont and Blue Ridge Mountains, all of whom have nourished and continue to sustain my body, consciousness, and dreaming. The places I've known and loved as home are a critical foundation for this offering.

Praise to my human teachers who helped me remember and activate my capacity for ritual and for relating with the ancestors. To mention a few: Ryan Bambao; Bryan Allen and the crew; Bekki and Crow of the Church of Earth Healing; Grant Potts, Clay Fouts, Amanda Sledz, and other members of the magickal tribe; Sarangerel Odigan; Jennifer Marchesani-Keyvan; Paul Rubio, Linda Held, Marco and Christine, David and Cheryl, the Native American Church, and relatives walking the Red Road; the Pacific Zen Institute, Joan Halifax, and other helpful dharma teachers; Martín Prechtel; Malidoma

Somé; Ginny Anderson; Meg Beeler; Graham Harvey; Luisah Teish, Ilé Ọ̀rúnmìlà Ọ̀ṣun, Awo Falokun, and other American teachers of Yorùbá ways; and Olúwo Fálolú Adésànyà, Ìyá Ifábùnmi, and the good people of the Adésànyà lineage of Òdè Rẹ́mọ, Nigeria.

Thanks to participants in ancestor rituals, trainings, and sessions from 2005 to the present: your dedication to healing and empowerment helped bring this book to its current form. Thanks to the staff at Inner Traditions for your trust, to my agent Anne Depue for the same, to Elaine Gast, Seyta Selter, and Julia Bernard for invaluable editorial support, and to all others who helped with edits. I had no idea writing a book was such a group undertaking, and I have no doubt that the final product is far better for it.

Finally, I thank my beloved wife, Sarah, for her dedication and encouragement and for having my back at each stage of this creation. May the blessings from this book also support the happiness, health, and longevity of our family for generations to come.

INTRODUCTION

When you think of the *ancestors,* who or what comes to mind? Ancestors are a biological and historical reality for each of us, irrespective of our religious, racial, or cultural backgrounds. Your blood lineage ancestors include the thousands of women and men whose lives weave a story back to the first human beings in Africa over two hundred thousand years ago. Even if you were adopted or orphaned and will never know your biological parents, the ancestors still speak through the DNA in each cell of your body. They are reflected in your physical features, your health, and many of your predispositions.

Beyond your bloodlines, you might also claim as an ancestor anyone whose life has inspired you, either personally or culturally. This list might include extended and adoptive family, beloved friends, and well-known people who touched your lives before their passing. Most religious traditions look to their human founders as an embodiment of core values and spiritual teachings that have been passed down through generations (e.g., Siddhartha for Buddhists, Muhammad for Muslims). Even in the ostensibly secular United States, Americans collectively celebrate the lives of inspiring human beings with holidays such as Martin Luther King Jr. Day, Presidents' Day, Easter, Memorial Day, Halloween, Thanksgiving, and Christmas.

Everyone knows there are certain physical and psychological realities to being dead. That said, most people on Earth also believe in some sort of afterlife or continuity of consciousness after physical death. Belief itself is a tricky thing. We might adopt a certain perspective and then have experiences that reinforce those views; other times, new experiences challenge our ways of seeing the world. For me it was a mixture of both. I was not raised with awareness of my family or lineage ancestors; however, through personal experience, clinical training in mental health, and two decades of immersion in diverse lineages of spiritual practice, I came to experience them as an important source of relationship and support. With that said, I assume in this book that some aspect of what we are continues after our death and that the ancestors are therefore "real" and worthy of our consideration and respect.

In the pages that follow, I share an in-depth framework to support those who want to improve their relationships with the ancestors. I'm offering this information both for those who are new to ancestor work and for seasoned practitioners. I've sought to present the material in ways that are relatively free from religious dogma, compatible with most spiritual paths, and accessible for those who prefer not to identify with a specific tradition. In places where this framework diverges from your personal beliefs and training, be curious about the differences, and trust your instincts about how to navigate the gaps.

Perhaps you are a psychotherapist, priest, psychic, shaman, ritualist, healer, family elder, educator, or someone in a position to support others in navigating relationships with their ancestors. In this book you'll find many perspectives and exercises you might incorporate into your practice, provided you are first grounded in healthy relationships with your own ancestors. If you're interested in genealogy or family history and would like a greater context for honoring ancestors, this book presents ways to convey respect and gratitude and to strengthen your direct channel of communication with them. Maybe you are seeking to make sense of spontaneous, unsolicited encounters with the spirits of the dead. If so, you'll find a context for navigating potentially confusing or frightening experiences. And if you simply want to better understand individuals and traditions that claim to directly relate to the ancestors, this book can serve as a window into ancestor reverence and ritual.

Benefits of Ancestor Work

As you begin reading, you might find yourself thinking: "Why seek to relate to our ancestors at all?" From personal experience and my work as a psychotherapist and ancestor-focused ceremonialist, I have found relating to ancestors to be healing and beneficial on at least three levels: personal, familial, and cultural.

On a personal level, research confirms that relating in conscious ways with your ancestors supports physical and psychological health in the following ways:

- Reflecting on your ancestors boosts intellectual performance and confidence.[1]
- Awareness of family predispositions, including behavioral health risks, may encourage life choices that benefit you and future generations.[2]
- Forgiveness, a common component of family healing and ancestral repair work, promotes greater physical and mental health.[3]

Ancestor work also encourages introspection and greater clarity about life purpose, which in turn creates more personal satisfaction and sense of meaning in life. In getting to know and love my family ancestors, I feel more confident, supported, and comfortable in my skin. Moreover, I maintain a sense of healthy pride about my roots and culture of origin. Because we are partly composed of family karma or consciousness, assisting blood ancestors who are still in need also improves our personal wellness and soul-level health.

On a familial level, sustained ancestor work can help heal intergenerational patterns of family dysfunction. By working with spiritually vibrant ancestors, you can start to understand, contain, and transform patterns of pain and abuse and gradually reclaim the positive spirit of the family. I've seen situations time and again where one person engages the ancestors, and it creates a ripple among living family members, who may suddenly reconcile after years of disagreement or restore overlooked blessings. When you engage your loving ancestors, you can catalyze healing breakthroughs in your family, including establishing appropriate boundaries with living relatives. Also, when you make yourself available for ancestral repair work, the recently deceased are in turn more able to help living family members navigate their journey to become ancestors after death.

Finally, on a cultural and collective level, the ancestors are powerful allies in transforming historical trauma relating to race, gender, religion, war, and other types of collective pain. Recent findings in epigenetics are showing that in a very real way, the pain of our ancestors can endure through generations. In a landmark 2013 study on the biological transmission of trauma, a team of researchers in Jerusalem showed that the children, as well as grandchildren and further descendants, of Holocaust survivors are especially prone to depression, anxiety, and nightmares. This tendency is tied to a biological marker in their chromosomes that is absent in those *not* descended from Holocaust survivors. This transgenerational transmission of trauma is a new field of study. In many ways it overlaps with the ancestral repair work presented in this book.[4]

When we reconcile with ancestors who experienced different types of persecution or who enacted violence and oppression, we make repairs in our personal psyches and family histories that, in turn, mend cracks in the larger spirit of humanity. This supports us in moving beyond identifying with victim/victimizer consciousness and in embodying what is beautiful and helpful from the past. Transforming generations of family and cultural pain also frees us to draw upon the support of the loving ancestors for prosperity in our vocation and service in the world.

How to Read This Book

This book is organized into three parts. Part 1, "Foundations of Ancestor Work," will give you an overview of different types of ancestors and ancestral engagement as well as ways that ritual and ceremony can help you connect with your ancestors. In chapter 1, I share from my personal journey of getting to know and love my family ancestors. Chapter 2 introduces different types of ancestors and challenges that relate to each. Chapter 3 explores types of spontaneous ancestral contact such as dream visits, waking visions, and synchronicities. Chapter 4 outlines a framework for ancestor reverence and ritual that establishes the foundation for the exercises and ritual work in the later chapters.

Part 2, "Healing with Lineage and Family Ancestors," presents a process for establishing lines of communication with supportive ancestral guides. This and part 3 are the "how to" sections of the book. Here you will learn to partner with wise and loving ancestors to assist the souls of any deceased family members who have not yet joined the ancestors. It's this very process—and my desire to share it—that motivated me to write this book. Chapter 5 speaks to genealogy and family research and offers ways to make first contact with your ancestors. Chapter 6 emphasizes connection with ancestral guides and teachers. In chapters 7 and 8, I share ways to assist both the forgotten or historical dead and the more recent and remembered ancestors. Part 2 concludes with ways to ground the work in family healing and presents rituals for ongoing relationship with family ancestors.

In part 3, "Honoring Other Types of Ancestors," I offer a broader picture of relating to the ancestors. Chapter 10 considers the ancestors' relationships to specific places. It includes an exercise for honoring the dead at a cemetery and suggestions for getting to know the ancestors near your home. In chapter 11 you'll learn ways to honor ancestors of affinity and spiritual lineage, including those capable of supporting your work in the world. This chapter also presents exercises for further integration of your work with different types of ancestors and explores the topics of multiple souls, reincarnation, and past lives. Chapter 12 focuses on funeral rites, the dying process, and the first year after death.

This book grew out of my training with human teachers, my personal relationship with the ancestors, and my experience in guiding others in ancestor work. Like other teachers, I share what works well for me; please take what helps you and leave the rest. There are some inherent risks in working with the ancestors, and I suggest reading through the entire book before deciding whether or not to engage them directly. If you do decide to engage your ancestors, keep it positive and reach out for support if you get in over your head. By writing a manual encouraging people I may never meet to engage both their supportive ancestors and the troubled dead, I've gone pretty far out on a limb. However, my experience tells me that anyone who is psychologically stable, has good intentions, and is willing to listen to their intuition can cultivate an empowering relationship with their loving ancestors. By *anyone*, I really do mean anyone. You don't need to be a traditional shaman, ghost whisperer, or trained medium. You don't need to be descended from Cherokee healers, African chiefs, or Taoist masters. Nor do you need to be Christian, Buddhist, Pagan, or identified with any religious or spiritual tradition. We all have loving and supportive ancestors and can draw upon these relationships for greater clarity about life purpose, increased health and vitality, and tangible support in daily life.

Despite the challenges, you should no more fear the ancestors than you do the living. Each of us, no matter how troubled our recent family may be, descends from lineages that include loving and empowered human beings. These ancestors are no further from us than our blood and bones, and they are waiting to be welcomed into our lives and to assist us in fulfilling our potential. I pray that this book will help you to draw on the support of your people to express your soul's gifts—for your own happiness and for the well-being of your family, the Earth, and the generations to come. I also pray that this book will lead to greater care and consideration in how we relate to the human dead and help to reestablish the ancestors as one essential force and community in the larger ecology of the sacred.

Part One

FOUNDATIONS
OF
ANCESTOR
WORK

This part introduces foundational teachings on:

- Different types of ancestors (e.g., family, historic, collective)
- Types of spontaneous ancestral contact
- Practices common to ancestral reverence
- Ways in which ritual and ceremony can facilitate ancestral contact

You'll also be invited to reflect on your own experience of your biological ancestors, including both recent family ancestors and those whose names are no longer remembered. Practices of ancestor reverence may call into question your beliefs about the afterlife and the relationship between the living and the dead. Allow space for personal reflection as you read, and stay open to helpful dream visits or other spontaneous contact from your loving and supportive ancestors.

ONE

MY PERSONAL JOURNEY
WITH THE ANCESTORS

Making Initial Contact

My recent ancestors were mostly early Lutheran and Methodist settlers to North America from England, Ireland, and Germany. All of them crossed the Atlantic at least four generations ago, some much earlier. They were farmers, mothers, coal miners, and soldiers from Pennsylvania and West Virginia whose lives seemed to be focused on hard work and caring for family. In the places my family ancestors emigrated from, major disruptions in the most recent historical strata of tribal European cultures began around two thousand years ago with the military expansion of the Roman Empire (40 BCE–230 CE). Rome introduced the indigenous peoples of Europe and many others to the imperial cult of emperors, and by the fourth century CE, Rome had adopted Christianity. Over the next eight hundred years, Christian leaders like the Holy Roman emperor Charlemagne (742–814 CE) carried out campaigns of military expansion and conversion throughout western Europe. Along some of my bloodlines, ritual engagement with the spirits of our ancestors may not have been practiced for over a thousand years, and nothing from my research into the last few centuries of family history and tradition easily accounts for my calling to focus on the ancestors.

Nor does anything about my early life explain my affinity for ancestors. Born in suburban Ohio to a sane and loving middle-class family, I was not raised with a strong awareness of my ancestors nor with any framework for relating to the dead. Unlike some naturally gifted psychics or mediums, I did not talk with dead people or see spirits as a young person, nor did I experience profound trauma that cracked me open to other realities. Nor have I ever been struck by lightning, had a near-death experience, or endured a truly life-threatening illness. I do know that long hours playing in the nearby woods and creeks as a boy helped me to feel at home in the natural world, and that reading fantasy novels as a young person established a foundation from which to explore ritual and other ways of seeing the world.

My first conscious contact with the unseen happened when, as a teenager, I put into practice basic ritual instructions from an introductory book on shamanism. Through these early experiments, I made contact with nonphysical beings or spirits that I experienced as quite real. I remember feeling like I had stumbled through a doorway to another dimension, and the pushback I received from these spirits left me scrambling for a way to make sense of my experiences. Fortuitously, by age eighteen, I responded to a flyer for a public workshop and began to learn from my first formal teachers in shamanism and earth-honoring spirituality, Bekki and Crow of the Church of Earth Healing.[1] Their mentorship, combined with my immersion in contemporary Pagan culture and the academic study of world religions, provided a critical context and grounding for my early experiences with ritual and spirit work.

I remember one pivotal day of training in 1999 that introduced me to relating directly to family ancestors. By this point I had been practicing shamanic journeywork, ritual magic, and other types of trance work for about four years. During the training, Bekki guided me to connect with a family ancestral guide, and I made contact with a spiritually vibrant but historically distant European ancestor from my paternal grandfather's lineage.

Later in the day, I was invited to ask this supportive ancestor if there were any among the recently deceased that could use healing. Immediately I knew I would visit with my father's father. When I was seven years old, he died from a self-inflicted gunshot wound. His death rippled through the family, especially for my grandmother, who was home when he took his life, and her sons, including my father, who was on duty with the local fire department at the time. As a child, I was shielded from much of this impact, and before this moment I had never sought contact with my grandfather as an ancestor or considered in any real way the possible effects of his death on the family. Fifteen years after his passing, the ancestral guides and I contacted my Grandpa Foor in spirit and determined that he was still in a state of relative confusion.* He appeared to me as fragmented and was missing part of his energy body in his abdomen, where he had shot himself. The guides repaired this damage and helped him to understand who we were and what had happened. He then shared a kind message for my grandmother that I later conveyed to her while we were standing together at my grandfather's grave. That pivotal day of ritual repair ended as the guides and I helped my grandfather start to assume his place among our loving and supportive ancestors.

Family Research and Personal Healing

My work with my grandfather and the guides sparked a longing to better understand my family history. This led to eight years of occasional genealogical research and family trips to visit with older relatives. In 2007 I shared a moment with my family at a small cemetery in rural Fayette County, Pennsylvania, that showed me how closely ancestor ritual, genealogical research, and family healing can interweave. In conversations with extended family members over the previous year, I had learned that my maternal grandmother's parents were buried in

---

*Individuals who die through suicides, murder, accidents, war, or other sudden and/or violent deaths are at greater risk for having difficulty in joining the ancestors.

an unmarked grave in a location remembered by only one living relative. Through ritual, I contacted these ancestors in spirit and asked them what kind of headstone they would like to mark their resting spot. Wanting to give this gift to them and feeling confident that I had received their request, I placed the order. Then something curious happened. Within days I noticed that online genealogy databases that I had checked numerous times in previous years were suddenly brimming with historical information on these specific Irish and English ancestors. It was as if these lineages, in response to my gesture of care, were opening up to me in ways that hadn't previously been available. Weeks later, when I was standing at the grave with my parents and a handful of other family members, this breakthrough enabled me to name the ancestors of these great-grandparents before formally placing the headstone. This honoring ceremony helped my mother and our older relatives to feel seen and appreciated for their knowledge of family history and brought my family closer.

My affinity for ancestor reverence also motivated me to understand my older European ancestors, who lived before Christianity and the Roman Empire. Pre-Christian Irish/Celtic and Norse cultures both have established traditions of ancestor reverence. The masks that millions of American children and adults wear during Halloween can be traced back to an older Celtic holiday called *Samhain,* brought to North America by Irish and Scottish immigrants. This traditional holiday was incorporated into the Catholic calendar as All Hallows' Eve in the ninth century, and it is still celebrated by modern Pagans and Christians alike as a time to remember, feast, and perhaps communicate directly with the ancestors. Modern practitioners of Norse Heathenry/Asatru have revived a ritual known as *seidhr* detailed in the thirteenth-century *Saga of Eric the Red.*[2] In both the text and the modern ritual, a trained ancestor medium ascends to an elevated seat and from there serves the community as an oracle or voice for the dead by responding to questions from the assembled. (For a more detailed description, see chapter 9, page 178.) Norse ancestor mediums and Celtic rituals of masquerade and feasting the dead help me appreciate just how recently my blood ancestors practiced some communal form of ancestor reverence and how some traditions continue today.

Before meeting my older ancestors in spirit, I never thought to see my family or cultural history as a source of spiritual strength and richness. Masking personal pain with unconscious egotism, I was undoubtedly hurtful at times to my family and others close to me. My training in world religion and healing arts helped me to gradually understand that the disappointment I had grappled with as a young adult was more about gaps in my education from the larger culture than about my family's shortcomings. These blind spots had been in place for generations and felt to me like a kind of systemic betrayal. For example, I was not raised with knowledge of traditional songs, stories, or rituals; I was not taught ways to consciously dialogue with the natural world; I received no framework for safely engaging the spirits or unseen worlds. Yet how could I expect my parents or grandparents to teach me these things when this knowledge had been largely missing from the culture for more than a thousand years? By seeing my personal healing in the context not only of *family* breaks but also of larger *cultural* breaks from Earth-honoring traditions, I could release old judgments about my family. I'm now able to view challenges that *do* arise from a larger historical context—reminding me that not all family issues are personal or sourced in the recent past.

Learning and Teaching Ancestor Work

In the nearly two decades since my first contact with ancestral guides and with my grandfather, I've been blessed to work with different spiritual teachers and traditions that consciously honor the ancestors. Among indigenous Earth-honoring traditions, my most important influences are European Paganism, Mongolian shamanism, Native North American ways, and the Ifá/Òrìṣà tradition of Yorùbá-speaking West Africa and the African diaspora.

Modern Paganism and revived forms of shamanism provided my earliest experiences with Earth-honoring teachings and community ritual. Immersing myself in the study and practice of ceremonial magic, Western occultism, and Pagan traditions inspired by pre-Christian Europe (e.g., Celtic, Norse, Mediterranean cultures) helped me to cultivate a habit of introspection, to learn foundational skills for relating with the spirit world, and to appreciate the deep roots of my own ancestry. I view the ancestor-focused teachings in this book as an extension of the Earth-honoring ways of my older European ancestors, and I feel great love and appreciation for practitioners working to rekindle the older ways of continental Europe and the British Isles. During my first visit in 2014 to megalithic sites of Scotland and England, simply standing at four-thousand-year-old stone monuments to honor the dead confirmed that ancestor reverence is nothing new.

Before her passing in 2006, Buryat Mongolian shaman, teacher, and friend Sarangerel Odigan encouraged my work with the ancestors and shared how her tradition would view some of my early experiences. She was the first representative of an intact indigenous tradition that I worked with in depth, and she was an exceptionally kind and generous mentor whose works I refer to throughout this book. Learning from Sarangerel expanded my understanding of the unseen, provided a living human model for a heart-centered embodiment of indigenous wisdom, and stoked my longing to learn as much I could from indigenous elders and traditions. Her sudden death also unexpectedly taught me how to continue a relationship with a spiritual mentor after her journey to the realm of the ancestors.

Regular participation in purification or sweat lodges, wilderness quests, and other traditions indigenous to North America over the past fifteen years introduced me to the beauty, dignity, and healthy pride of peoples whose connection to place and ancestral wisdom remains relatively intact. Most of my experience with Native ways has been with Lakota-style ceremony and with the Native American Church. As a participant in these sacred spaces, I've learned how to pray from the heart and to honor traditional protocol as a gift from the ancestors. Time in circle with Native teachers and communities also taught me a lot about forgiveness. I have witnessed the tremendous resilience and open-heartedness of tribal leaders who share traditional ways with non-Native individuals, many of whom are direct descendants of the colonists who carried out genocide against indigenous peoples. Better understanding of this aspect of American history also helped me to understand on a heart level the painful histories of my earlier European ancestors and the mandate to participate in healing legacies of racism and oppression in the United States.

Over the past decade I've also been a student, and more recently an initiate, of the Ifá/Òrìṣà tradition. Originally brought to the Americas through the transatlantic slave trade, diverse branches of Yorùbá culture now include over fifty million practitioners worldwide in places such as Nigeria, Cuba and the Caribbean, Brazil, Venezuela, the United States, and even Europe. During four pilgrimages to Nigeria, I have been privileged to step into the tradition as an initiate of Ifá (the deity of destiny and divination), of Ọbàtálá and Ọṣun (deities of wisdom and love), and of Egúngún (the collective spirit of the ancestors) in the lineage of Olúwo Fálolú Adésànyà Awoyadé from Òdè Rémọ.

Being welcomed into the society of ancestral mediums was particularly meaningful and served as the culmination of years of work with my own ancestors as well as my search for elders who could help me bring out this calling to ancestor reverence. Of course, initiation is only the beginning of a new cycle of learning and growth, and I continue to seek learning from other practitioners, in both the United States and Nigeria, about their approach to ancestor reverence.

Although I refer to these traditions and others throughout this book, *I make no claim in this book to represent any specific tradition or lineage.* The teachings and practices shared in this book emphasize cross-cultural similarity. They aim to be widely accessible and free from the constraints of any specific tradition. When I draw upon a specific cultural lineage to highlight some aspect of ancestor reverence, I refer to established sources and representatives of that tradition. I realize that many readers will not be deeply called to any one spiritual path, and I firmly believe that you as the reader don't need to adopt any particular religious identity, nor do you need to see yourself as a particularly religious person in order to deeply love and honor your ancestors. Furthermore, I also accept full responsibility for any shortcomings in the teachings and practices presented.

In addition to work with spiritual teachers and traditions, my training as a doctor of psychology and a marriage and family therapist informs my approach to ancestor work. As a therapist, I have seen firsthand how ancestral wounds are transmitted across generations, as well as some means by which these cycles can be healed. As someone committed to inner work, I've also seen how many ways there are to procrastinate or avoid the discipline necessary for cultivating wisdom and an open heart. Some traditional cultures designate a living family member to tend to relations with the ancestors on behalf of the rest of the family; sometimes the ancestors choose this individual themselves. Since assuming this role in my family about a decade ago, I have sought to study family poisons and medicines in the context of my own life and relationships. Accepting responsibility for my psychological health and happiness, including my relationships with family and community, is foundational to my ritual work with the ancestors.

In the decade since guiding my first ancestor-work weekend intensive in 2005, I have led this training over a hundred times for over a thousand people throughout the United States. In this same time, I've spoken with several thousand others through talks, monthly circles, and personal sessions. In holding a space for others to contact their ancestors, I have witnessed profound transformations that also convey benefit to living family members. Three key lessons I have learned are: (1) the work is about relationship; (2) everyone has loving ancestors; and (3) relating to our ancestors is entirely normal. First, getting to know and love them requires a deep and sustained reckoning with our family, our culture of origin, and ourselves. This process takes place over years, not months; it is certainly not finished in one weekend. The ancestors are not a "subject" we can master or complete; the point is building a relationship with the collective spirit of family in ways that help us grow into wise and loving human beings. We are never done with the ancestors until we join them after our death, and even this is merely the beginning of a new cycle. Ancestor work is both deeply personal and inherently relational.

Second, we all have ancestors who lived, loved, and worshipped in intimate relationship with the Earth. Getting to know them can heal and empower people of any background, including adoptees who do not know their biological family. Even though I have no recent family members who have practiced ancestor reverence per se, I have come to understand my affinity with Earth-honoring spirituality in the context of my European roots. My point is this: you don't need to have some kind of spiritual calling from the ancestors themselves; it's fine just to go knock on their door. In my case, I trusted my first teachers in Earth spirituality when they said it would be a good idea for me to do the ancestors workshops they offered, and I'm extremely glad I listened. Although it makes for a better story, I don't necessarily believe that my ancestors were somehow leading me along a trail of bread crumbs to connect with them. You don't even need to feel an emotional longing to know your ancestors; sometimes you just decide to engage, and a new kind of relating begins. We are all unique and blessed, and no one is more special, more human, or more deserving of respect.

Finally, I've realized that, contrary to fear and popular misconceptions, working with the ancestors may actually make you less—rather than more—strange. In my case, although supporting others in talking with dead people is one part of my day job, I am a down-to-earth, straightforward Midwesterner who loves and respects his family, his country (mostly), and his cultural roots. I pay taxes, read the news, and vote. I sometimes eat fast food, like going to the movies, and struggle to make it to the gym. I'm also a Western-educated psychotherapist and doctor of psychology with a deep love and respect for the physical sciences. Sometimes people assume that having a relationship with the ancestors requires quitting your job, making pilgrimages to Egypt or Peru, eating magic mushrooms, or adopting some kind of new, weird identity. To the contrary, ancestor work has functioned in my life as an antidote to spiritual snobbery by helping to ground me in this reality and to value my family and myself. I have seen similar effects in the lives of others who take it to heart. There is nothing unusual about having a healthy, ongoing relationship with our ancestors; in fact, it's one of the most inherently human things we could do.

TWO

WHO ARE THE ANCESTORS?

Genetics, family, and blood lineage are ways to approach the question "'Who are the ancestors?" Blood kin are the first way in which most people think of and experience the ancestors, and they're also the focus of much of this book. Like Russian nested dolls, our experience of recent family ancestors rests within larger patterns of lineage, culture, and human prehistory. Our oldest ancestors lived in Africa at least two hundred thousand years ago. In this way, the ancestors express the collective wisdom of humanity. They are elders who remember our full evolutionary journey as human beings, and they are custodians of our genetic and cultural memory.

This chapter introduces key beliefs shared by many different cultures about the ancestors and their relationship with the living. You'll learn to distinguish between recent family ancestors and the older, collective dead, and to tell the difference between healthy ancestors and troubled ghosts. You'll also learn about challenges and positive effects you're likely to encounter when engaging with ancestors. Chapter 2 concludes with an exercise to reflect on your perception of family and older ancestors. As you read, assume that some of these souls are deeply at peace, while others may still be working things through. Unless you already have a practice of relating directly to your ancestors, again I encourage you to read through the whole book before seeking intentionally to make contact.

The Dead Are Not Dead

I believe that most indigenous peoples, animists, shamans, pagans, spiritual healers, and others who intentionally relate to the dead would agree with the following four assertions. These beliefs are the foundations of my approach to ancestor reverence and ritual, and they inform the exercises and rituals in this book. As you read, see which perspectives feel natural to you, and where your beliefs and experiences may differ.

1. Consciousness continues after death.
2. Not all of the dead are equally well.
3. The living and the dead can communicate.
4. The living and the dead can strongly affect one another.

Consciousness Continues after Death

Traditions of ancestor reverence assume that the ancestors are as metaphysically real as you or me. Like far-off galaxies or microscopic bacteria, the souls or spirits of the deceased exist whether or not you believe in them or can perceive them. Several factors influence a person's degree of openness to the subject of the ancestors: *religious or spiritual views, direct personal experience,* and what I would call *gut feeling* or *instinctual belief.* Any one of these is enough to foster a stance of openness toward the spirits of the dead. As you read, notice how open you are to the reality of the ancestors and where this receptivity comes from.

When people think of the ancestors, they often picture older people, black-and-white photographs, and deceased family members. It's true: the ancestors include those who have lived and died before us; however, as religious scholar Graham Harvey writes, "To be an ancestor is to continue relating."[1] When a loved one who has died pays a visit to the living, this is an event, an encounter *in the present moment* between an incarnate human and an ancestral spirit who previously walked the Earth. From this perspective, the dead are still alive. Ancient Egyptians sometimes referred to their beloved dead as "the living ones" and to Osiris, steward over of the dead, as "Lord of the Living." Why emphasize that the dead are in fact alive? If we allow that the souls or spirits of the dead can relate to the living, it's worth being clear about what we mean when we describe someone or something as "dead." Could this mean that this soul continues to exist while we have ceased to consciously relate to them, and that they may be in that way dead *to us*?

Insofar as ancestral spirits may continue to relate with the living, they are no more "dead" than angels, gods, the spirits of plants and animals, or other unseen forces. Instead of thinking about the living and the dead, it may be more accurate to distinguish between human souls who are currently incarnate (the living) and souls who were previously incarnate but whom we may still relate to in the present (the ancestors). Like incarnate humans, the ancestors live and dwell in the present, even if they have their own communities and places of dwelling distinct from our lives on Earth. In the words of Senegalese poet Birago Diop in his poem "Spirits," "The dead are not dead."

The existence of ancestral spirits hinges on the fact that some aspect of what we are continues after death. Nearly all faiths affirm some type of postmortem continuity of consciousness. This doesn't necessarily mean that all "believers" have direct, personal experiences with the dead. Research shows that 64 percent of Americans believe in life after death and 45 percent believe in ghosts, even though most haven't had a near-death experience and many report never having seen a ghost personally.[2] If your faith tells you that some aspect of the soul continues after death, belief in the ancestors naturally follows. Likewise, if you've personally experienced contact from the ancestors, then "belief" in the spirits of the dead is a function of direct knowing. But why do millions of Americans who don't identify as especially spiritual or religious *and* who don't report direct encounters still act as if the ancestors are real?

Consider the multibillion-dollar funeral and cemetery industry in the United States as one example of what I would call *gut feeling* or *instinctual belief* in the ancestors—acting as if they are real. People invest in funerals, cremation urns, and grave plots to honor the memory of the deceased and also to show love and respect to them as ongoing realities in the present. U.S. laws prohibiting the desecration of cemeteries and human remains enforce the widespread taboo against disturbing human remains, a view that hinges upon a presumed link between the remains and the soul of the deceased. Hollywood understands the power of belief in this topic. Films like *Poltergeist,* in which construction over a cemetery leads to paranormal trouble, and the idea of the "curse of the pharaohs," believed to kill anyone who disturbs the tombs of ancient Egyptian rulers, play on the association between the spirit of the deceased and their remains. Popular TV shows like *Ghost Hunter, Medium, Ghost Whisperer,* and *Crossing Over* rest on the widespread belief that soul or consciousness—in some form—continues after death. Stories like this continue to sell because most Americans tend to act as if the ancestors are real. Just in case.

Not All of the Dead Are Equally Well

When we accept that some aspect of what we are might carry on after death, then questions naturally arise about where exactly we're headed. Most religious traditions assert the existence of an unseen or spirit world: some other aspect of reality (and of who we are) that is not fully circumscribed by the physical world. This is closely related to belief in continuity of consciousness after death: if some part of what we are endures when the body dies, there must be at least two places or dimensions, a metaphysical "here" and "there." Where we go after life on Earth would be the existential "there," the place where other ancestors dwell, the spirit world or otherworld.

Many traditions describe this "otherworld" in ways that imply structural integrity of the overall system. The Yorùbá people of southwest Nigeria and other practitioners of Yorùbá traditional religion (also known as Ifá/Òrìṣà) sometimes use the image of the spherical calabash or gourd to convey duality within a greater wholeness. In observable reality, the upper half of the calabash is the dome of the sky (*òrun*), and the lower half that of the earth (*ayé*). Often translated as *heaven,* òrun also refers to the unseen realm that surrounds and intersects the physical world or ayé. The journey from the ancestral realm (prebirth) to incarnate life and back again (post-death) is a journey from òrun to ayé to òrun. One divination verse (*odù Ìrosùn-Ìwòrì*) from Yorùbá culture states, "People will continue to go to heaven and return to earth after death until everyone attains the good position."[3] The verse implies that at any given moment some human souls reside in the otherworld and some on Earth, but all participate in the greater story of human consciousness that is playing out in the great calabash of the world, both seen and unseen.

The pairing of heaven (there) and Earth (here) also runs throughout Judaism, Christianity, and Islam and can be viewed in terms of the following dichotomies:

The Living — The Ancestors
Earth — Heaven
This World — The Otherworld
Physically Perceivable Reality — The Unseen or Spirit World

Many traditions also believe that the condition of the dead mirrors or parallels that of living humans on Earth. Some people are wise and kind, while others are dangerous and tormented; depictions of the otherworld often reflect this full spectrum. To account for these differences, maps of the ancestral realms often elaborate two or 'more locations, with some being distinctly more comfortable than others. For example, Christian sources depict heaven and hell in radically different ways, yet both are dwelling places, and perhaps states of consciousness, for souls after death. Buddhism recognizes the existence of a hungry ghost realm populated by suffering souls; it also acknowledges the existence of benevolent ancestral teachers. Sometimes traditions say that the troubled dead remain here among the living as earthbound spirits, ghosts in need of assistance to make their belated transition to join the ancestors in the otherworld.

The teachings presented in this book are consistent with traditional lore by acknowledging that the levels of awareness among the souls of the dead run the full spectrum from loving, wise, and inspired ancestors to dangerous and ill-intentioned ghosts. This fact requires practitioners of ancestor reverence to demonstrate discernment like that required when meeting new living humans. If we fail to distinguish between levels of awareness among the dead, we risk viewing the ancestors either as entirely frightening and dangerous or as an idealized source of love and light, when the reality is more nuanced. Throughout this book I refer to "the ancestors" interchangeably with "the dead" (meaning all human souls not incarnate on Earth at this time), but I sometimes use the term ancestor more narrowly to refer to those souls who are well in spirit. In the second usage, ancestor is a kind of compliment. It refers to an earned or acquired status and contrasts with ghosts, the troubled dead, or those who are not yet ancestors.

A related, and important, assumption is that, like us, the souls of the dead change. When a parent or relative dies, our memories and psychological filters may distort the connection or attempt to freeze the relationship in the past. Malidoma Somé, a teacher and ritual leader from the Dagara people of Burkina Faso, West Africa, spoke to this problem:

> In this dimension, once you make a mistake you are always referred to from the perspective of that mistake. There is an unspoken assumption of the irredeemability of the human being. That is why criminals remain criminals the rest of their lives. That is why people live their lives trying to avoid having a record. The problem with that is that this eventually stretches itself to the other world, so that ancestors, the dead forebears who during their lives were less than wise, made mistakes that a lot of other people paid for, are still kept within that kind of framework as if even death didn't redeem them.[4]

Some emphasized how the same ancestors whose lives were most troubled during their time on Earth may actually be highly motivated to work for good after their death. The ghost of Jacob Marley in Charles Dickens's *A Christmas Carol* beautifully embodies this wisdom by warning Ebenezer Scrooge to change his ways and avoid making Marley's mistakes. Even Christianity and Islam, which tend to view heaven and hell as relatively enduring states, recognize that after death the soul undergoes purification, reckoning, or some type of further refinement or growth.

In my experience of supporting others in making repairs with recent ancestors, I have encountered situations in which the spirit of the deceased seemed to be bright, loving, and available for connection, while the living—often adult children of the deceased—were not able to move beyond memories of their parent during life. Ideally, people work through their issues with a family member in life or in the period of time after the individual's death. However, unhealed emotional pain from a past relationship can keep a living person from relating to supportive ancestral spirits in the present.

The Living and the Dead Can Communicate

Contact between the living and the dead can take many forms. Sometimes the deceased come unsolicited as visitors in our dreams. Sometimes they speak through waking visions or synchronicities, or at times when our psychological defenses are thin (e.g., near-death experiences, altered states). When people who have no framework for this contact have such experiences, they may be unsettled or wonder if they're "going crazy." In most cases, experiences of spontaneous ancestral contact are no more a sign of psychosis than are spontaneous interactions with living humans here on Earth. In fact, some people engage in spiritual traditions precisely because they're seeking to make sense of spontaneous, unsolicited, or even unwanted contact from the dead.

Many also seek to contact the dead through practices of ancestor reverence. These can include ancestor-focused prayer, meditation, inspired song, and creative expression; psychic and mediumship practices; some types of divination; and any other practice that facilitates communication. In nearly every ancestor-focused ritual I have participated in over the past two decades, living participants have attempted to communicate with the deceased. Of course spontaneous contact and intentional contact with the ancestors are not mutually exclusive. Those who intentionally relate to the ancestors also tend to report occasional instances of spontaneous contact (e.g., dreams, synchronicities). For those who do succeed in making contact, it's important, over time, to seek to refine the accuracy of the communication.

When thinking about communication between the living and the dead, remember what you know about relationships between living humans—that contact is not necessarily either conscious or beneficial. People may be aware of you before you are aware of them, and they may have helpful or harmful intentions toward you. For example, many people enjoy the support of loving ancestors whether or not they are aware of or even believe in the existence of these unseen friends and protectors. Contact in this case can be considered unconscious but beneficial. When the dead who are not yet at peace weigh on those with no awareness of the unseen, this would be an instance of unconscious and unhelpful contact between the living and the dead. Practitioners of ancestor-focused ritual also know that it's possible to turn our attention toward beings in the unseen realm, including the ancestors, without drawing their attention to us. In brief, we can reach out intentionally to the ancestors, or they may communicate with us by their own volition. The resulting contact may, for either party involved, be helpful or harmful, conscious or unconscious.

The Living and the Dead Can Strongly Affect One Another

Of the four key assumptions, this is perhaps the most foreign to modern Western people. Yet without this consideration, practices to engage the ancestors wouldn't be important. Practitioners of ancestor reverence generally assume that the ancestors influence us to a degree that truly matters and that we also affect them in important ways; mutual impact is more than just a given. What *is* an option is whether the influence will be conscious or unconscious, beneficial or harmful. Many rituals focus on maintaining positive relations between the living and the dead precisely to ensure that their influence is beneficial rather than harmful. In a conversation, a Haitian Vodun priest, Manbo Maude, gave me the image of one of the Guédé (ancestral spirits) digging your grave while another tries to fill it in. The ancestors can confer blessings of health and longevity, or they can send us to an early grave.

Consider first some of the helpful ways in which the ancestors may influence the living. On the most fundamental level, healthy ancestors can bestow a legacy of good health, prosperity, and rootedness in place and culture. Ancestors who embodied kindness and integrity during life can serve as sources of inspiration and motivation for living relatives. The loving dead can also work to guide, uplift, and protect their descendants, whether or not the living family is conscious of this support. In my experience, the ancestors who are strong and bright in spirit are also the best guides and allies for living family members who seek to transform and end difficult intergenerational burdens. We are their eyes and hands in this dimension, and they are deeply invested in good outcomes. Ancestors who are well in spirit bring added blessings to major life events like birth, weddings, and the return of the living to their ranks at the time of death. In brief, when we enjoy the active support of our loving ancestors, life tends to go more smoothly, with higher levels of luck, ease, and vitality.

We on Earth can also benefit the ancestors. Like any other type of being in any dimension, they need to eat. When we speak well of them and feed them through heartfelt offerings (e.g., food, drink, flowers), they receive the pleasure of nourishment and remembrance. We also bring honor and joy to our ancestors when we heal intergenerational challenges, support healthy families, and live as good and ethical people on Earth. Remember that death in our world is the start of a rite of passage for the recently deceased. This journey is completed only when they fully join the ranks of ancestors. The living can play an important role in this transformation. When we assist the recently dead and those who are not yet well in spirit to complete their transition, we support the ancestors' health. Generally, any act of service that encourages healthy families, children, and a future for humans here on Earth also reverberates in positive ways among the ancestors. Can you think of other ways in which you benefit from ancestral support or bring honor and blessings to your people?

What about the dead who are "digging your grave," the ones who are not yet at peace? Remember, the three maxims given above assert that the ancestors are real, they're not all equally well, and they can communicate with us (even if we don't seek out the contact). Good news: if you ever have the sense that a beloved grandparent or parent is looking out for you, there's a good chance they are. Bad news: if you get the sense that the souls of family ancestors are not at peace or are interfering with the living family, there's also a good chance that you're right. We can't have it both ways, any more than we can believe that only nice, friendly people exist on Earth. When the ancestors are not well in spirit, living elders may often feel physically and psychological unwell, and so on down the generations. Manifestations may include legacies of illness, addiction, physical and emotional abuse, isolation, poverty, and early death. Destructive actions by recent ancestors can reverberate through the living family for generations, functioning as a kind of ancestral curse, oppressive intergenerational karma, or pervasive bad luck. What are your beliefs about the troubled dead and their effect on the living? The impact of ghosts or the unwell dead will be explored at length in following chapters, and the repair process at the heart of this book emphasizes ways to transform and heal these difficult legacies.

Although living family members are often downstream from ancestral trouble, actions taken (or avoided) by the living can harm the ancestors. As in many types of relationships, the most common way that living people do this is by failing to observe basic respect or to show up for the connection. Many contemporary communities (religious and otherwise) reject the existence or relevance of the ancestors; this lack of consideration functions as a kind of ancestral amnesia with respect to family, heritage, and culture. When we forget our origins, we're more likely to enact and reinforce unhelpful intergenerational patterns, if only because no one has warned us about family burdens. Insofar as the ancestors look to us to heal the troubles passed down along the bloodlines, unwillingness to heal can keep them from fulfilling their role in the repair work. Repeating old, harmful patterns can keep the ancestors stuck along with us. Lack of consideration for family members after death also increases the risk that they will fail to be fully elevated and arrive as ancestors. Moreover, the living may also cause disruption for the dead when desecrating places important to them, such as cemeteries, ancestor shrines, and natural sanctuaries. Can you think of other ways that people on Earth have an unhealthy relationship with the deceased?

Building on those four underlying assumptions or tenets of ancestor reverence and ritual, the following section explores:

- Different types of ancestors based on how recently they lived on Earth
- Distinctions between individual ancestors, lineages, and the collective dead
- Common challenges when relating with different types of ancestors

When reading, reflect or make notes on how these perspectives align or differ from your personal beliefs and experiences. The chapter concludes with an invitation to personal reflection on how you feel about your ancestors.

Family and Remembered Ancestors

Family can be a source of great joy as well as devastating pain, and our family, whether by presence or absence, profoundly shapes our identity and outlook on life. Your experience of family likely also informs your perception of your much earlier ancestors.

Family Ancestors

When you think of family, maybe you think of your birth parents—particularly if they are the ones who raised you from childhood. For adoptees, individuals who have never met their birth parents, and those from blended or chosen families, the subject of family ancestors can be complicated. Perhaps the narrowest lens through which to think about ancestors is DNA—blood relation. Many physical features and health predispositions derive directly from blood ancestors, and their impact can be life-altering. The ancestors can bestow gifts such as longevity, fertility, and an even temperament, just as they can pass along vulnerabilities to physical and mental illness. Individuals who are adopted, orphaned, or estranged from their blood relatives may not know their genetic predispositions. They may also lack access to the stories of their biological ancestors. Nevertheless, those with no living connection to blood family can engage with the spirits of their beloved dead and blood ancestors through practices of honoring and ritual. In addition to direct lineage elders (e.g., grandparents, parents), family ancestors can include children, siblings, aunts and uncles, cousins, and anyone linked through the same blood lineages.

Family can also include *chosen family,* even if we are not always the one making the choices. In this sense, genetically unrelated individuals become blood relations, often through formal adoption rituals. For example, some North American Native tribes have ceremonies for making relations, after which adopted individuals are understood to be family, with all the accompanying privileges and responsibilities. Legal adoption can function as a kind of contemporary ritual of making relations, and some adoptees find that their new family and ancestors carry the same psychological weight as biological ancestors. In my own experience of becoming "blood brothers" with a childhood friend, I continued to dream of him years after ceasing to be in regular contact. Blood in this way is also symbolic, and the family you choose or are chosen by may influence not only your identity but also your blood and body. Family ancestors may also include genetically unrelated loved ones who at some point transitioned from friend to family member. Although this book emphasizes lineage repair with our biological ancestors, you can extend some of those same principles and practices to other types of ancestors and lineages.

The Remembered Dead

No matter whom we consider family, it's our memory of those people that determines the reach of the remembered ancestors. The recent or remembered dead include deceased parents, grandparents, children, siblings, and other kin who knew us during their lives on Earth. They may also include earlier generations of ancestors remembered through family lore or genealogy research. Think of these ancestors as those remembered by name, face, or deed.

Practitioners of ancestor reverence sometimes encourage knowing the names of ancestors back to seven generations. If this is taken to heart, seven generations along every bloodline calls for memorizing the names of 254 ancestors. Most people I meet know the names of their grandparents and maybe one or two great-grandparents. This lack of knowledge is understandable, as family research is not for the faint of heart. For example, Native Americans and people of African ancestry who are able to trace their family history through recent generations inevitably confront a historical wall where documented names give way to the less personalized records of slavery, forced occupation, and genocide. Those with recent disruptions in ancestral knowledge (e.g., adoption, war and dislocation, conception through violence, sudden migrations) often have even more limited knowledge of family history. In my case, years of research revealed names and knowledge of family ancestors back more than three hundred years along a few bloodlines, but for others only to four generations. If you know the names of your ancestors, even along just one lineage, to seven generations, that's a blessing! Remember that any effort to understand family history or research your genealogy can help awaken your relationship with ancestors, both known and unknown (see chapter 5 for research suggestions).

Relating to Family and Remembered Ancestors

What obstacles can come up around relating to recent ancestors? First, you may simply have little or no information about them. Second, you might have negative experiences and perceptions of family members that hinder your enthusiasm for engaging that family line. Third, there may be problems that source from the ancestral spirits themselves.

Let's look at each of these three challenges. Although you may feel discouraged because you have limited information about your recent family ancestors, you can still connect directly with them in spirit. Genetic ancestors are no farther from you than your blood and bones. In fact those with no experience of a biological family are less likely to project memories of the deceased onto their present relationships with the ancestors. To adoptees and those in similar circumstances, I suggest trusting your intuition and ability when interacting with both your blood and your adoptive ancestors.

Another common question I hear goes something like this: "If my living family or recent ancestors are abusive, unloving, dysfunctional, absent, or otherwise uninspiring, why in the world would I want to connect with them?" One reason is to make sure that they're not already connecting with you unhelpfully. Until the deceased join the ranks of the loving ancestors, they can weigh on the living relatives' connections with each other and with the older ancestors. Conversely, their successful transition may free up old blockages and support personal and family healing. *But at no point does relating with your ancestors call for opening yourself to harmful or abusive energies from your family, living or deceased.* To the contrary, positive change may call for you to establish healthy boundaries, both with your living relatives and with any of the deceased who are troubled in spirit.

Another reason to communicate with recent ancestors is to help facilitate a better way for them, for your living family, and for yourself. The family we knew during their lives on Earth are also the ancestors most likely to affect us in the present. This makes it in our self-interest to be sure that all is well for them. Occasionally people realize that their beloved dead are already well in spirit, even though our perception of them remains negative and rooted in the past. (For more on ways to determine if your ancestors are well, see chapter 5, pages 88–95.) Malidoma Somé has encouraged those seeking family healing through ancestor work to "detach themselves from the thought that ancestors who once had a record [of harmful behavior] in this dimension are still carrying that same frequency in the other world."[5] Ancestors whose lives on Earth were troubled may be strongly invested in making repairs in our world as part of their own journey of healing, and they may have already joined the wise and loving ancestors sometime after death. When any given family ancestor is well in spirit, the conditions support forgiveness and reconciliation between the living and this ancestor, and we have the opportunity for a mutually supportive relationship that may not have been possible during life. If all of your recent ancestors are already bright and well in spirit, you can work with them to maintain the health and vitality of your family and community.

Unfortunately, not all those who have died have fully settled into their status as supportive family ancestors. Without proper precautions, relating to the troubled dead or not-yet-ancestors can cause disruption and disequilibrium for the living. Unless you feel confident that any given family ancestor is well in spirit, consider first relating instead with older ancestral guides and initiating the lineage repair process described in chapters 5 through 9. In this way, any of the recent dead who are not yet well may "graduate" over time to become elevated ancestors themselves.

Some signs that this process of engagement is "working" include more conscious relationships with your living family members, a greater connection to lineage and ancestral support, and the elevation of the spirits of the remembered dead. Feeling the support of loving ancestors can help you update old perceptions, establish healthy boundaries, forgive past harms, and show up in more conscious ways with your living family. Even if you have no contact with or knowledge of your biological family or you are the last of your lineage, you can still call upon the assistance of loving ancestors and strengthen this relationship over time. Loving and forgiving our recent blood ancestors also helps them arrive at peace and, in turn, better support us from their world.

Older Ancestors and the Collective Dead

Contrast the light of a candle to a bonfire. With little knowledge of family history, the night beyond memory dwells close to the present, while for those with extensive records or oral history, memory burns brighter and reaches farther back in time. Even so, along all lineages, there is a threshold beyond which names, faces, and family stories are forgotten. Bloodlines among the older, collective dead include the most recent ancestor along any given lineage whose name is lost to memory (usually someone in the last few generations), through the last few thousand years of history, back to the first humans who walked the Earth at least two hundred thousand years ago. The dead whose names are forgotten include the vast majority of our ancestors.

No longer tethered to Earth by name or living memory, these older ancestors often appear to living people as a group or a collective energy. Nonetheless, you may experience ancestors from any period of time as individual spirits, as a distinct lineage, or as a collective presence. Ideally you will feel loved and supported by your older ancestors; however, accessing their support can call for healing and repair with living family and with recent ancestors. If you feel connection with older lineage ancestors whose names are now forgotten, how far back in time does this reach? Even practitioners of ancestor reverence seem to relate mostly to ancestors from the past two to three thousand years.

Consider the following four categories as a generalized starting point for distinguishing the ancestors whose names are forgotten:

- Ancient human ancestors: 200,000–10,000 years ago
- First agriculturalists and urban folk: 10,000–2,000 years ago
- Earlier ancestors known to history: 2,000–500 years ago
- Recent ancestors known to history: 500 years ago–named family

My comments above are not meant to imply that agriculturalists, urbanites, or those who write history are somehow better or that human culture progresses in any particular direction. Rather I am emphasizing that, as memory recedes into the past, specific knowledge gives way to broader and broader strokes of history and prehistory. The following section addresses some of the obstacles and the indicators of healing when relating with older ancestors.

Ancient Human Ancestors

Evolutionary biologists and paleoanthropologists generally place our emergence as a distinct species as far back as two hundred thousand years ago in East Africa,[6] and our arrival at full behavioral modernity around fifty thousand years ago, also in Africa.[7] This refers to the time when human beings established cultural universals such as language, story, art, toolmaking, cooking, dance, jokes, and music. According to this dominant "out of Africa" theory, all of our human ancestors originate in ancient Africa, as do the qualities that we most associate with humanity. Roughly fifty thousand to ten thousand years ago, some humans migrated out of Africa to inhabit most other regions of Earth. For thousands and thousands of years, nearly all of our ancestors, all around the world, lived in communities of a few hundred to a few thousand people and practiced some form of hunter-gatherer, seminomadic, or small-scale agricultural lifestyle. What do you know about the lives of your ancestors during this early span of time? In my case, I know that the earliest known human remains in Europe date to about forty-five thousand years ago[8] and that at least some of my personal ancestors migrated from northern Africa into southern Europe sometime after. I also know that, like others of European ancestry, I am 1 to 4 percent Neanderthal by genetic composition, meaning that some of my early human ancestors had children with and lived alongside our Neanderthal relatives in Europe until the extinction of the latter about twenty-five thousand years ago.

Over the past ten thousand years—only the most recent 5 percent of our history as a species—cultures around the world underwent major changes through adoption of large-scale agriculture, written language, and intensive mining and metallurgy. These innovations led to the emergence of larger cities and modern civilizations. As of 2014, over half of all human beings now live in urban areas.[9] Although some of our lineages shifted away from tribal ways of life thousands of years ago, a small handful of indigenous cultures to this day still lack a written language and live close to the land in more traditional ways. How long has it been since your people lived in a tribal culture or practiced an indigenous way of life? What do you know about the tribal, preimperial, precolonial strata of your blood ancestry?

As someone of northern European ancestry, my people ceased to practice tribal, Earth-honoring ways of life roughly one to two thousand years ago. Although I relate in spirit to these older ancestors who would have been "indigenous" by today's standards, I do not claim to be an indigenous person; rather, I am a practicing animist, cultivating Earth-honoring wisdoms.

Ancestors of the Past Two Thousand Years

When do your older ancestors first emerge in your awareness of history as distinct peoples? For me, this transition centers on the conquest and conversion of pre-Christian Europe by the Roman and later Christian empires. Before this, my ancestors lived by and large as tribal, indigenous people, and this is the stratum of my history that I most resonate with. If you are African-American, what do you know or imagine of the lives of your ancestors in the generations before the disruptions of the transatlantic slave trade? What about those ancestors who lived before the arrival of Christianity and Islam to sub-Saharan Africa? If you are a member of one of the hundreds of Native North American nations, do you have knowledge and a felt sense of the lives of your people before the arrival of Europeans to the continent? If your people hail from Asia, how much do you know of their history before regular European contact with Asia began in earnest in the sixteenth century?

The most psychologically influential of the forgotten dead are often those just beyond the reach of remembered names. You might consider these ancestors as forgotten by name but known to history. Their impact reverberates through shared culture and habits, historical and national identity, and body-level epigenetic influence. Insofar as the legacy of European colonialism over the past five centuries has been challenging for much of the world, this period of trouble continues to reverberate and inform many peoples' experiences of their ancestors in the present. But even if your people have experienced acute hardship over the past few centuries, be sure also to remember those who lived before these troubles and to not allow hardship to fully define your perception of your ancestors. Each of our bloodlines includes thousands of years of human history, with plenty of time spent as oppressor, oppressed, and every other configuration.

Individual, Lineage, and Collective Ancestors

Individual ancestral spirits are most often people we knew during their life on Earth. My grandparents and several friends who have passed are like this for me. Usually when people claim to talk to dead people, this is how they are experiencing the ancestors—as individual spirits who died sometime in the last century. Any ancestral spirit may be in a loving and peaceful state or in a state of restlessness and pain. The troubled dead usually appear as individual spirits. They may or may not be considered ancestors, as some reserve the term *ancestors* for those who are aware that they are dead and are reasonably well in spirit. The important distinction here is that you're relating to the spirit of one specific ancestor as opposed to a collective.

Lineage can be experienced as a kind of collective consciousness composed of the individual ancestral spirits in any given line. Recent family ancestors may take on the quality of lineage, such as a deceased parent who seems connected in spirit with their parents and grandparents. When the spirit of a recent ancestor merges with the greater lineage, communication through that ancestor, for example during a dream, can appear to be infused with the weight or authority of lineage and the feeling of being in the presence of a larger energy.

Lineage can also include older ancestral guides who present themselves as individual spirits. The family lineage repair process at the heart of this book (see chapters 5 through 9) calls for connecting with ancestral guides and working with them to make any needed repairs among both older and more recent family ancestors. For example, I have experienced connection with an ancestor along my paternal grandfather's line who lived in northern Europe about two thousand years ago. For me, this guide embodies lineage as a group consciousness, a face that the lineage puts on to facilitate dialogue with me. Behind the mask of the individual ancestor is the spirit of the lineage.

Just as individual spirits can present themselves as the face of a larger lineage, different ancestral lineages can be further harmonized into a collective embodiment of ancestral consciousness. In this way, lineage can function as an intermediate concept between the souls of recent individual ancestors and the collective dead. When the individual ancestors along your family bloodlines are vibrant and well in spirit, you have the possibility of harmonizing these different lineages in your body and experience (see chapter 9). Throughout this book, I weave relatively freely between a focus on individual spirits, ancestral lineages, and the collective dead. Different traditions and practitioners have their own styles and protocols for honoring these distinctions. If your family has a recent history of ancestor reverence, how do you understand the different types of human ancestors? If you practice a tradition that includes ancestor reverence, how does your path view the ancestors whose names are now forgotten?

Relating to Lineages and Older Ancestors

We can experience challenges when relating to our older ancestors. These include distrust in our ability to communicate safely with them, negative perceptions of our history, and unresolved issues among the ancestors themselves.

Because few people in the modern West were raised within a framework of relating to ancestors, I often hear questions such as: "How do I know I'm not making this all up?" This is an important question. Even those who talk to dead people on a regular basis recognize that it's possible to make things up, to think you're in connection when you're not, or to just be intuitively off the mark. One common concern centers on distinguishing imagination, fantasy, or daydreaming from spirit contact—a refinement that I've found comes only with a balance of faith and healthy skepticism, combined with practice over time. Remain patient as you gradually learn to trust your intuition when relating with the unseen realms, and see chapter 6 for further suggestions.

Another common concern is the fear of not being able to close a door once it is opened—a worry that talking with dead people either will lead others to see you as crazy or will actually destabilize your life. Talking to dead people, even if they're *your* dead people, does tend to raise a few eyebrows. And although it's not usually the case, it is entirely possible that such work will destabilize your life. Certain psychological conditions or backgrounds may not blend well with direct ancestor work; however, I rarely see people destabilized merely by engaging in practices to honor and get to know their loving ancestors.

Seeking to relate with older ancestors can bring to awareness previously unconscious, multigenerational avoidance of painful periods of family history. This can manifest as the rejection or devaluation of personal history and past, including holding certain groups as unforgiven and perhaps even unforgivable. Holding negative perceptions of ancestors (e.g., abusive people, soldiers on the wrong side of history, slave owners, zealots, conquistadors) highlights an opportunity for personal and cultural healing. Those we hold in judgment or contempt may already be well in spirit, in which case the work of forgiveness and reconciliation can proceed more easily. If you have reason to believe these ancestors whom you take issue with may be in a state of suffering themselves, connect first with loving and wise ancestral guides (see chapter 6).

What are the signs of healing and improved relations with your collective ancestors? For one, you may be more able to perceive their lives with greater clarity and compassion. In your own life, you may feel a greater sense of ancestral support and a willingness to engage and mend family and collective wounds. Remember: your loving and elevated ancestors have a vested interest in your well-being, and the more you begin to know them in the spirit of forgiveness, the more you can access (or draw upon) their support.

One of the best ways to honor these older ancestors is to transform inherited pain and dysfunction and to embody instead the blessings and gifts you inherit from your people. This includes mending collective wounds as they live in your family and communities and inside your own body and soul. Those committed to inner healing already know that family patterns, including the less helpful variety, can sometimes seem like "a gift that just keeps on giving." For example, the men along my father's lineage have not always been the most emotionally expressive people on Earth, and I am still reminded at times that I need to express my feelings more. Addictions or tendencies toward violence can also function as intergenerational legacies. If your ancestors struggled with alcohol, chances are someone in your family, or even you, will confront that same issue—and will either overcome it or succumb to it.

This chapter began with the question "Who are the ancestors?" To summarize, our ancestors include both the remembered dead and those ancestors whose names are forgotten. Both our recent and our older, collective ancestors influence our identity and sense of place in the world; ideally we will include both in our practices of ancestor reverence. While this book focuses on relationships with family ancestors, it's important to remember that we are all kin and that we all share common ancestry in Africa.

⟨∞⟩

EXERCISE ONE
How Do You Feel about Your Ancestors?

INTENT: Reflect personally or with a friend on what you know and how you feel about your ancestors

WHAT YOU NEED: A journal, someone you can talk with, or some way to express your reflections

Give yourself plenty of space to reflect on each set of questions, pausing also to make space for feelings, intuitions, and insights. This process of reflection and "taking inventory" is the groundwork for any subsequent engagement with your ancestors.

⟨∞⟩ Recent Family Ancestors ⟨∞⟩

Do you know the names of your ancestors? How many generations of your ancestors' names do you know? How does this knowledge or lack of knowledge feel? Are their names available to you from family members or through research?

What stories have you heard about your recent ancestors? Who from your family has shared stories about recent generations with you? How do these stories affect the way that you view these ancestors?

Have you visited the graves of your recent ancestors? If you know where they were buried (or memorialized) and you have visited these sites, did you take the opportunity to connect with them in spirit as well? If so, how was this for you?

Do you have any physical objects from their lives? Is there anything in your home or storage that physically links you to recent family ancestors? If so, how do you feel about these objects and their place in your life today?

How well do you know the history of your people over the last few centuries? Have you sought to better understand the life and times of your recent ancestors? From your knowledge, in what ways has recent ancestral history shaped your family, circumstances, and worldview?

Is there anything that needs to be forgiven between you and your recent ancestors? Are your feelings toward your ancestors mostly positive, mostly negative, or somewhere in between? How would you feel about the opportunity to meet with them directly? Are there issues that feel unresolved, unforgiven, or otherwise in need of repair?

∞∞ Ancestors of History and Prehistory ∞∞

What do you know of the story of your ancestors over the past two thousand years? At what point does your record of names give way to groupings of people and historical speculation about lineage? Among the people you claim, how well do you know their story? Have you explored the time when your ancestors lived in traditional, tribal ways?

What do you know of your ancestors' traditions and ways of life? Have you connected on an intuitive, heart level with the ways of life your people practiced before industrialization and modernity? How about before the time of the major organized religions? Do any of these older ways still inform your approach to spirit or to life in the present?

Have you visited or do you live on the lands of some older ancestors? If you traveled to some of your ancestral lands, how was this for you? If you still live there, how does this inform your experience of home, your sense of place, and your feeling of rootedness?

Do you have anything in your daily life that connects you to these ancestors? In addition to the DNA in each cell of your body, what physical things, practices, symbols, movies, songs, or interests still connect you to these older ancestors?

How do you feel about being descended from these people? Do you feel proud, ashamed, inspired, or indifferent about your older ancestors? How do your current culture, community, and family view your ancestral people? If you got to choose your ancestors, would you choose the same ones?

Is there anything that needs to be forgiven between you and your older ancestors? Are there historical actions that cause you to judge them? Do you identify more with certain ancestors because of these judgments? If so, have you ever explored the possibility of forgiveness and reconciliation with your less valued ancestors?

THREE

SPONTANEOUS ANCESTRAL CONTACT

Communication between the living and the dead can be intentionally cultivated, or it can happen spontaneously. Either type of contact can be helpful, harmful, or both. The ancestors contact people who affirm their reality, but the dead may also appear to those who don't believe in ancestors or an afterlife.

In this chapter, you'll learn about different types of unsolicited contact from the dead, including dream visitations, synchronicities, and waking encounters in both ordinary and nonordinary states of consciousness. Examples include both helpful and harmful types of contact, as well as some ways to respond to them. The exercise at the end of this chapter can help you assess your own experiences and beliefs about the ancestors and their role in your life.

Dream Contact

Many people who have lost a loved one eventually dream of their beloved dead. Some of these dreams are accompanied by the impression of actually meeting with the spirit of the deceased. When uplifting, they can center on reconnection with the ancestors, personal healing, and receiving helpful messages about the present. Unfortunately, not all dreams of the dead are uplifting. If you accept that some of the dead—most likely including some of your own ancestors—are not yet at peace and that they too may contact you in dreams, you have the perfect recipe for a nightmare involving creepy dead people.

If you have dreamt of a departed loved one and felt that you were in contact with their spirit during the dream, it's possible that you were. If they seemed well in spirit, simply being open to positive contact supports ongoing relationship and is a way of honoring them. You may want to acknowledge the encounter in some way while you are awake and in this way continue to work with the dream. For example, you might make a simple offering to them (e.g., prayer, candle, libations) or experiment with following their guidance, provided it does not radically contradict common sense. If you remain receptive to contact with the loving ancestors during your dreams, you will keep at least one channel of communication open with them.

Not all dreams of the dead involve a sense of actually meeting the deceased. When you have such a dream, ask yourself upon waking if it was accompanied by a sense of direct contact. If not, what might the dream be asking you to see? Are you being asked to understand, forgive, or celebrate something about your connection with the deceased? Is this person appearing as a reflection of some aspect of you? If so, what are your dreams inviting you to understand about yourself and about your relationship with this person?

What happens if you dream (or have nightmares) of the troubled dead, those who have not yet joined the ancestors? Unsettling dreams might include a sense that the deceased is lost, suffering, or somehow threatening the living. Strangers or spirits connected to a specific location may also appear more as ghosts than as elevated ancestors. If dreams such as these come with a sense of contact, after considering what may be your own unresolved issues with the figure in the dream, you may choose to make prayers, dedicate offerings, direct positive energy, and even conduct healing rituals for the elevation of these ancestors (see chapter 8, page 148). If you meditate or pray, see the deceased in the light of clarity and compassion, and visualize them surrounded by healing light, receiving whatever they may need from their supportive ancestors. If you do these or similar practices, notice your dreams and try to intuit what actions or offerings can help resolve the situation. If you choose to dedicate offerings and ritual to such souls, respect your own energetic boundaries and personal space and know how to close the door to their energy when you need to. Helping the dead become elevated ancestors is honorable work, but you want to do it in a way that is both effective for the deceased and safe for the living. Seek the help of an experienced guide or teacher when you need it.

Synchronicity

Popularized by the Swiss psychiatrist Carl Jung, the term *synchronicity* refers to two or more events that are meaningfully related but which otherwise would be unlikely to occur.[1] Suppose, for example, that your deceased partner loved lilacs, and on the anniversary of her death you're on the front porch having a drink and feeling sad. At that moment your new neighbor walks over to share with you, out of the blue, that she's thinking of planting a lilac bush and asks if you like lilacs. You feel a wave of energy pass through your body and sense that something magical is happening, a temporary drawing close of the worlds. You reply that yes, you like lilacs. Even though you have not experienced your partner as a spirit, after the conversation you're left with a sense, against all logic, that she has reached out to comfort you.

In this example, the ancestors are speaking through an unlikely event that involves a striking convergence of meaning. Songs on the radio, written signs and messages, spontaneous animal encounters, and signs in nature are only a few of the ways in which the world around us can respond to some aspect of our inner life and generate a meaningful event. For me, noticing a synchronicity feels like déjà vu in that it's never anything I can predict, and the initial feeling doesn't tend to last too long. Nevertheless, I am more inclined to ascribe meaning to synchronicities than to déjà vu experiences. Synchronicities for me are also more likely to be accompanied by a sense of contact with or communication from another being or force, such as the ancestors.

Sometimes dream contact and synchronicity can blend, or a series of synchronicities can unfold in a short span of time. When I was getting to know my mother's ancestors, I received an old Bible in the mail that belonged to my great-uncle John and included a death certificate for his niece Maude. This led to conversations with living family members about their relationship, and I learned about a child born from the complicated union of these two related ancestors. This prompted me to do ritual healing and prayer for their well-being, which seemed well received. Around this time I also dreamt of this great-uncle John's father, my great-great-grandpa Ressin Litton. In the dream he had a distinctive handlebar moustache. Several days later, to my surprise, photos arrived of him in the mail from relatives back in Pennsylvania. Recalling the dream, I paused before I opened the envelope. When I saw the picture of Ressin Litton with a handlebar moustache, it was a magical moment—one that aligned the family research I had done with my experiences of dream contact, ancestor ritual, and of course synchronicity.

One way to support contact with the ancestors through synchronicity is to develop a shared vocabulary of symbols with them. For example, if you associate your favorite grandmother with crows and ravens, the color red, the Virgin Mary, the direction of south, and the number six, this creates common symbols or associations that your grandmother can use to get your attention. You can't force synchronicities, but having this shared symbolic language with the ancestors can encourage you to stay open to this type of contact over time.

Keep in mind that there are also risks when reading too deeply into signs and events in the world around us or focusing too much on synchronicity. One way to reduce the risk of confusion is to have several different ways in which you can reliably communicate with your ancestors (e.g., dream contact, waking meditation, divination). This allows you to more easily cross-check the guidance and messages you receive.

For example, if you believe your ancestors are telling you to buy a new house or end your marriage, you will want to first run this suggestion by your own common sense. It also helps to talk with trusted friends and advisors, ask your ancestors for a confirmation dream, or use any other way to get a second opinion before acting.

Waking Contact in Nonordinary States

Ordinary waking consciousness is the type of awareness in which you likely spend most of your time. It enables you to navigate physical reality and operate as a functional person. The distinction between ordinary and nonordinary or altered states of consciousness is blurry at times, and there are many types of nonordinary states of waking consciousness. These shifts in awareness can be associated with physical exertion (e.g., sports, exercise, dance), intoxicants (e.g., alcohol, psychoactive medicines, pharmaceuticals), meditation, states of artistic and scientific inspiration, sex, hunting, combat, and some types of ritual. Such states are occasionally accompanied by an encounter with some kind of presence or force. Sometimes this presence is clearly identifiable as the spirit of the ancestors.

Clinical death is one type of nonordinary state often associated with spontaneous ancestral contact. Accounts from those who have near-death experiences (NDEs) suggest that consciousness and memory may continue after brain activity and other vital signs have ceased—which some regard as evidence for continuity of consciousness after death. Many who have NDEs report encountering beings of light, angels, or some kind of benevolent presence, and some of these accounts include meetings with family ancestors.

If you have had ancestors spontaneously visit you while you are in some nonordinary or altered state of consciousness, the first thing to know is that this is a relatively common experience (and usually doesn't mean you're going crazy). Second, you want to be sure that you're mostly engaging with loving, evolved ancestors and not with the troubled dead.

How can you tell the difference? If your sense of the encounter was positive, you're likely relating with the supportive ancestors or elevated dead. You can then attempt to extend that energy to an ordinary waking state of consciousness by reconnecting with these ancestors or with what was positive from the original encounter. For example, if you have had an NDE and now feel at peace about dying, you could draw on that experience to comfort others who feel afraid to die. When you can extend the goodness from one state or experience into other aspects of your life, it helps ground your contact with spirit by improving your life and the lives of others.

If you have an unexpected meeting with the spirits of the dead and you feel ambivalent or disturbed about it afterward, it's possible that you encountered the troubled dead. Consult your personal instinct to determine if any spirit is basically loving and well intended. As a general guideline, if your contact with a spirit doesn't feel intuitively right to you or feels as if it's hindering you from becoming a better person, consider stepping back from the connection and getting a second opinion. Again, it's important to establish clear boundaries with not-yet-ancestors, as their energy can be a source of disruption. To learn more about ways to accomplish this, see "Considerations before Working Directly with Your Ancestors" in chapter 5 (page 79).

Waking Encounters in Ordinary States

Sometimes, at the strangest moments, even for those who don't believe in spirits, the dead just appear. No grand entry; they're just lying in bed next to us in the morning, sitting next to us in the car, beside us while we're working. Sometimes these encounters can be subtle and are dismissed as imagination or fantasy. Often they are not even visual or auditory—it is merely a matter of feeling their presence for a moment. For those with a strong link with the unseen realms, such visits may be relatively common and are not necessarily charged with any more meaning than a phone call from a friend. For those who don't have a habit of talking with dead people or don't believe they exist, unsolicited visits from the ancestors can be frightening.

Children in particular are well known for talking to the dead as if it's no big deal. Popular movies like *The Sixth Sense, Poltergeist, Casper, Pan's Labyrinth,* and the Harry Potter films, as well as TV shows such as *Psychic Kids* and *Medium,* all feature dialogue between children and the dead. Many people in spiritual circles view young children as being more intuitive and open to the otherworld because they are recent arrivals to Earth. Some of these children grow up to be talented psychics and mediums, and many well-known intuitives (e.g., George Anderson, Sylvia Browne, José Ortiz, Danielle Egnew) claim that their gifts were present from an early age, even if there was little support for them from the surrounding culture.

In some cultures, community elders recognize children's ability to communicate with the ancestors early on and encourage the children to develop this gift over the course of their lives. Part of the magic of the Harry Potter series is the way in which children with an aptitude for magic are recruited and trained for relationship with other realms. The series also warns against repressing the magical aspects in the lives of children and in ourselves. If you find yourself in an environment that condemns your experience of communicating with the ancestors, you can continue to honor your personal truth and seek supportive human and spirit allies. If you are a parent or if you work with children, stay open and curious if they report talking with the dead.

Another group of people who tend to report lucid contact with the dead is people who know or believe they are imminently dying. Accounts of the dying process commonly mention the dying patient being in dialogue with those who are already deceased. Those who die in a lucid state sometimes say that they are being joined before their passing by departed loved ones and ancestors. Those with dementia or debilitating illness may also experience moments of speaking with or for the dead, at times with striking accuracy.

If you find that dead people are talking to you (and you're not doing lots of drugs), here are my suggestions for how to proceed:

1. Start by ruling out any kind of mental or physical illness, and make sure you feel good about exploring the connection.
2. Identify at least one person in your life with whom you can share your experiences without fear of judgment.
3. Remember that contact with ancestors is recognized by many different religious systems. If you follow a tradition that does this, it may be a source of support for relating to the ancestors.
4. If your contact with the ancestors feels supportive, loving, and helpful, find ways to honor them.
5. If the dead people contacting you are not friendly or if you want the contact to stop, you can clearly request that it stop. That is often sufficient to close the door.
6. If this doesn't work, reach out for support and do whatever helps you stay grounded, healthy, and in balance while you sort out your relationships with the ancestors.

Although you may not personally experience spontaneous contact with the ancestors, you may find yourself in the position of supporting others who have. For example, health professionals of all sorts may have contact with children, the dying, those in altered states of consciousness, and practitioners of traditions that honor the ancestors. The more supportive and open-minded you are when someone confides in you about such an experience, the more helpful you can be.

∽

EXERCISE TWO
What Are Your Experiences with Your Ancestors?

INTENT: Reflect personally or with a friend on ways that you already relate with your ancestors

WHAT YOU NEED: A journal, someone you can talk with, or some way to express your reflections

Give yourself plenty of space to reflect on each set of questions, pausing also to make space for feelings, intuitions, and insights. This process of reflection and "taking inventory" is the groundwork for any subsequent engagement with your ancestors.

怀 SPONTANEOUS ANCESTRAL CONTACT 怀

Have you ever dreamt of the dead in ways that felt like contact? If so, what helps you distinguish between dreams of contact and personal, noncontact dreams of the deceased? Has the quality of the dreams been uplifting, troubling, or both?

Have you ever felt that the ancestors are trying to get your attention through events? If so, are there certain associations they speak through (e.g., songs, animals, plants, places)? When you feel they are speaking to you, do you respond and engage in dialogue or just notice? Are these moments peaceful, upsetting, or mixed?

Have you ever had a near-death experience, serious accident, or life-threatening illness that was accompanied by a sense of ancestral contact? If so, what role do you feel the ancestors played in this process? Have you ever felt that the ancestors protected you from danger? Has anyone close to you ever shared this kind of experience with you?

Have the ancestors ever spontaneously contacted you during your waking life? If so, were you in an altered or an ordinary state of consciousness? Was this frightening, comforting, or something normal for you? Have you ever felt that the ancestors were guiding you to a certain location or acting to influence events in your life?

怀 WAYS OF RELATING TO SPONTANEOUS 怀 ANCESTRAL CONTACT

How do you feel about the possibility of unsolicited ancestral contact? On a basic level, are you at peace with the possibility of the dead contacting you? What messages have you received about this from your family, religious tradition, and culture of origin?

If you believe they have contacted you, how did you respond? After initial contact, did you express openness to further contact, set a clear boundary, or do neither? If you requested that contact stop, why? If you are open to further contact, have you pursued this actively?

Have you shared your experiences of ancestral contact with anyone? If so, how was it received? Do you have a friend or mentor you could share with if needed? Has anyone ever shared these kinds of experiences with you? If so, how did you respond?

Have you learned skills for navigating contact with the dead? Has anyone, in person or through books, ever shared with you ways of safely responding to ancestral contact? If so, did these skills help you know how to respond to your own experiences?

FOUR

ANCESTOR
REVERENCE
AND RITUAL

There are many ways to relate to your ancestors. Many of these fall into the category of ancestor reverence. *Ancestor reverence* refers to ways of living and worshipping that recognize and honor the human dead as one important type of person or force in the larger web of relations. Traditions of ancestor reverence are especially prevalent in animist, shamanistic, and indigenous communities. Religions such as Christianity and Buddhism (as well as many secular cultures) also communicate respect to the spirits of the deceased, even if these groups do not always identify themselves as practitioners of ancestor reverence per se.

Ancestor rituals are practices or events that often bring the living and the dead into a state of heightened contact. These rituals or ceremonies are often guided by those with both an interest in and a common ritual language for relating to the ancestors. Although contacting your ancestors does not require you to adopt any specific belief or identity, studying established traditions of ancestor reverence and ritual can give you more context and support for making contact yourself.

Common Intentions for Ancestor Rituals

We are bonded with the ancestors as life to death, light to shadow. The choice is not whether or not to be in relationship with them, but whether or not these relationships will be conscious and reciprocal. Ancestor-focused rituals are one way to relate more consciously to the dead and to advocate for our interests and for the well-being of our family and our world. One reason for engaging the ancestors is to more fully receive their support in our everyday lives. Another reason is to extend support to the troubled dead. Furthermore, the ancestors can play important roles in maintaining religious or secular traditions as well as in navigating the transitions of human life. Although styles and forms vary from culture to culture, even among practitioners within the same tradition, this section surveys some of the most recurrent types.

Rituals to Seek and Maintain Ancestral Support

The loving and wise ancestors (also called *ancestral guides* or *elevated ancestors*) wish well for their living descendants, and many ancestor rituals emphasize bringing blessings, healing, and guidance from these ancestors into this dimension. (See chapters 6 and 9 for examples of these types of rituals.) Rituals that connect us to ancestral guides promote healing and alignment with personal destiny. Staying open to the ancestors also functions as an early warning system that protects the living from unnecessary hardship, illness, or premature death. Rituals to maintain these relationships feature in holidays such as the Celtic Samhain, the Mexican Day of the Dead, and the Japanese Obon festival. At other times of the year, communities may call upon ancestors for guidance and healing during rituals of mediumship, possession and embodiment, oracular work, or divination. Drawing down (or raising up, if you prefer) the loving ancestors may occur in regular maintenance rituals or in times of crisis or celebration. Tending to the relationship in an ongoing way is probably the most common reason for calling upon them.

Rituals to Assist the Troubled Dead

Ghosts, the troubled dead, earthbound spirits, and other types of not-yet-ancestors can be a source of illness, distress, and other problems for the living, so there are rituals to address these concerns. Chapters 7 and 8 detail ways to elevate and assist the spirits of the dead when they are not already well in spirit. If ghosts have become attached to a location, the living can perform house blessings and other rituals to address the disturbance. They may also help the spirit of the deceased join the loving ancestors.

At the more intense end of the spectrum, when the troubled dead attach themselves to a living person rather than to a specific place, a full exorcism may be needed to untangle the spirit of the deceased from the living. A ritual to enable the deceased to make the transition generally follows, and the energy body of the living client may be cleansed and repaired if necessary. Exorcism practices in Christianity, Islam, Hinduism, and many other traditions typically acknowledge that one common type of troublesome spirit may be that of a human ghost. Communal ceremonies such as the annual Hungry Ghost Festival in traditional Chinese culture seek to convey care and compassion to the less peaceful dead through remembrance, offerings, prayer, and other practices.

Rituals with Ancestors of Lineage and Place

My emphasis on blood and family leads me to view engagement with nonfamily ancestors as ritually distinct. Nevertheless, some individuals may find the distinctions between ancestors of family, spiritual lineage, and place to be blurred or even irrelevant.

Most religions have some element of spiritual lineage that is not necessarily based on blood ancestry (e.g., the dharma lineages of Buddhism, the chain of transmission in Islamic Sufi orders, the guru lineages of Hinduism). These ancestors embody the tradition's teachings. They may be called upon during regular spiritual practice as well as during rites of passage and initiations. Lineage may also revolve more around vocation than religious identity; for example, woodcarvers may call for inspiration upon famous woodcarvers, scientists may be visited in dreams by deceased scientists, and living leaders may experience themselves in a succession of previous leaders, most of whom are now ancestral advisors. (See chapter 11 for rituals to honor ancestors of spiritual and vocational lineage.)

Ancestors of place include the spirits of anyone who has lived and died in a specific area. Even if they are not related by blood or culture, these ancestors are relevant because of their proximity and their relationship with the land. Cemeteries and burial grounds are natural places to contact ancestors of place. For example, in the San Francisco Bay Area, ancestors of the land include California Indian peoples (e.g., Ohlone, Coast Miwok, Bay Miwok, Mishewal Wappo), as well as Spanish, Russian, British, African, Asian, and other immigrants from the past 250 years. Ritual work with such ancestors may include respectfully calling upon those who lived and died in a place as a source of wisdom about local medicines and other issues that affect the land. Rituals may also invite local ancestors to participate in acts of remedy and repair in places of historic disturbance. (The peace tree ceremony shared in chapter 10 is one example from Buryat Mongol culture of a ritual focused on ancestors of place.) Also, for any individual or group entering a new place—especially to settle or conduct a ritual—indigenous protocols encourage people to relate as consciously and directly as possible with both the earlier and current human inhabitants. These protocols may include approaching the living elders of local communities or, if this is not possible, humbly seeking ritual permission directly from the ancestors. At the very least, one should humbly acknowledge the spirits of earlier human inhabitants.

Life Transition Rituals

Life transitions include births, rites of passage into adulthood, marriages, possibly transitions into elder status, and deaths. Nearly all cultures acknowledge these transitions with ritual. People may call upon the ancestors to bless or preside over these transitions, as each transition is a kind of symbolic (or literal) death and change of communal status. Children are a recent arrival from the realm of the unseen or the ancestors, and as such, birth-related blessings may include a ritualized release of the newborn from the realm of the ancestors into this earthly dimension. Marriage is an act that draws two lineages closer, and the union may proceed more easily when the couple or family consults with the ancestors of each partner and secures their blessings. Death is perhaps the most common time for rituals that explicitly invoke the ancestors. The living may call upon wise and loving lineage ancestors to escort the recently deceased through the post-death realms and may imagine or sense the recently deceased to be reunited with already transitioned loved ones. Chapter 12 includes suggestions for crafting rituals to call upon ancestral support for the dying and recently deceased, as well as ways to incorporate ancestral support into funeral practices.

Practices to Sustain Ancestral Connection

Ancestor-focused rituals include living humans, the spirits of the deceased, and potentially any number of other beings. This section outlines some of the most recurrent types of practice that comprise the bulk of the rituals in this book. In the kitchen of ancestor reverence, these are the ingredients that I see as staples, and they appear in most rituals that I cook up.

Ancestor Altars, Shrines, and Consecrated Spaces
Setting sacred spaces for ancestors may include setting a place at the dinner table or keeping a chair or space in the circle open for them. Symbolically, among other things, this communicates, "We (living humans) recognize that you (ancestors) exist, and we welcome you." Such sacred spaces may be individual or communal, and they may be permanently established or may exist only for the duration of one ritual. Permanent communal spaces to honor the dead include cemeteries and

any sacred space that arises around the remains of a famous ancestor (e.g., the Mosque of the Prophet (al-Masjid an-Nabawi), in Medina, Saudi Arabia—see plate 10—or the Buddhist Temple of the Sacred Tooth Relic in Kandy, Sri Lanka). Monuments to important groups of ancestors (e.g., those who died in the transatlantic slave trade, the unknown war dead, those who died in the Holocaust) also function as places to seat or remember the ancestors (see chapter 10).

On a personal or household level, ancestor shrines may be as modest as a special shelf in a small closed cabinet, or they may be as elaborate as a separate ceremonial room or structure. Ritually, the household shrine serves as a focal point for communication with family ancestors and as a reminder of their presence in everyday life. Personally, I have tended an ancestor shrine the size of a small table for over a decade. The surface of my altar includes such offerings as fire, incense, flowers, and water, along with prayer bundles and ancestral *ongons* (see chapter 6, page 112 for more on this), some divining tools (e.g., Tarot cards, runes, shells), instruments, and other miscellaneous medicines. If you decide to dedicate a space to honor your people, try to avoid locating the shrine in your bedroom or, if you have no other choice, to find some way to contain the energy when sleeping (for example, a closed cabinet, a cloth over the shrine). If you have photographs of the dead, I personally only recommend including them on your altar if you know those ancestors are well in spirit, the photos don't also include the living, and your ancestors say that they'd like their photos on the shrine. Ultimately, trust your guidance and intuition about what will inspire you to connect with your loving ancestors.

With respect to community ritual, necessity often drives creativity and is informed by materials available at the time. In rituals in which I have taken part, we have used a simple table or even a patch of earth covered with images of the dead, as well as candles, incense, offerings, and other consecrated items to serve as the ancestors' place of honor. In nature, special trees, stones, or other exceptional formations may function as living shrines for generations stretching back through time—or for the duration of an afternoon. In all cases, the principle is the same: the living tell the ancestors that they are welcome and that they continue to live and speak in this dimension.

Inspired Speech, Prayer, Invocation, and Song

It's not a party unless the guests show up, so effective ancestor-focused ritual requires that the spirits of the dead attend in some form or another. On the most basic level, simply asking them to be present can go a long way. Even if I have no shrine and have nothing physical to offer them, if I just start speaking to my ancestors, telling them how much I love them, and how nice it would be to have them join me for ritual, this heartfelt invitation greatly increases the chances of their arrival. When they feel present in spirit or even when they are simply in my field of awareness as memories, I may speak aloud in a spontaneous and inspired way. (Of course it's necessary to keep in mind the reactions I may get from nearby living humans who hear me talking to dead people.)

Prayer involving the ancestors may include words of praise and appreciation as well as specific requests. Some styles of invocation follow an established pattern of naming lineage ancestors and may include traditional, formulaic ways of calling the dead that are repeated from one ritual to the next and from one generation to the next. Songs and chants for the ancestors have the same underlying intent. Song may invoke their presence and function as a direct prayer, or it may simply enhance the felt intimacy and connection with the beloved dead. Many traditions have a body of ancestor-honoring songs. Many practitioners, including me, believe that the ancestors respond to emotional energy and sincere intent. Hence popular songs, songs the deceased may recognize, and heartfelt improvised vocalization can all open pathways of connection with the ancestors.

Offerings of Substance and Beauty

At the heart of the practice of making offerings is the spirit of reciprocity and remembrance: we give to acknowledge the gift of life and to ensure the flow of ongoing ancestral support. Whether through elaborate feasts or by simply pouring out a little of our drink to the Earth as a libation, many cultures honor the ancestors with food and drink. Other traditional offerings include candles, incense, flowers, stones, shells, ash, pollen, seeds, baskets, bones, currency, photographs, beautiful cloth, and handmade creations. Those with an established practice of ancestor reverence often present offerings to the dead at places of heightened ancestral contact, such as personal altars, community monuments, the location of deaths (e.g., roadside shrines), or places of burial. Less physical offerings may include songs, stories, poetry, prayers, inspired actions, vows, ritual performances, dedicated acts of service, charitable contributions, or any other gesture of beauty, love, and respect. As with gifts for the living, offerings to the ancestors tend to include some type of explanation, personal sharing, or other way of addressing the dead.

One specific way in which I invite group ritual participants to make offerings to the ancestors is through the South American practice of the *despacho*. Originating among the indigenous Quechua-speaking peoples of the Peruvian, Ecuadorian, and Bolivian Andes, despacho ceremonies include heartfelt prayers and abundant offerings layered into a ceremonial bundle that is then typically delivered to the spirits by burning it in a sacred fire. The intention of the despacho ceremonies can vary widely, and in my experience with ancestor-focused despachos the coupling of specific prayers with and for the ancestors together with nourishing offerings and ritualized beauty seems to be especially well received by the beloved dead. When possible, favor local, thoughtful, and ecologically sensitive offerings for your ritual work. (See plates 2 to 5.)

Communication through Meditation, Trance, and Direct Intuition

As stated in chapter 3, the living may experience direct contact with spirits of the deceased at any time, with no prior intent to connect and no context for speaking with them. Rather than waiting for the ancestors to approach us, practitioners sometimes seek contact with them in a variety of ways, any one of which may be combined with the ritual elements explored above. One strategy includes quieting the heart and mind in order to trigger a shift in consciousness, which allows us to hear ancestral spirits more clearly. Practices that can support this shift include meditation, contemplation, vision quests, fasting, retreats, and other ways of removing external distractions. Sensory overload may achieve a similar purpose. Examples of practices on the ecstatic end of the spectrum include sonic driving (e.g., drumming, rattling), intensive song and dance, psychological and physical ordeals, and the intentional use of psychoactive substances.*

I suggest experimenting with different practices to gain a greater understanding of the perceptual channels that are naturally strongest for you—and the ones that could benefit from further development. In my case, I am naturally visual and fairly strong with dreaming, I am moderately empathic, and I tend to get information through a kind of direct knowing that, if I'm not careful, I can overlook as simply random thoughts. Through effort and practice, I have developed the ability to quiet my mind and more fully access the wisdom of my body as another intuitive channel.

Those who relate regularly to the ancestors may more simply engage in shifts of attention while remaining in ordinary states of consciousness as they converse with the dead. Psychics, mediums, and those with years of experience often report little to no alteration in their baseline awareness when in contact with the spirits. Just as I do not need to be deep in trance to talk with a friend on the phone, I don't necessarily need to be in an altered state to talk with my ancestors. At this level, the practice is simply that of noticing, testing, and trusting over time the clarity of the connection—and then, in the moment, just picking up the receiver to listen and speak. Intuitive multitaskers may converse

---

*Consciousness-altering substances are not necessary for ritual work or ancestral engagement. In addition to legal and health risks, entheogens, psychoactive plants, and similar substances are a poor choice for some temperaments and settings.

with the living about mundane topics while carrying on silent conversations with the ancestors. Individuals with this capacity often favor simpler, less formalized styles of ritual.

Divination, Dreamwork, and Interpreting Signs

Divination can vary in meaning. Some use the term to refer to any process of consulting with spirit allies, while others associate divination with predicting the future. For others still, divination is an elaborate symbolic system for diagnosing and treating all manner of life challenges. The ancestors may speak in any of these ways. In any event, we can communicate with the dead through symbols with culturally predetermined meanings, including established systems of divination. For example, when asking yes-no questions, practitioners of the Ifá Òrìṣà tradition of Yorùbá-speaking West Africa and the African diaspora often use either the divided parts of a four-lobed kola nut or a substitute (e.g., pieces of coconut or cowrie shells). When the diviner determines that a question is best directed to the ancestors, after asking them to be present and clarifying the question, the diviner throws the four pieces of kola or kola substitute to arrive typically at one of five to eight possible outcomes. Some outcomes or throws are interpreted as a type of "yes," and others as a type of "'no." Other common examples of yes-no divinations methods include coin flips; pendulums; some stone, bone, or card systems; and plucking petals from flowers ("she loves me, she loves me not").

Most divination systems involve far more complexity than yes-no questions, and more elaborate practices may involve invocations, prayers, offerings, shrines, and spontaneous spirit contact. For example, the Tarot has seventy-eight cards, the *I Ching* sixty-four hexagrams, and the Norse oracle twenty-four commonly used runes. Mayan, Aztec, and other indigenous traditions from Central America use elaborate day-keeping and world-ordering systems, some with 260 (13 × 20) primary energy configurations. The Ifá/Òrìṣà system works with 256 (16 × 16) different energy patterns or outcomes. Each system has certain patterns that refer more strongly to the ancestors. When these energies speak, it falls to the diviner to understand what the ancestors wish to convey.

Dreams can also give rise to rich practices of interpretation and ritual. Carl Jung and other depth psychologists agree with indigenous elders that dreams can be cultivated as a potent avenue for insight as well as for direct contact with larger forces such as our ancestors. In addition to learning to interpret dreams on a symbolic level, some teachers encourage the cultivation of lucid dreaming (becoming conscious of dreaming during the dream), as well as the practice of meeting with ancestors or guides during dreams. Dreams of the dead may serve to confirm ritual work performed while awake, bring attention to concerns that need to be addressed during the waking time, or simply function as another type of ancestral contact.

As mentioned in chapter 3, the ancestors may speak through unsolicited synchronicities—meaning-charged events that include the felt presence of the dead. The same skills used in dream work can apply to interpreting these signs and events. Those seeking ancestral contact can make themselves more available for these types of synchronicities during waking consciousness by emphasizing "as if I am dreaming" awareness at certain times or places. Ritual spaces inherently attract such meaning-charged events. For example, wilderness or vision quests are increasingly popular in North America and often include multiple-day solo retreats in the natural world with periods of fasting from food, water, and/or contact with others. During quests, events such as animal encounters, weather, or other movements of nature often take on heightened meaning. A branch that falls or a bird that appears while a quester is thinking about a deceased family member may be a way for that ancestor to confirm their presence and initiate a waking dialogue. Visits to places special to the ancestors (e.g., burial places, former dwellings, sacred sites), dedicated time with family, and events surrounding the birth and death of family members are all more likely to attract ancestral contact. If one adopts a more relaxed attention that allows for symbolic communication with the ancestors, any moment can become a time of direct and intimate contact. This capacity to read the movement of spirit and the presence of the ancestors into waking events is something that develops slowly over many years of ritual, dream work, and introspection.

∞

EXERCISE THREE

RITUAL TO INITIATE CONTACT WITH YOUR ANCESTORS

INTENT: Offer a ritual to thank and invite more conscious contact with your ancestors

WHAT YOU NEED: A quiet space and whatever helps you connect with your ancestors

∞ SETTING RITUAL INTENT ∞

As with any ritual, **clarifying your intent** is critical and informs everything that follows. In this case, I suggest setting an intention to initiate conscious contact with loving and supportive family ancestors, at a level of intensity that is helpful for you at this time. If you already feel that you are in contact with your ancestors, you may modify the intent to renewing relations and inviting their ongoing support and guidance. I suggest staying open about whether the contact will come from recent or more distant ancestors (or both); however, be clear that you are only seeking contact at this time from loving and helpful ancestors.

After settling on the ritual intent, I often follow a **basic progression** or plan that supports spontaneity, creativity, and spirit contact. For this ritual, I suggest the following:

1. Choose a sacred space.
2. Directly address your loving and supportive ancestors.
3. Make offerings.
4. Spend time in open, receptive awareness.
5. Bring the ritual to a close.

You can move through this progression in a focused half hour or expand it into a half day. You can offer the ritual alone or with family and friends.

⠶⠶ Initiating Contact ⠶⠶

1. **Choose a sacred space**—a quiet place in nature or somewhere clean, private, and peaceful in or near your home. If you already have a place for honoring your ancestors, you can focus the ritual there. If not, the space you choose does not need to become your permanent ancestor shrine. It can simply serve as a focal point for the duration of the ritual. You can form the base of a simple altar with a colorful cloth, a candle, a glass of water, incense, or a special stone. You may include photographs of the ancestors, but if you're not sure that those pictured are well in spirit, don't include any images.

2. Center yourself physically and emotionally. This may include meditation, personal prayer, or unstructured movement, or it may just be a pause to remember your intent. When you feel ready, **directly address your loving and supportive ancestors**, aloud if possible, silently if necessary. If you are not sure that your recent ancestors are well in spirit, call out only to older generations, whose personal names are now forgotten. Introduce yourself and speak from the heart about why you are reaching out to them. You may want to invite their support into your life and the lives of your family, asking them to help heal family troubles or to elevate the recently deceased. Or you may simply wish to get to know the ancestors for the sake of relationship and intimacy. Your invocation could include spontaneous singing, toning, or chanting. Continue until you feel complete or sense that they have heard your call.

3. In circle now with the ancestors, **make offerings** on or near the altar space you have established. Common offerings include any food or drink you believe they may enjoy, flowers, incense, personal artwork or crafts, and natural objects. Offerings may be made before invocations, during the heart of a ritual, or toward the end. In this particular sequence you are invoking the ancestors before making a gesture of goodwill and sincerity. When you present the offerings, you may share why you brought what

you did. Remember that a glass of water offered from the heart will have greater impact than an elaborate ritual meal lacking in emotional connection.

4. After presenting your offerings, **spend some time in a receptive and open awareness**. This could consist of five minutes lying on the ground with your eyes closed, a half hour of some kind of creative process, or an afternoon of solo time in nature. The point is to assume an open and curious mind that allows for any echo of response from the ancestors. If being still is a relatively new practice for you, I recommend taking a little time to do nothing on an outer level, to daydream while gently listening to your intuition. If messages come through, you may record them for later review.

5. When you feel complete, **bring the ritual to a close** with a simple prayer, thanks, or acknowledgment that you are done for now. This may include extinguishing a candle or returning any natural, biodegradable offerings to the Earth. If you have a regular shrine, you may let the offerings rest there for a few days or until you sense they are complete before returning them to the Earth, if possible. In the days or weeks after ritual, stay open to further communication from the ancestors—through dreams, synchronicities, and other kinds of contact. Sometimes a ritual may seem relatively simple but sets in motion forces that play out in our lives for years to come.

Part Two

HEALING WITH
LINEAGE
AND
FAMILY
ANCESTORS

P art 2 presents a framework and exercises to support direct engagement with loving and wise ancestors for the intention of personal, family, and lineage healing. In part 2 you will be invited to:

- Greet ancestral guides and other elevated ancestors
- Practice transforming ancestral burdens and claiming ancestral gifts
- Seek emotional healing and forgiveness with your ancestors
- Assist the dead who are not at peace to join the loving ancestors
- Embody the support of ancestral guides while praying for the living family

The middle third of this book is a guidebook for relating directly and safely to the ancestors as well as to the troubled dead. Please read all of part 2 (chapters 5 through 9) and check in with your own intuition before initiating lineage repair work or attempting the exercises. If you do choose to work with this approach, take it slow, stay grounded, and reach out for help when you need to. If in doubt, focus only on relating with your loving and wise ancestors.

FIVE

FAMILY RESEARCH AND INITIATING ANCESTRAL HEALING

It can be helpful to begin by gathering what is already known about your family history before directly engaging the spirits of your ancestors. Step one begins with gathering information from living family members, genealogy research, and/or personal reflection. Using any available knowledge as a foundation, you can then draw on direct intuition to determine the spiritual health of your four primary bloodlines. At that point you can choose where to focus your lineage repair work.

Gathering What Is Remembered

To begin with, evaluate your current experience and knowledge of your family and your ancestors. How do you feel about them? (See exercise 1, page 43, if you're still not sure.) Are you in touch with the culture, skills, and practices of your people? Are you in touch with what's not working in your family?

Western psychology and neuroscience teach us that imprints from our earliest years give rise to personality patterns that may endure for a lifetime. By reflecting on your relationships and family dynamics, you can gain powerful insights into both the gifts and the challenges that you have inherited. Remember: when you act to heal any harmful legacy of your ancestors—including patterns in your personal life—you bring honor to the ancestors and, hopefully, more happiness to yourself.

Ready to start your research? There are many ways to go about it. First, look for information about your living family and ancestors. This can include full names (including maiden names for women), birth and death dates, photographs, letters, stories, newspaper clippings, court records, family symbols or lore, and inherited objects. The best ways to acquire this information are conversing with family members and doing some basic genealogy research. This process may take many years, but it does not require any special skills. All you need to begin is a sincere desire to better understand yourself and your family.

Engage the Living Family

If you have elders whom you believe are close to passing, now is the time to ask them about your ancestors. Sadly, both my mother's parents and my father's father died before I became interested in my family history. On multiple occasions while I was dreaming, my Grandma Howell has tried to show me a black-and-white photograph of her mother (I have not been able to locate any such picture in waking life). My Grandma Foor was a tremendous source for my knowledge of her and my grandfather's people before her passing in 2008. Talking at length with her started me down an eight-year path of genealogy and family research that included meetings with my grandparents' siblings and other extended family, cemetery visits, and extensive online research. This culminated in a self-published book through which I shared what I had learned about our people.

I was fortunate. My living family supported my research. But sometimes asking about family history may provoke defensiveness or a desire to shield younger generations from old pain. In addition, adoption, conception through sexual violence, having a sperm or egg donor as your biological parent, or other kinds of cutoffs may make it impossible to directly ask relatives about the ancestors.

If your relatives already practice some form of ancestor reverence, respectfully approach those who already work with the ancestors to see what they're doing and if they're open to collaboration. Other living family members may also claim to speak for the ancestors, and their views warrant consideration. If possible, offer prayer and celebratory ritual with them. Guidelines I find helpful when talking with family include:

- **Respect boundaries and requests of living family.** If approached with respect, relatives are often willing to share personal experiences and knowledge of family history. Nevertheless, some people have no interest or belief in talking to dead people. If family members are not open to hearing about this subject, honor their requests. If you feel it's important to convey a message to them from the ancestors, you could frame the message as a dream (e.g., "I had a dream that so-and-so wanted me to tell you . . .").

- **Seek out extended family.** Sometimes aunts, uncles, cousins, and grandparents are knowledgeable and happy to help. They can also provide a fresh perspective on older generations, as siblings may have radically different memories of the same parents.

- **Meet in person when possible.** In-person meetings allow for more involved and nuanced discussions. When approaching family elders, a simple gift can help initiate dialogue. Be sure to respect your personal safety as well as the cultural sensibilities of any new extended family members that you meet.

- **Record full names; dates of birth, death, and marriage; places of burial; and any life stories.** Factual information serves as the skeleton on which the flesh of story and meaning hangs. If closely examined, seemingly dry facts can reveal relationship patterns, family gifts, and rich stories. Make careful records of what you learn, including copies of any photographs, and back these up for yourself and for future generations. If you add to existing family knowledge, consider sharing it with interested relatives.

- **Follow up on leads and synchronicities.** Unexpected synchronicities and leads will inevitably arise during family research. Stay open to following this trail and to receiving guidance through dreams and waking events.
- **Allow time for emotional integration and self-care.** Getting to know extended family and researching your ancestors can unearth intense information that takes time to integrate, emotionally and spiritually. Be kind and patient with yourself, let the process unfold in stages, and be sure to engage your research and family from a place of respect, positivity, and wellness.
- **Invite the support of the loving ancestors in your research.** Consider making simple prayers and offerings to invite the support of your vibrant ancestors (see exercise 3, page 67, for suggestions). Ask them to show you what you need to know at the right time, in the right way, and for the highest good of all involved.

Use Online and Professional Resources

Genealogy research has blossomed into a distinct branch of historical research. Although genealogy research in the United States has historically emphasized European-American men and Mormon families, there are now extensive (and often free) databases with greater access to historical records for maternal lineages and individuals with non-European ancestry. As someone of European-American early immigrant ancestry, I have been able to trace most of my bloodlines back to the 1700s and, along a few lineages, several centuries earlier. I found sources for information on my family ancestors who lived earlier than the 1850s almost entirely from online databases.

If your living relatives are unsafe, problematic, or in any way obstruct your quest, online research can provide a way to bypass them. Just remember that when you're using online databases, accuracy can vary widely, because it is not always possible to verify primary sources. Consider cross-referencing names in another database, taking note of their references, and, when possible, including primary sources.

As you gather information over time, you may come to know more about your family ancestors than anyone else alive. This knowledge can confer on you a kind of status as family memory keeper—a potentially awkward role if you are younger than many of your relatives. The sheer volume of information may also start to feel overwhelming. When I was conducting my research, I found it helpful every year or two to compile the information (e.g., full names, birth and death dates) I had gathered onto one large page or piece of poster board. The most common visual presentation of names is called a *pedigree* (see page 78).

Personally, I prefer a mandala, wheel, or other radially symmetrical way of organizing the treasure from genealogy research, as this geometry implies equal importance among different bloodlines. The sample mandala on page 79 includes space for the names of the eight great-grandparents. If your grandparents are still alive, simply omit their names from the ancestor chart, and if your parents are deceased, you can add their names in the small generational ring between you at the center and your four grandparents at the cardinal directions. This organization also supports new associations and connections for those who have a prior practice of honoring the cardinal directions and elements (see exercise 11, page 187).

Even if you encounter difficulties with your research, don't be discouraged. Individuals who will never meet or know the names of their biological parents can still enjoy a profound and transformative relationship with their ancestors. Our ancestors speak through our bones and the DNA in each cell of our bodies, and as long as you are physically incarnate, you are inseparably linked to them. Now modern genetic technologies offer a third avenue for ancestral research: DNA testing. Several types of relatively inexpensive tests can provide useful information, especially on the directly maternal and paternal lineages (using testing for mitochondrial DNA and Y-DNA, respectively).

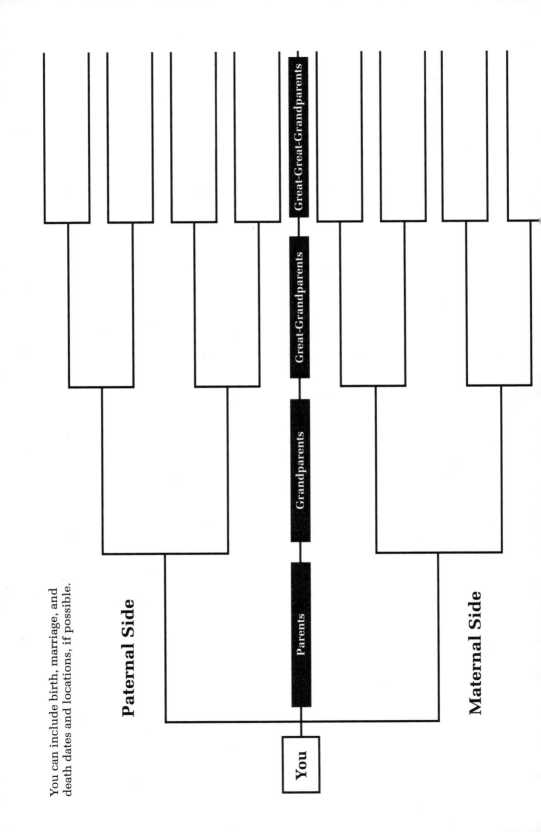

You can include birth, marriage, and death dates and locations, if possible.

Paternal Side

Maternal Side

You

Parents

Grandparents

Great-Grandparents

Great-Great-Grandparents

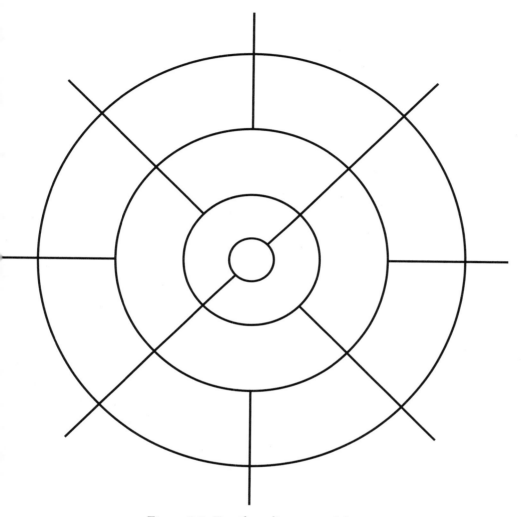

Figure 5.2. Family pedigree mandala

Considerations before Working Directly
with Your Ancestors

The next step is to directly engage the spirits of your ancestors (meaning: this is where I invite you to start talking to dead people and listening for their responses). Because most readers, like me, have probably not been trained from a young age to navigate spirit contact,

I have included six important skills and reminders that I find useful in this area.

Establish and Respect Personal Boundaries

Personal boundaries are essential in relationships, and ritual work with the ancestors is no exception. The underlying premise, again, is that the ancestors are as real as we are, so we need to respect their reality and space rather than collapsing our identity into theirs. Establishing healthy boundaries can prevent energetic intrusion from the troubled dead, as well as enable you to decline an invitation from the loving ancestors to merge with them. To retain full choice with respect to our personal space and bodies (both physical and energetic), we must be able to say "no" to requests the ancestors are making of us, and to be open to hearing "no" when we ask a question or make a request of them. As in any relationship, declining invitations from the ancestors may have consequences for trust and intimacy. However, it is critical to know that we have choice and, conversely, that we acknowledge their choice with respect to our own agenda.

Most traditional practitioners I have met agree that it is not appropriate or desirable to blur the distinction between oneself and the ancestors. One exception might be in a ritual context with a distinct beginning and ending. Individuals who have long-term relationships with their ancestors are still 100 percent responsible for their actions. "The ancestors told me to do it" or "I was possessed by the ancestors when so-and-so happened" is not an excuse and does not reduce personal responsibility. If you feel confusion about where you end and where the ancestors begin, these blurred boundaries can lead to trouble. They may indicate that you need more introspection, grounding, and inner work before contacting your ancestors.

We receive information and play out our relationships through many different perceptual channels (e.g., sight, sound, touch, smell, empathic awareness, intuition), and the same is true when relating with nonphysical beings. The channels we favor are largely a function of style and temperament, and certain habits or styles may be cause for extra concern. Specifically, having porous or open personal boundaries is a common trait among people who are highly intuitive. If this describes you, before embarking on your work with the ancestors, you will ideally learn to gain access to intuitive information in alternate ways that are still effective but are more contained and boundary-affirming. As we have seen, not all of the dead are equally well in spirit. Think of greeting your ancestors like getting to know mushrooms in the forest. Eating any mushroom you find will result in direct and intimate knowledge, but it may also result in a speedy and painful death.

One tool you can use to establish boundaries—in new relationships with both living humans and spirits—is to envision a protective barrier between you and them. You can still see and hear each other, and yet a boundary prevents you from merging with any potentially harmful energy, especially while you are still in the process of getting to know each other.

Maintain a Witness State

A related skill is the ability to maintain a state of emotional neutrality, even when the content makes this difficult. This ability to witness or "look but don't touch" is the same as it is when you're communicating with beings in the physical world, but it can be easier said than done. Common reactions that can make it difficult to maintain a witness consciousness include fear of harmful spirits or forces, strong judgments about what is being witnessed, and the felt need to help or intervene.

If you've established healthy personal boundaries and clear intent and are engaging respectfully with spirits, you will greatly reduce the risk of attracting harmful or dangerous forces into your sphere. Nevertheless, fear can be an important reminder that some situations are potentially dangerous. When necessary, practice caution, protect yourself, disengage with the spirits, and reach out for support to trusted allies or those versed in relating with the unseen.

The fact that strong judgments can compromise your ability to do spirit work does not mean you should throw your discernment out the window. It merely means that you can bear witness to something without condoning it or rushing in to try to change it. For example, I am conscious that there are people being murdered all around the world as I write this, and I am also clear that it is not my personal role to physically stop that from happening. To do so would distract me from attempting to fulfill my unique destiny in my brief time here on Earth. Furthermore, it is simply impossible.

In other words, focusing on personal responsibilities will yield a better long-term outcome than rushing around frenetically, which ultimately adds to the energy of crisis. Bad things happen in the world without our permission, and just as there are mean-spirited people, there are mean spirits—some of whom happen to be our ancestors. Whatever our most despised human behaviors may be (e.g., sexual violence, race- or religious-based persecution, harming children), it's safe to assume that some of your ancestors at some point in history have engaged in them. If you're not willing to accept the reality of shadow material or unevolved forms of behavior, you are probably not ready to get to know your ancestors.

Another common reaction that is in some ways more insidious than judgment or fear is the impulse to help. This type of intrusion into another's personal space (be they corporeal or spirit) is a problem precisely because it masquerades as being *helpful* and therefore as entirely justified. I'm not talking about the spontaneous desire to extend care and compassion to others, but rather the hubris of assuming that our help is invited or that we understand what actually constitutes help in any given situation. Imagine a doctor who feels so distraught at seeing people suffer that he distributes strong medicine, without a clear diagnosis, to individuals who are not even aware of being given the drug. In ancestor work, when encountering the spirits of the less peaceful dead, people sometimes immediately jump in with some kind of energetic healing or ritual repair for them. Although this may be helpful under certain circumstances, to intervene in a knee-jerk way oversteps a boundary.

If you find yourself drawn toward the tendency to help or "do something," you might instead work to increase your capacity to sit with others' suffering, and double-check that you're allowing the older ancestral guides and teachers to drive work with the troubled dead. Seek to respect the autonomy of all beings encountered through ritual.

Avoid Psychological Meltdown

The ancestors are both separate and inseparable from us. By ritually feeding and elevating their collective spirit, we also raise our own awareness and vibration. In doing so, any number of personal issues may surface for healing, completion, and transformation. When the gnarled roots from generations of family abuse or disconnect start to untangle, some individuals may experience a reactivation or aggravation of past trauma. This can be serious business, but as long as you have sufficient psychological support and resilience, you will probably be able to regulate the intensity of the work in ways that are healing and cathartic rather than unhelpful and overwhelming. In those times when work with the unseen stirs up more intensity than people can handle, they may need to reach out for support. Psychological meltdown and destabilization are almost never desirable. If you find that you are losing your center, turn down the volume on the spirit work. Focus on practices that keep you grounded, sober, and in your body, and, again, reach out for reliable help.

Here's the good news: over the last decade of helping others relate to their ancestors, I have found that Spirit tends to provide people with only as much as they can handle at any given time in their lives.

I also suggest finding an ally in your work—a spiritual buddy. Early on in the lineage repair process, if possible, identify someone you can talk with and, if needed, go to for emotional and spiritual support. This could include a close family member or friend, a spiritual mentor, a supportive therapist or healer, or any helpful elder. Track your personal well-being throughout the work and remember to take it all at your own rhythm. If possible, try to connect locally with groups, teachers, and other practitioners who honor their ancestors. Stay open to being part of a healthy community if you are blessed enough to have kindred spirits in your area.

Access Traditional Teachings

There are many communities that still maintain robust practices of ancestor reverence and ritual. The teachers within these circles know many of the challenges that can arise when you're cultivating a direct relationship with the ancestors, because relations with the unseen are a part of everyday life for them. If you have access to such trustworthy elders and teachers, take full advantage of this opportunity. Otherwise, consider doing research on the historical culture of your people. What is known about how your ancestors related with the ones before them? What from this inherited wealth of knowledge can support your ancestral tending today?

Even so, I offer some cautions here. First, not all traditional ancestor veneration practices are relevant for modern times. For example, some of my ancestors, like many people's ancestors, lived in cultures that performed human sacrifice, sometimes accompanied by ritual consumption of at least parts of the human sacrificed. This is one example of many that illustrates why it's important to trust your judgment if practices don't sit right with you. Second, I have found spiritual teachers to be just as fallible, complicated, and capable of ethical shortcomings as anyone else. If you do work with a living teacher or community, maintain support outside this community if possible, and be certain to maintain your own discernment, center, and sense of personal responsibility. If you find that any teacher or tradition feels contrary to what is right for you on a heart and gut level, use your discernment, get reliable outside opinions, and, when needed, part from that teacher or tradition. Finally, a person's relationship with his or her ancestors is inherently personal. Be sure to follow your intuition and try to strike a balance between adhering to tradition and finding your unique expression and style.

Stay Humble

People don't tend to see themselves as arrogant or inflated, and yet some of the greatest atrocities in human history have manifested from what I would call "ancestor ego inflation," or in psychological terms, a displacement of primary narcissism onto the ancestors.[1] In less technical language, this sounds something like, "My people are better than your people (and I am just a humble member of my superior ancestral group)." Conversely, there is the even more convoluted stance of "Your people are better than my people (and I seek to identify with or gain the approval of *your* superior ancestral group)." Either way, this is a big problem.

Race, however historically constructed and biologically suspect as a category, is often one factor in ancestral ego inflation. Atrocities fueled by delusions of racial supremacy include the European colonization of North America, the transatlantic slave trade, and the crimes of Nazi Germany and Imperial Japan during World War II. Global casualty estimates from racially motivated war and homicide in the twentieth century alone easily exceed ten million human lives. In addition to race, ancestry also informs religious, national, ethnic, and tribal identities, any of which may be invoked to justify brutality. A few examples from recent decades of ancestral ego inflation that revolved around some of these other factors include:

- Shi'a-Sunni tensions in the Iran-Iraq War (1980–88, an estimated one million people killed)[2]
- Christian-Muslim rifts in the war in Bosnia and Herzegovina (1992–95, an estimated one hundred thousand people killed)[3]
- Hutu-Tutsi ethnic tensions in the Rwandan Genocide (1994, an estimated eight hundred thousand to one million people killed)[4]
- Tamil-Sinhalese tensions in the Sri Lankan Civil War (1983–2009, an estimated eighty thousand to one hundred thousand people killed)[5]

In these and many other examples, one or more groups constructed a narrative about a neighboring group and then proceeded to demean and dehumanize these others as a pretext for aggression and brutality. In other words, "Our people are inherently better than your people." This kind of violence is entirely preventable and gains little traction without the valuation of some ancestors over others.

Although the spiritual seekers I meet are not engaged in guerilla warfare or genocide, many of them do engage in some degree of largely unconscious ancestral favoritism. In the United States, European-identified people often devalue or deny their Native American, African, or Asian ancestry. Correspondingly, people with non-European ancestry may, for a variety of reasons, downplay their European backgrounds. On a personal level, this means rejecting parts of yourself that don't feel congruent with your cultural identity, often from a belief that "my people (the ancestors I celebrate) are better than those other people (the ancestors in my own bloodlines that I reject)."

I have heard stories of individuals of predominately European ancestry rejecting factual evidence that their physical and culture heritage includes Africans or Native Americans. Similarly, in the powerful PBS television series *African American Lives,* created by the distinguished scholar and educator Henry Louis Gates Jr., some African-American guests share complex feelings that can arise when learning of their European ancestors. In any event, choosing to claim some parts of your ancestry while rejecting others sets the conditions for an inflated sense of self—and also denies the fact that many if not most individuals at this point in history are multiracial.

Reverse/negative ego inflation, or the "your people are better than my people" syndrome, is also present in the United States, and this stance is also problematic. Here one's sense of self may have diminished rather than being "just the right size." For example, people of predominately European bloodlines, especially those that practice indigenous traditions or shamanism, sometimes idealize or identify with indigenous or other non-European cultures. This identification, which looks strange to the cultures being imitated, can include taking new names, adopting styles of dress, and adopting a bad attitude toward one's European ancestry. For example, one prominent spiritual teacher of indigenous ways is a very small percentage Cherokee by blood and only learned about this part of her ancestry as an adult. Yet in promotional materials she claims to be Cherokee without mentioning her European heritage. Although this claim is not entirely false, why value Cherokee over European heritage? What makes one's Cherokee ancestors in some way superior to one's European ancestors (or vice versa)?

Nonetheless, becoming deeply involved in a different culture, even to the point of adoption and ritual initiation by that culture, does not necessarily mean that you are showing ancestral favoritism. Having participated in rituals of diverse cultures—both from a place of avoiding my past and inner work and also from a place of self-respect and respect for my ancestors—I know how this distinction feels for me, and how clarifying one's motivation makes a world of difference. All of our ancestors include amazing and praiseworthy people, but the story that any one person or group's ancestors are somehow superior to the ancestors of others is a view that may give rise to racism, nationalism, war, and other causes of human suffering.

Keep Your Intent Clear

Finally, with respect to communicating with the dead: if you are at all hesitant, take time to honor your process of inquiry and introspection. Consider how simple practices to convey respect to your ancestors may harmonize better with your personal traditions and relationships. If you decide to reach out to them in a more focused way, try to be as clear as possible about your reasons. A few wholesome motivations include wanting to heal yourself, wanting to heal your family, wanting skills for communicating with the dead, and wanting to satisfy curiosity about your ancestors or traditions. Whatever brings you to the work, be clear about your original intent, share it with your ancestors at the outset, and reaffirm and revisit it as needed.

Choosing a Focus
for Lineage Repair Work

Attempting to relate with all of your ancestral lineages at the same time can be chaotic or overwhelming, especially if you're just getting to know them. I've found that an approach of considering your four primary bloodlines provides enough breathing room to get to know and appreciate different lineages. Think of each of your four grand-parents, whether living or deceased, as the most recent faces of the lineages before them. In the case of your two grandmothers, *lineage* here refers specifically to the line of women before them; for your two grandfathers, it refers to the line of men before them (e.g., your father's father's father's lineage, your father's mother's mother's lineage, and similarly one lineage of men and one of women on your mother's side). Of course these are only four specific bloodlines of many; however, I've found consideration of these four lines to be plenty as a foun-dation in ancestral reverence. Once these four lines are vibrant, you can of course include another four lineage lines (such as your moth-er's mother's father, etc.) or beyond. Even if you already have an idea about which side of the family you want to focus on, try to refrain from deciding until after you check in directly, because the side of your family that you have felt closest to may not necessarily be the most beneficial place to begin. If you stay with the work over time, you will come into more conscious relationship with each of your four primary bloodlines. So there's no need to rush.

There are two important questions to hold in your awareness when determining where to begin the work. The first consideration is how well the ancestors are in spirit. I work with a 1–10 scale, with the higher the number, the more at peace the ancestor or lineage:

- **One to three** refers to troubled ghosts—the dead who are clearly fragmented or lacking in shine. At the lower end of this range are frightening and potentially dangerous spirits. If you encounter spirits in this range, ask your loving guides to assist you in holding a firm boundary with them until they have gone through their own processes of healing and elevation. Remember that although many of the dead may be in a condition of need, this does not make them bad people.

- **Four to six** refers to those who are more or less intact in spirit but are not yet radiant or connected to the loving and bright ancestors. Many of those who die, at least in the United States, seem to reside in this limbo state between their life on Earth and full reception by their ancestors. Because they are not yet ancestors in their own right, they could be considered well-intended or common ghosts.

- **Seven to ten** applies to the dead who are well, the "true ancestors," who are now sources of support, love, and guidance for the living. These are the beloved dead—people with whom you would feel instinctively safe if they were paying a visit to your children or standing at the foot of your bed while you slept. They may have colorful personalities, but they are rooted in love and strongly connected to other well ancestors.

I encourage holding a boundary with any spirit ranked below a seven on this 1–10 scale.

Remember that this exercise is merely about observing what *is*, without judgment or a need to fix or heal. Positive change begins with the ability to objectively perceive the dead as they are.

The other important factor at this stage is the level of influence each ancestral lineage has on you and your living family. Consider ancestral influence in basic terms of *high, medium,* or *low*. This influence may be harmful or helpful. Worst-case scenario: your ancestors are both troubled and influential. Best-case scenario: your ancestors are both well in spirit and influential. When determining the most important place to focus the healing work, level of influence may trump level of wellness as a factor. For example, one lineage may be quite troubled (e.g., a two on the 1–10 scale) but only moderately influential in your present life, while another lineage may be less acutely troubled but more impactful by virtue of a close connection. Although these distinctions may seem somewhat clinical, these two factors, *level of wellness* and *level of influence on the living*, can be a way to track changes over time.

Before proceeding, please take a moment to reflect on assumptions you may hold about the relationships between biological sex, gender identity, and ancestral lineage. Although the approach to ancestral healing presented in this book emphasizes two maternal and two paternal bloodlines, this does not imply anything about the gender identity, sexual orientation, or even the genitalia of your ancestors along any given lineage. You may be descended from women who were hunters, builders, travelers, or warriors. Your grandmothers may have held vocations or expressed any number of other personality traits that modern societies more often associate with men (and vice versa for the men). Both male and female ancestors may have preferred sex and long-term relationships with people of the opposite sex, the same sex, or a bit of both. And some of your people along the way were almost certainly intersex, meaning that they were born with ambiguous or atypical genitalia in ways that blur even the binary distinction of male and female. All this diversity may have been embraced, judged, or a bit of both during the times in which they lived on Earth. In other words, your people include ancestors whom we would today consider gay, lesbian, bisexual, transgendered, queer, intersex, or otherwise variant from heterosexual and cis-gendered norms, and it's important to stay open as you get to know your ancestors.

The following exercise is a guided visualization to assess the condition of your four primary bloodlines. You can modify it as you proceed through the stages of ancestor work (see chapter 9). For now, the intent is to give you a preliminary sense of how healthy each bloodline is and to help you decide where to begin the lineage repair process.

EXERCISE FOUR

Attuning to Your Four Primary Bloodlines

INTENT: Greet your four primary lineages and decide where to focus the ancestral repair process

WHAT YOU NEED: A quiet space and whatever helps you connect with your ancestors

For this exercise, you will first record your own voice (or a friend's) reading the guided visualization below. Alternatively, you could ask a friend to read it aloud for you while you listen. Speak slowly and clearly, incorporating pauses as suggested below. Once you have done this, find a space conducive to ritual work. When you are there, do whatever helps you **establish sacred space and ritual intent** (e.g., light a candle, offer incense, make prayers). If possible, identify the cardinal directions (east, west, north, south) and comfortably settle in near the center of the space. Play back the recording, or ask your friend to begin to narrate.

1. (*Begin recording.*) Start by taking a few minutes to **get grounded and centered** in your body. Let your eyes close or settle into a soft gaze, and let your soul's light fill and shine forth from your body, knowing that you will stay present in your body for this entire visualization and will remember afterward whatever you perceive. Bring your breath to your belly center. Feel your bones, your heart and blood pumping. (*Brief pause.*) When you feel present in your body, **call in any supportive guides** with whom you already enjoy relationship. If you're not sure who your guides are in spirit, simply call on divine love, light, and positivity. When the guides or the felt sense of divine support are present, **reaffirm your intent** to better understand the condition of your four primary ancestral lineages. (*Brief pause.*)

2. Centered in your body, with your spirit helpers present, **ask your guides to establish a layer of protection around your personal space**.

You might picture this as a protective sphere or circular house with walls or windows like a two-way mirror, from which you can see out, but those outside can't see in. Remember your intent to merely observe, not to connect with your ancestors or to change anything. See if it's possible throughout the exercise to observe without calling attention to your presence. Reconfirm that your guides are with you and that the protection is in place. (*Brief pause.*)

3. In your circle of protection, with your awareness anchored in your body, and with the support of the guides, **turn your attention to the east**. You may remain still in body and visualize the east, or you may physically turn your body to face that direction. (*Brief pause.*) In the east, see your father's father, if he has passed, and the lineage of men before him back through time. Form first impressions of these ancestors, *as they exist in the present,* without judgment or need to change anything. (*Pause for one minute.*) Is the energy here bright or dark, present or absent, peaceful or conflicted? Are there colors, symbols, or images that appear? Even if ancestors appear who seem well in spirit, for now just observe. Allowing for differences between the recent dead and older ancestors along the lineage, try to rank the overall level of wellness of your father's father's lineage on the 1–10 scale. (*Pause for one minute.*) Now be curious about the impact of this lineage on you and others in your living family. If heavy energies are present, how strongly do they affect you or other relatives? (*Pause for one minute.*) When you feel complete, **thoroughly clear any heavy or disruptive energies from your personal space, shift your attention away from your paternal grandfather's people, and bring your attention back to a neutral state.** (*Pause for one minute.*)

4. In your circle of protection, and with the support of the guides, **turn your attention to the south** and notice your father's mother and the lineage of women before her. Form first impressions of these ancestors, *as they exist in the present,* without judgment or need to change anything. (*Pause for one minute.*) Is the energy here bright or dark, present or absent, peaceful or conflicted? Are there colors, symbols, or images that

appear? Even if ancestors appear who seem well in spirit, for now just observe. Allowing for differences between the recent dead and older ancestors along the lineage, try to rank the overall level of wellness of your father's mother's lineage on the 1–10 scale. (*Pause for one minute.*) Now be curious about the impact of this lineage on you and others in your living family. If heavy energies are present, how strongly do they affect you or other relatives? (*Pause for one minute.*) When you feel complete, **thoroughly clear any heavy or disruptive energies from your personal space, shift your attention away from your paternal grandmother's people, and bring your attention back to a neutral state.** (*Pause for one minute.*)

5. In your circle of protection, and with the support of the guides, **turn your attention to the west** and notice your mother's mother and the lineage of women before her. Form first impressions of these ancestors, *as they exist in the present,* without judgment or need to change anything. (*Pause for one minute.*) Is the energy here bright or dark, present or absent, peaceful or conflicted? Are there colors, symbols, or images that appear? Even if ancestors appear who seem well in spirit, for now just observe. Allowing for differences between the recent dead and older ancestors along the lineage, try to rank the overall level of wellness of your mother's mother's lineage on the 1–10 scale. (*Pause for one minute.*) Now be curious about the impact of this lineage on you and others in your living family. If heavy energies are present, how strongly do they affect you or other relatives? (*Pause for one minute.*) When you feel complete, **thoroughly clear any heavy or disruptive energies from your personal space, shift your attention away from your maternal grandmother's people, and bring your attention back to a neutral state.** (*Pause for one minute.*)

6. In your circle of protection, and with the support of the guides, **turn your attention to the north** and notice your mother's father and the lineage of men before him. Form first impressions of these ancestors, *as they exist in the present,* without judgment or need to change anything. (*Pause for one minute.*) Is the energy here bright or dark, present or

absent, peaceful or conflicted? Are there colors, symbols, or images that appear? Even if ancestors appear who seem well in spirit, for now just observe. Allowing for differences between the recent dead and older ancestors along the lineage, try to rank the overall level of wellness of your mother's father's lineage on the 1–10 scale. (*Pause for one minute.*) Now be curious about the impact of this lineage on you and others in your living family. If heavy energies are present, how strongly do they affect you or other relatives? (*Pause for one minute.*) When you feel complete, **thoroughly clear any heavy or disruptive energies from your personal space, shift your attention away from your maternal grandfather's people, and bring your attention back to a neutral state.** (*Pause for one minute.*)

7. Before bringing your attention fully back, take an extra moment to be certain that your personal energy is in the clear and that all pathways of curiosity that may have been opened with the ancestors are now closed. Also, pause to give thanks to any supportive guides. (*Brief pause.*) When you are ready, open your eyes and anchor your attention in your physical body and your surroundings. To ensure that you recall all that you were shown, consider making notes about what you observed. (*End recording.*)

After you have completed exercise 4, make notes that you can later refer to. Include how you ranked the relative vitality of each of your four primary lineages from one to ten. If you have children or siblings who have preceded you in death, consider moving through the exercise a second time on a different day to also ask about their condition in spirit. Include questions about the condition of brothers or male children when considering your father's father's lineage and sisters or female children when considering your mother's mother's lineage. Although there is tremendous variation, among clients I have supported in the United States, I would say that an average ancestral profile would have one lineage relatively bright and healthy, one acutely troubled and disruptive, and the other two somewhere in the middle range. Remember that a primary goal of the lineage repair cycle is to be certain that all of your recent ancestors and the lineages before them are bright in spirit (in this framework, at least a seven or above). Also, you ideally want their influence to be both high in degree and positive in nature. If this is already the case for one or more lineages at the outset of the work, congratulations!

With some exceptions, I've found that it's ideal to stay focused on one bloodline in order to complete the lineage repair work in manageable stages. When deciding which of your four primary lineages to focus on first, consider several factors. Starting where things are in worse shape may yield the greatest benefits; however, many find it best to first focus on lineages that are already relatively well in order to open up additional sources of support and to get used to engaging with the ancestors. Saving the most troubled lineages for last also helps to ensure a safe and grounded container in which to metabolize more intense forms of ancestral trouble. If none of your lineages are having an actively harmful effect on your life, you have a bit more breathing room. You may consider starting with your father's father's lineage if you are male, and your mother's mother's lineage if you are female. Ultimately, trust in where the bright ancestors, any spiritual guides, and your intuition direct you to begin.

Once you have settled on a lineage, consider memorizing the names of your ancestors of this lineage. For example, if you've chosen to focus on one of your grandfathers' lineages, learn the available names of the men in this line. In addition, learn by heart the names of the women in the lineage before your grandmothers. Learning their names conveys respect and helps when you are invoking the ancestors during the rituals of repair and reconnection. Before moving on to the next step, take a moment to give a brief nod of respect to the other three lineages. And of course, while you are focusing on one of your lineages, you can continue to show respect and acknowledgment to all your ancestors as you are moved to.

SIX

MEETING WITH
ANCESTRAL GUIDES

In stage one, you gathered what could be readily known about your ancestors from the living family and other forms of genealogy research. You also decided which quarter of your blood ancestry to focus on in the lineage repair process. In stage two, you will learn how to connect with wise and loving ancestral guides and how to access the blessings and gifts of these ancestors more directly. This chapter also presents ways to converse with bright and elevated ancestors through practices of trance work and guided visualization. At the end of this stage, you will be able to connect with supportive ancestral guides along your lineage of focus. You will also be able to partner with them to direct healing intent to any in your lineage who have passed and are not yet at peace.

Ancestral Guides

So who are these ancestral guides, and how do you contact them?

In lineage repair work, the guides are the spirits of those who previously lived on Earth as our blood ancestors *and* who are willing and able to support our lives and assist any of the dead who may be troubled. The guides are the defining lives—the *highlights,* so to speak—of human incarnation that set the bar along any given bloodline, and they are our elders in spirit. Think of them as bright points along the tangled line of our DNA—points at which human potential harmonized most clearly with love, wisdom, beauty, and service. As ancestors, these guides mirror back to us our own potential and responsibility to be exemplary human beings.

Even if such ancestors are part of our lineages, why make the effort to seek them out? Why not call upon other benevolent, capable, and readily available spiritual forces who are *not* blood ancestors? Furthermore, since our experience of family is so often the source of our troubled mind and need for healing, why not go to the source of the problem—our recent ancestors—to seek a solution? Martín Prechtel, a ceremonial leader and author who trained with the T'zutujil Maya of Guatemala, wrote:

> While of course our blood ancestry is a real thing and must be given its due, unless you descend from an immediate line of openhearted humans with intact forms of origination as a way of life, dependence on Ancestors for an identity will usually be the den of a lot of doctored and unmetabolized grief, hidden behind nonsense and still more intentional habitual Amnesia and mental lockdown. For in all probability, your ancestors for the last millennia or so were suffering just as much from a lack of origins as yourself. These are the "recent" ancestors.[1]

Martín articulated the need for most modern people to reach further back along our bloodlines in order to contact ancestors who lived before the cultural disruption and colonialism that have led to our dissociation from the natural world. Speaking about these earlier ancestors, he continued, "The real, real 'old' ones are the indigenous ones, and they are not going to be tribalist, because they are in the story of all mythic things and have merged into the submolecular awareness in the sap and bloodstream of all living things that feed the present and do not value small-thinking isolationist ancestral prejudice." Simply by being who they are, these older ancestral guides have greater authority to restore the vitality and integrity of the bloodlines than any other type of guide. As insiders to the ancestral and family system, they can understand and treat dysfunctional family patterns at the source, no matter how far back in history the troubles are rooted.

Just how far back along the bloodlines do you need to go in order to connect with sufficiently awake ancestors? As far back as necessary. Time in the realm of spirit is not as linear as our everyday consciousness would lead us to believe, and ancestors who lived hundreds or even thousands of years ago may speak naturally and with authority in the twenty-first century. Millions of human beings implicitly affirm this truth by relating to the inspiring spirits of human beings who died well over a thousand years ago (e.g., Muhammad, Jesus, Moses, Siddhartha, Lao Tzu). I personally tend to work with ancestral guides who lived on Earth from 1000 BCE to 1000 CE. When I have supported others in making these connections, I have seen some make contact with even more historically distant guides, while others meet with more recent ancestors (e.g., from 1000 to 1800 CE) whose names are still beyond the reach of history. The older the disruptions to any given lineage, the further back you will need to vision to meet with ancestors who lived before those troubles.

If your recent ancestors practiced ancestor reverence or were unusually aware and evolved people, they may comfortably embody the vitality of the lineage before them. In this case, you may not need to contact earlier ancestral guides. For example, in his autobiography, West African healer Malidoma Somé described his paternal grandfather as a highly developed Dagara medicine person. Very likely he can count on his grandfather to embody the blessings of earlier ancestors along his father's lineage.

Occasionally ancestors are present during visioning practices who, for whatever reasons, may be either willing or capable of helping, but not both. Most commonly, these are well-intended and helpful ancestors who simply lack the vitality needed for lineage repair work (think of these ones as sevens on the 1–10 scale: generally well but not vibrant). When people are seeking ancestral guides, I ask them to be realistic about whether or not they feel that the ancestor in question embodies a truly spacious, awake, and loving presence. This is not a question of whether you like the style of the guides; their personalities may rub you the wrong way, but they may be quite awake. On the other hand, you may enjoy their energy, but they may not be particularly elevated. The ancestors may be blunt, crafty, flamboyant, and confrontational, and they may embody every other kind of human quality. But for lineage repair work, the guides *do* need to be basically wise, loving, and able to wield a certain amount of vitality. If you're not sure that you've contacted a guide who is "on the level," one test question is to ask to see the ancestral guide's connection with his or her earlier ancestors. Remember that the dead who are well in spirit tend to function as a collective energy. If you have any doubt about whether or not this is the case, respectfully continue further back along the lineage until you meet an ancestor who is not only willing but also capable of providing the necessary support.

When an ancestral guide seems capable with respect to presence and vitality but is otherwise unwilling to support the lineage repair process, he or she could be responding to too much goal-directed or linear energy coming from you. In other words, if you demand the guide's attention or if you approach with pushy or needy energy, this can have a chilling effect on the initial meeting. The ancestral guides are literally and spiritually our elders, and this calls for deference and patience in our approach to them. If you are working with a spirit who is indeed a vibrant blood ancestor, try slowing down and seeking to know this ancestor on his or her own terms before asking for help. If you get the message that you personally are not ready to engage in lineage repair, respectfully ask the ancestral guides for appropriate ways for honoring and celebrating your vibrant ancestors. In some cases, you may need to find an earlier guide along the same lineage and seek understanding about the nature of the initial difficulty.

Using Ritual to Contact Ancestral Guides

Often, although not always, relating to helpful nonhuman powers or spirits takes place during ritual or ceremony. How to craft and carry out rituals is a subject worthy of several full-length books and ultimately is only learned through direct experience. To begin with, this kind of work depends on establishing a safe and supportive ritual space. Several protocols in this book, including exercise 5 in this chapter, will help enable you to do this. But if, even after reading this chapter, you don't feel confident in setting up the vessel needed for ritual work, consider reaching out to trusted living teachers and taking your time to develop your comfort level with basic ritual practice before doing the exercises.

This section explores ritual structure, energetic protection, the use of nonordinary states of consciousness, ways to distinguish imagination and fantasy from authentic spirit contact, and what to do if "nothing happens." Pragmatism trumps perfection. In fact, whatever serves your particular temperament and style in communicating with your loving ancestors is perfect.

Ritual Structure

Begin by having a clean and safe space, free from disturbance, where everything you may need is readily available. If you are new to leading ritual, consider the basic progression:

1. Cleansing or purification (of self, the ritual space, and other participants)
2. Opening prayers and invocation
3. Heart of the ritual
4. Giving thanks to the powers you've worked with and completion prayers
5. Relaxing and releasing of ritual vessel

After the ritual space is physically organized, you may perform a cleansing with smoke (e.g., burning sage or incense), sound (e.g., toning or rattling), liquid (e.g., sprinkling blessed water), or whatever else helps clear distractions and make the space sacred.

Next is the ritual opening. It can involve something as elaborate as a lengthy invocation and call to the ancestors, or it can be as simple as lighting a candle and offering a prayer. I recommend somehow using voice to welcome the ancestors and to speak or sing aloud your reasons for asking them to be present. Continue with your opening invocation until you feel that your call has received a response, that the ancestors are present, and that the energy in the space is bright. The more effective your invocation, the more you will find that the work that follows will be spirit-guided and will proceed in flow.

Energetic Protection

During ritual, participants sometimes work with nonordinary states of consciousness or access strong emotion. This can lead to a kind of vulnerability to outside disruption, like the condition of someone deep-sea diving, absorbed in states of meditation, or having a strong dream. For this reason, around the time of the opening prayer or invocation, ritual leaders often establish some type of energetic containment or protective boundary around the sacred space. Typically they will cleanse or purify the space and participants and will then contain the space in this state of protection. If you are leading a ritual, you will want to protect the space on a physical level by securing a place relatively free from outside interference, and if possible, by having a human ally who is versed in spirit work present to assist. On a subtle level, you can also increase the degree of protection by visualizing protective light and spirit allies surrounding the space. If you feel the need for more containment, consider surrounding your ritual space with a circle of stones, salt, ash, or other protective medicines. Trust your instinct and intuition here, and continue until you feel the necessary level of safety and spiritual protection when in ritual space.

Work with Nonordinary States of Consciousness

It's critical to have a clear intent at the start of a ritual—both to inform ritual content and as a way to gauge its success afterward. If you intend to communicate with ancestral guides or other spirits of the dead, then you will likely need to enter into a state of awareness that is conducive to this type of dialogue. As we noted in chapter 4, this may happen in an ordinary state of consciousness, or it may include entering into some type of lightly altered state. These states are often entered through moving consciousness toward stillness, moving consciousness toward sensory overload or flooding, or some combination of the two. Some practitioners alter their body physiology before entering ritual space, either through practices that optimize physical vitality, balance, and intuitive abilities or, more rarely, by ingesting consciousness-altering substances. The more ways in which you can relate to the unseen and shift your attention into states conducive to spirit contact, the more easily you can engage in effective ritual under any conditions.

There are plenty of ways to shift your body physiology before entering ritual space *without* using consciousness-altering substances. Some examples include mindful and medically safe fasting or eating lightly; making sure to get enough sleep before ritual (or, on the contrary, intentionally forgoing sleep); and engaging in exercise or disciplines like yoga, dance, chi gong, and martial arts. Optimizing your health and vitality will enhance your intuitive abilities.

If you do partake of consciousness-altering substances (e.g., alcohol, cannabis, peyote, ayahuasca, psychoactive mushrooms) prior to ritual, take caution: in addition to the risks of medical complications and legal trouble, there is no guarantee that any of these medicines will actually enhance your ability to relate with your ancestors. I have been fortunate to work with some of these medicines in ways that felt beneficial, but they are not a regular part of my practice. In any case, they are unnecessary—and are even a potential hindrance—when doing this kind of ritual work. Many indigenous cultures with highly developed practices of ancestor reverence use no psychoactive medicines.

If you do work with these substances, please observe proper precautions, attempt to honor the medicine in its traditional context, and cross-check the results of your ritual work when you are not under the influence of the medicine. If you become dependent upon any substance, take this as a strong call to develop pathways of communication with spirit that do not require intoxication.

The two practices for shifting consciousness that I recommend for beginners are meditation and drumming. As I mentioned in chapter 4, both of these practices allow for the rational, thinking mind to take a back seat—whether through the stillness of meditation or through the sensory stimulation of the drum. Meditation may be the more challenging approach unless you have cultivated a regular practice and find that your everyday mental activity can subside relatively easily. Repetitive rhythms using a frame drum are popular among contemporary shamanic practitioners and can be effective live or, if needed, from a recording. In addition to drumming, I have found some kinds of rattling and the sound of the Native flute or recorder to be supportive for light trance. Experiment with what works best for you.

Distinguish Imagination from Spirit Contact

Let's return to one of the most common questions from individuals who are new to spirit work: "How do I know I'm not making this up?" My first response is often to tease apart two different concerns. The first is: "How do I know I'm not making *all* of this up? How do I know if it's even possible for me to relate with spirits?" This goes back to the core assumptions outlined in chapter 4: that there is some kind of continuity of consciousness after death and that living humans and the spirits of the ancestors can, at least under certain circumstances, communicate directly. Those who do not accept these propositions as potentially true are not likely to attempt ancestral contact, unless perhaps they are struggling to make sense of some unsolicited contact from the dead. Nonetheless, our ability to relate to the other world in general and to our ancestors in particular is innate, an ancient and universal human gift.

The second concern is more nuanced and goes something like this: "How do I distinguish my mental chatter, personal fantasy, and imagination from actual spirit contact? How can I tell when I'm really connecting in any given moment versus 'making it up'?" The issue here is accuracy—a legitimate concern. Over time, a few guidelines I've found useful for discerning authentic spirit contact from personal thoughts include:

1. **Trust your instincts and body wisdom.** We can sometimes tell when someone is watching us. We can also sense things, for better or worse, about the people we meet. In the same way, we often instinctively know when we're in the presence of a genuinely different being in ritual. If we listen to the wisdom of our body, we can often start to notice a certain body-based feeling associated with personal imagination and a different feeling connected to authentic spirit contact.

2. **Cross-check your information.** Even if you feel confident in what you hear or see from the ancestors, it's good to double-check your information from time to time. This can include any kind of reliable yes-no divination to confirm your conclusions, asking for a confirmation dream, consulting with a trusted spiritual friend or teacher, or just waiting a day before checking in again to be sure you heard the message correctly. This is the equivalent of "I want to make sure I heard you right" in our interactions with living humans.

3. **Experiment with trusting and track the results.** Consider taking calculated risks to trust what's coming through. If putting the ancestors' guidance into practice helps you and those around you feel happier, healthier, and more in alignment with spirit, chances are you're actually making contact. Even if you are a professional psychic, shaman, or other kind of ritualist, one of the only guarantees of accuracy when relating with the unseen is the evidence of tangible benefit in this earthly dimension. Highly gifted mediums sometimes have an off day and may

be totally off the mark, even if they truly believe what they are sensing and seeing. Humility and openness to being wrong are essential when communicating with the ancestors.

Be Patient, Creative, and Tenacious

People occasionally have the experience that "nothing happened" during ritual. This is common. It can happen for many reasons, and it need not be a cause for discouragement. If you feel this happens with the exercise that follows or with any of the rituals in this book, first go back to what exactly *did* happen. Often people report that "nothing happened" when in fact they received a great deal of information. Especially for those new to spirit contact, the voice of inner knowing can begin as a whisper or "still, small voice" that we gradually learn to trust more and more over time.[2]

Sometimes people discount direct spirit contact by overvaluing the visual and auditory channels of perception. Each of us has stronger and weaker pathways of intuition, and this can change over time, even from one day to the next. For example, some people experience spirit contact through body sensations, dreams, or just a direct knowing. Be mindful of any pressure to have something specific happen, relax, and notice what you *are* experiencing during ritual.

Other times it's actually true that nothing in particular happens. This can occur for a multitude of reasons. You may simply be distracted or sleepy, having a rough day, or otherwise not in your most intuitive state. Be kind with yourself, don't make a big story about it all, and try again on a different day. Also, the ancestors may take a moment to respond to your request for direct contact. Remember that centuries may have passed since a living relative has sought ancestral connection, so it's sensible to allow your people some time to reply. When they do reply, the contact may come during waking ritual or through a dream visit, waking synchronicity, or some other kind of spontaneous contact. If staying receptive and tenacious doesn't yield results over time, reconfirm that you're where you need to be with the lineage of focus and that you're fully on board personally with the work. If needed, consider reaching out for support, but stay hopeful, as we all have loving ancestors, even if they're far back along the lineage.

The exercise that follows presents a ritual progression for connecting with an ancestral guide. In addition to the more general guidelines given above, keep the following considerations in mind:

- **Relate to the ancestors in the present.** When seeking to connect with ancestral guides, you're not just imagining the past or exploring personal memories. Even though the ancestors may present themselves through the life and times they experienced while on Earth, this appearance may simply be for our benefit. The connection itself plays out here and now, in the present moment.

- **Bypass more recent heaviness to connect with the older guides.** Our linear minds would suggest passing through the span of the recent lineage to arrive at older guides, but in this case it's important to intentionally sidestep those who are not yet well in spirit. Go above, below, or around them—whatever serves the purpose—but bypass those among the dead who are not yet at peace.

- **Seek a connection that is decisively healed and vibrant.** You're seeking a lineage ancestor who is not just well but *exceptionally* well—an eight or above on the 1–10 scale. The guide should clearly embody the blessings of those who came before—he or she should be a representative or avatar of the earlier lineage. Think of this guide as embodying the last time the line was in excellent, self-aware condition.

- **Stay open to meeting with ancestors from much earlier times.** If our recent ancestors and family were already vibrant and healed, we wouldn't need to engage in ancestral repair work in the first place. To make a sufficiently strong and helpful link with ancestral blessings, remember that you may need to extend your vision centuries or even thousands of years before remembered names and history.

∞

EXERCISE FIVE
Seeking an Ancestral Guide

INTENT: Connect with a bright and supportive ancestral guide along the lineage of focus

WHAT YOU NEED: A quiet space and whatever helps you connect with your ancestors

As with exercise 4, you will first record your own voice (or a friend's) reading the following guided visualization and then play it back. Or you could ask a friend to read it aloud for you while you listen. Once you have made these arrangements, find a space conducive to ritual work. When you are there, do whatever helps you **establish sacred space and ritual intent** (e.g., light a candle, offer incense, make prayers). If possible, identify the cardinal directions and consider sitting near the center of the ritual space. Play back the recording, or ask your friend to begin to narrate. If needed, repeat the process, typically on different days, until you feel you're able to make a solid connection.

1. (*Begin recording.*) Start by taking a few minutes to **get physically and emotionally centered.** This may include some meditation or breathing, personal centering prayer, unstructured movement, or just a pause to remember your intent for the ritual. Do what you need to do to calm your mind and connect with your heart. (*Pause for one minute.*)

2. **If you have any supportive guide(s) with whom you already work, call on them now.** Invite the support and feel the loving presence of your guide or guides. They will be your main source of spiritual support—your allies. Some people call on angels, deities, or animal or plant spirit helpers; others may simply envision themselves surrounded in spiritual light. (*Pause for one minute.*)

3. When you feel centered and well supported in spirit, **bring your awareness to the specific lineage you decided to work with and set your intent for this ritual**: to connect with a guide along

your chosen lineage who is both willing and capable of helping you with ancestor repair work. Confirm that your spirit guides support you in this work before proceeding. (*Brief pause.*)

4. To connect with a bright and available ancestor guide, **track back along your chosen lineage**. Maybe you envision following this specific bloodline along a path, a river, or a thread of connection back through time. Use your intuition here as you picture this particular family line, and see how it shows itself. As you go back, be sure to bypass (in whatever way is easiest) any heaviness that may be present along the more recent span of the lineage. You will likely need to travel back before remembered names, sometimes back a thousand or more years. Keep going as far back as is needed and only **stop when you sense or see a clear, bright, and loving guide.** (*Pause for about three minutes.*)

5. **When contact begins, check in with your intuition about this guide**. On the 1–10 scale (ten being the brightest, safest, and most helpful guide), how would you rate this particular ancestor? Seek an eight or above—a big, bright, and vibrant energy. If you meet a guide who is helpful but not too bright in spirit, go back farther to connect with one who is in better shape. Make certain that you are clear about your guide. Trust your gut and your heart here, and if you're unsure, ask your supportive guides to cross-check your choice. Go further back along the lineage if needed. (*Pause for one minute.*)

6. When you get a clear and positive impression from the ancestral guide, approach him or her with deference and humility, knowing that you are greeting a respected elder. Introduce yourself and let this one know why you've come. Confirm that this is an ancestral guide along your lineage of choice and that this one is willing and able to assist in the repair work. If not, respectfully part ways and take your vision farther back. If so, there is no need to rush or drive this process—let the guide lead this initial encounter. **Take some time to simply be in each other's presence and get acquainted**. (*Pause for one to two minutes.*)

7. Consider asking about the guide's relationship with ancestors who came before. Think of this guide as embodying the last time the lineage itself

was in excellent condition. (*Brief pause.*) Be open to any information about what it was like when this guide was alive on Earth. Be curious about what his or her life was like, and about any particular medicines or blessings or qualities that this guide brings. Again, don't rush it. Relax, and take in the quality of the connection. **If it feels right, you might ask the guide for a blessing from the lineage and be sure to truly receive that blessing**. (*Pause for about three minutes.*)

8. You might also ask: **what simple offering or gesture of respect can I make to acknowledge this connection?** This might be a physical offering—water, wine, food, flowers, fire, incense—or it may be a song, some drumming, or just spending more quality time. Listen to what, if anything, comes through. (*Pause for one minute.*)

9. Before you shift your attention back, take a moment to **see these bright and well ancestral guides between you and any recent lineage ancestors who are not yet at peace**. In this way the healed ancestors can function as an ongoing buffer between you and more recent ancestors who are not yet well in spirit. Invite the support of the guides in maintaining your healthy energetic boundaries as needed until the entire lineage is deeply at peace. (*Brief pause.*) Take a final moment to thank these ancestors and any other guides who helped you to make connection. (*Brief pause.*)

10. **Bring your attention all the way back to your body and surroundings**. (*Brief pause.*) When your attention is fully present in your body and your immediate surroundings and your eyes are open, take a moment to notice the energy of the guide you have just contacted. Know that this connection is available to you anytime, even when you are not in a ritual space. To ensure that you recall all that you have been shown, often it's helpful to make some notes immediately after the visualization. (*End recording.*)

As with any new undertaking, don't be discouraged if you're not able to make decisive contact on the first attempt. Be both patient and tenacious, adapt the exercise to your personal temperament while preserving underlying principles, and stay open to responses coming from the ancestors in unexpected ways, such as dreams or synchronicities.

Ways to Deepen Relationships with Ancestral Guides

Once you have made contact with an ancestral guide and are able to honor this connection as a real and meaningful relationship, you may wonder how to nourish this type of relationship over time. Just as relationships with physical beings all have their own unique contours and needs, so it goes with relating with ancestral guides. Several important practices already mentioned in chapter 4 for nourishing relationship include offering inspired speech (e.g., prayer, song, and invocations); establishing an ancestor shrine or other place for honoring; actively working with dreams; and making physical offerings, possibly at your ancestor altar. Below are four additional suggestions.

Spend Quality Time with the Ancestral Guide

After initial contact, consider returning through meditation or visioning to get to know this guide more fully. Remain curious about this ancestor's life on Earth and how his or her gifts and spiritual medicines may help you in the present. If you are open to hearing this ancestor's perspective, ask how he or she sees you and your living family. Consider bringing something challenging in your life to this ancestral guide for support. You can also ask how to honor and convey respect to this ancestor and lineage. If you follow the guidance of this ancestor and find it to be helpful, be sure to follow up with acknowledgment and some expression of gratitude. Perhaps most importantly, return to ask for blessings from this one and get used to feeling this resource and source of support.

Meet Helpful Spirits Associated with This Lineage

You may find that you have unseen allies that you can call upon by virtue of the relationships between them and your older ancestors. These other-than-human spirits may include the collective spirits of animal and plants, deities, elemental powers, or spirits of place. For example, if some of your ancestors were Muslim, they likely spent long hours of their lives reading and reciting verses channeled by the Prophet Muhammad from the archangel Gabriel (that is, the Holy Qur'an). In this way the relationship not only with Muhammad as an ancestral teacher but also with the archangel Gabriel may come more easily to you. Similarly, many tribes of North America recognize that specific medicines, gifts, or spirit connections travel along family lines and that the spirits connected to the bloodline may demand recognition or catalyze initiatory ordeals for the living. The European coats of arms often depict animals like the bear, wolf, eagle, or mythical beings, like dragons and griffins. In this way, multigenerational affinities with specific powers are honored and conveyed to future generations.

Powers connected to lineage express something about the spiritual qualities of the human ancestors. They can also provide critical support for the lineage repair process. The presence or absence of these multigenerational lineage allies may be one criterion for assessing the vitality of the bloodline (see chapter 7). If, for example, a particular family lineage has been associated for centuries with Mount Shasta in northern California, the powers associated with the mountain may help determine which points along the lineage need care and attention. They may also be important to invite in to restore health to the lineage. To use a more familiar example, if a specific bloodline has a strong historical connection with the Virgin Mary, even if the living family or recent ancestors are not Christian, calling in the Virgin's underlying qualities of love, compassion, and sacred feminine energy may help restore that lineage's vitality. In any event, when you assess the health of the lineage, try to determine if and to what degree these forces still speak, and if they wish to play an active role in lineage repair.

What relationships do you already enjoy that you have inherited from your ancestors? With what animals, plants, metals, sacred places, deities, and other spiritual forces did they interact? Which of these relationships are most deeply rooted in your family history? Are any of them still part of your daily life? If so, recognize the ways in which you and these other-than-human relations are connected through your ancestors. Ask your ancestral guide if there are helpful spirits associated with this bloodline that wish to become known to you at this time.

Consecrate Something to Honor These Ancestors

One important teacher of mine, the late Buryat Mongol shaman Sarangerel Odigan, shared in her trainings and writings the Mongolian practice of consecrating an *ongon*.[3] An ongon is a physical object used to enhance and concretize important spirit relationships—such as a connection with an ancestral guide. Throughout history, different cultures have recognized the power of ongons. For centuries, Vajrayana Buddhists persecuted Mongolian shamans, and when not killing them outright, some Buddhists would specifically confiscate and burn ongons as an act of desecration, control, and defilement. This history illustrates the importance the ongon can have as a house or vessel for the energy of the ancestors.

Making and consecrating an ongon is relatively simple. You can use simple natural materials like carved wood, fur, shaped metal, fabric, feather, stone, or decorated bone.

MAKING AN ONGON

Begin by creating the physical form of the ongon itself according to ancestral guidance and intuition. Sit quietly with the questions: "What type of ongon would my ancestors most enjoy? What would it look like?" If you do not receive an answer right away, you might ask to receive a response within three days, either in waking life or in a dream. Over the course of these three days, pay attention to what comes to you.

Once you receive your answer, take the time to lovingly craft your ongon, using the materials you are called to use.

When the physical spirit house is ready to consecrate, enter into a receptive space with your ancestors and ask them to enliven and infuse it with their spiritual energy. This may include offering prayers, songs, or any other inspired ritual elements. You might envision the ancestral guide you are inviting to inhabit the ongon as surrounding you and the spirit house with love and support. Sarangerel gives these directions: "Hold the ongon upward in front of you. You may feel a flow of spiritual energy into the ongon as the spirit takes hold of it. You will be able to tell the difference between 'alive' and 'dead' ongons, for the spiritual essence in them will be directly perceptible through your hands." Stay with this process until you feel that the ancestors have received and blessed the ongon, at which point the consecration is complete.

Finally, begin to relate with the consecrated ongon as a link between you and these ancestors, a manifestation or extension of their spirits in this dimension. You may, for example, wish to keep it on your ancestor altar or wear it on your person when you want to feel closer to these ancestors. You can also make offerings to the ongon. Following Mongolian custom, Sarangerel suggested feeding ongons "by putting a dab of milk, alcohol, or grease on them from time to time."[4] At the heart of the practice, you are designating something physical—something tangible in this world—to serve as an empowered link between you and the ancestors. This can be as subtle as having a consecrated piece of jewelry or article of clothing that you wear in order to remind you of these ancestors and feed the relationship over time.

Pray with the Ancestors for the Lineage Between

Once you have established a strong connection with the ancestral guides, you can work with them to surround the lineage ancestors between you and them with healing intent and positive energy. This practice is beneficial for several reasons. By calling the attention of the guides to the ancestors between their lives and your own, you set in motion the vision of this span of the lineage eventually arriving at a whole and healed condition. By asking the older, well ancestors to extend healing energy to those who came after them, you affirm that the guides are the ones who carry out the repair work, that it is they who will do the heavy lifting, so to speak. Finally, by working with the guides to wrap the not-yet-vibrant ancestors in a net or cocoon of healing prayer, you help contain any heavy energy along the lineage and reinforce your boundaries with the dead who are not yet at peace.

SURROUNDING THE LINEAGE BETWEEN YOU AND YOUR GUIDES WITH HEALING ENERGY

To begin, focus on the connection with the ancestral guides and confirm that they support this practice at this time. If so, invite a space to open between you and the guides—a space for a third between you and them. In this space, envision the lineage between you and the guides. Here you're not calling in any of the heaviness or unhealed energy. You're merely noticing the inseparable link through the generations between you and the guides. However the connection appears to you, ask the guides to direct healing energy and intent to the lineage between. See the span of the lineage between your most recent ancestor (likely your parent or grandparent) and the children of the guides surrounded in prayer and positivity, not in an invasive or pushy way, but as a net of healing and beneficial energy. Once you find your groove and are able to hold the lineage between you and the guides in your awareness, simply sink into this practice for a bit. Allow the guides to be the source of that energy without drawing on any of your personal reserves. If you are able to feel your way into this practice, modify slightly the form of the prayer by asking the guides and the well ancestors before them to hold both ends of this net of prayer, to effectively surround the lineage between you and them. This should allow you to step back and to feel these older, well ancestors entirely surrounding the lineage in healing energy and intent. When you feel complete, ask that the ancestors continue their work with the lineage, take a moment to confirm that no troubled energy remains in your space, and allow whatever doorways of connection were opened between you and the lineage to now close. This practice of prayer is a safe and noninvasive way to extend the blessings and healing energy of the guides to the lineage between you and them.

SEVEN

LINEAGE ANCESTORS AND THE COLLECTIVE DEAD

As you enter into relationship with your ancestral guides, you might wonder about the span of time between their lives and your own. Family patterns of disconnection and pain often originate in the lifetimes of ancestors between the vibrant guides and the more recent and remembered dead. This chapter focuses on practices to get to know and, when needed, make repairs with those ancestors who are beyond the reach of remembered names and faces. In this work, you will learn to identify ancestral gifts and challenges and enliven stories about yourself and your family. Work with the lineage ancestors beyond living memory also sets the stage for effective work with the more recent and remembered dead.

Ancestral Lineage

As you'll remember, in chapter 2 we explored differences between the remembered and collective dead; we also distinguished among the experiences of individual, lineage, and collective or group-level ancestors. Now we're going to go deeper into lineage. Like strands or filaments, our bloodlines consist of individual ancestors whose lives and spirits weave and combine to form sturdy fibers. The intricate weave of these fibers in turn expresses the beautiful and elaborate cloth of the ancestors as a singular collective consciousness. The quality of the raw materials and individual lives informs the integrity of the fibers, and by extension the quality of the overall garment. Each level of scale, every individual life, is inseparable from the whole.

I've heard people describe their experience of distinct family lineages in many different and beautiful ways. Even for the same person, each bloodline tends to have specific associations, a feeling or tone, and an energetic signature. For example, I tend to experience my paternal grandfather's lineage as a bright current of electricity—birdlike, mercurial, and angular, like lightning—while my maternal grandfather's line feels heavier, more like iron, the night sky, pine trees, and snow. During trainings, participants have described lineage as a vine or tree with many branches, a winding river or stream, a series of fires with each flame a single lifetime, a rope or golden chain with many links, a particular color or quality of energy, or a blessed wind passing from breath to breath, lifetime to lifetime. Finding ways to experience and embody different bloodlines is enjoyable, spiritually potent, and useful in repair work with ancestors (see the section in chapter 9 titled "Embodiment, Channeling, and Mediumship," page 176).

To facilitate the overall cycle of lineage repair, I distinguish between five basic spans along our blood lineages, each of which can call for different sensibilities and raise specific concerns.

These are:

- Lineage before the guides
- Lineage from the guides to the remembered dead
- Remembered dead
- Living family members, both elder and junior
- Descendants: those not yet born

Visually this can be conceived as:

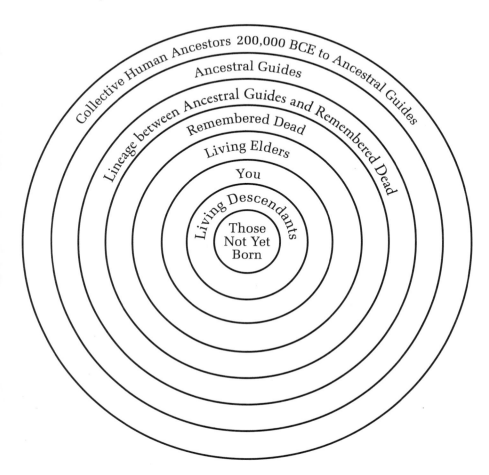

Figure 7.1. Layers of lineage through time

The earlier span of the lineage corresponds to work with ancestral guides (see chapter 6) and provides the vitality and wisdom to guide the ritual repair work. The next three spans of the lineage are the focus of chapters 7, 8, and 9, respectively. Practices to extend blessings to the living family, living descendants, and those not yet born are included in chapter 9. These different types of ancestors, as well as the living family and descendants, all contribute to the collective energy that is *lineage*.

Lineage before the Guides

Our lineage before the lifetime of the ancestral guides extends back through prehistory to the origin of our species, the beginning of life on Earth, and the birth of our universe. Indigenous peoples often view themselves as descendants of specific powers, deities, land spirits, stars, natural forces, or exceptional and ancient human beings. When they say they are children of Raven or the Sun or a specific mountain, this is not just a pretty story. The original powers of any given tradition are generators, batteries, and portals of energy that, when honored and respected, generously feed the forms of our world, including specific lineages. Like an underground root system, stories that anchor the bloodlines in sacred time and divine personalities link human ancestors with the vitality of these old powers, and thereby feed the well-being of the lineage. This wiring of human origins directly into the lives of the gods or primordial powers can add tremendous vitality to lineage repair work.

In practice, however, I find that working with the ancestral guides is functionally similar to (and perhaps a bit safer than) working with even older, primordial powers. In my experience, the guides are the faces or avatars of the ancient lineage, and they express the blessings of the beings that went before them. In doing so, they can also regulate the intensity of otherworldy energies into a human face and form conducive to relationship. Imagine traditional Chinese dragon dancers; if the head of the dragon is the ancestral guide and those dancing the body of the dragon are the earlier lineage extending back through time, relating with the head of the dragon is respectful, efficient, and safer than just climbing on the dragon's back. For this reason, I encourage first working at depth with ancestral guides before seeking direct contact with deities, archetypal forces, or prehuman ancestors.

Lineage from the Guides to the Remembered Dead

Ancestors between the ancient guides and the remembered dead are no longer remembered by name. Therefore they can be counted among the collective dead; however, they may or may not be vibrant or elevated. Martín Prechtel wrote on the post-death journey:

> The Tzutujiil [Maya] believed that the dead rowed themselves to the other world in a "canoe made of tears, with oars made of delicious old songs." Our grief energized the soul of the deceased so it could arrive intact onto the Beach of Stars where the dead go to the other side of the ocean, the salty Grandmother Ocean who tossed and surged between us and the next world. On this beach of star souls our dead were well received by the "last happy ancestor" and then further initiated in that world into the next layer of life. After four hundred days, these dead would graduate into the status of ancestors.[1]

He says that the dead join not their last ancestor but rather their last *happy* ancestor. Thus the guides consist especially of happy ancestors, and the dead in the lineage who lived after them are hopefully also in the process of "getting happy." The intent of this third stage of ancestral repair work, then, is to bring happiness in the form of a vibrant and intact lineage to the doorstep of the remembered dead. The intent of the *entire* lineage repair process is to make sure *all* your family ancestors, distant and remembered, graduate to become happy ancestors and that the blessings of your ancestors are well seated in your living family and in future generations.

In chapter 6, you made intent to contact the most recent point along the bloodline where everything was decisively well, and to greet there an ancestral guide who both embodies the goodness of the ancient lineage and is able to assist with the more recent dead. Unless your family is especially bright in spirit, odds are that this "last happy ancestor" resides beyond remembered names and living memory, in the realm of the older, collective dead. This approach assumes that the ancestral guides are not only well in spirit but that the lineage before them is also well and at peace. In this way the "last happy ancestor" is also the last time when the lineage as a collective energy was well and intact.

Once you have made connection with this guide, the lives that followed immediately after the guide comprise the more distant end of the bloodline still in need of healing. This repair process eventually arrives at your mostly recently forgotten ancestor—the one just beyond the reach of family memory and genealogy research. For example, along my maternal grandmother's line, this is the mother of my great-great-grandmother Mary Fitch. Mary's mother rests for me just on the other side of a veil of forgetting, and her daughter Mary is my most distant ancestor in that line remembered by name. I have met in spirit with an ancestral guide in Mary's and my lineage that lived in pre-Christian Wales. At our time of meeting, the ancestors before this guide were already decisively bright, as this ancestor had consciously worked with them during her lifetime as part of her healing and spirit practice. The lineage from the guides to the remembered dead is therefore from this guide to the mother of Mary Fitch, the span from about 300 to 1870 CE.

Lineage among the Remembered Dead

Often the most challenging type of ancestors to engage, the recent dead can have a tremendous impact on the living. In addition to names and photographs uncovered by genealogy research, these ancestors include deceased grandparents, parents, children, grandchildren, and, potentially, adoptive family that we claim as blood. This is the point in the line where tens of thousands of years of history and life experience step out from the fog of forgetting to intersect living family, old emotional pain and nostalgia, and the complicated truth that we are now the living, breathing face of our lineage. The recent or remembered dead also rest directly between the present and the more ancient ancestors. This does not mean that recent ancestors can block our connection with elevated ones, who are much like a river that flows around a large stone. Nevertheless, the spirit of a not-yet-elevated relative in our immediate space can alter the course of our lives if not addressed. For most people, personal experiences or unresolved emotional pain with the last two generations will profoundly overshadow, often in unconscious ways, their perceptions of and openness to relating to their ancient and ultimately blessed lineages. Please see chapter 8 for guidance on ways to work with the remembered dead.

Assessing the Lineage

To catalyze positive change within any system—be it an individual life, an organization, an ecosystem, or one of your lineages—you first need to form a clear picture of the current state of affairs. So in order to begin repairing your lineage, try to understand the major themes and areas of disconnection along your lineage of focus as well as the condition of the recent dead.

To assess the health of any ancestral line, you may ask what gifts and burdens have been transmitted across the generations and what sources of spiritual power feed this lineage (see "Meet Helpful Spirits Associated with this Lineage," page 110, and "Lineage before the Guides," page 118). Lineage assessment also includes identifying who among the recent dead has yet to fully join the elevated and bright ancestors. As a kind of ancestral doctor, seek to know some basic indicators of both health and illness along the lineage.

Understanding Ancestral Blessings and Burdens

Every human being inherits blessings and burdens from their blood ancestors. Many of our most cherished gifts and our most tenacious life challenges are a continuation, conscious or otherwise, of not-yet-transformed ancestral burdens and family karma. Struggles that may be rooted in ancestral suffering include physical afflictions; predisposition to addiction and mental illness; financial scarcity; legacy of physical or emotional abuse; unresolved karmic debt from murder, war, or exploitation of others; loss of traditions or healthy cultural pride; or an intergenerational disconnection from the natural world, from a sense of home, or from intuition and spiritual vitality. Ignoring family history encourages an unconscious replay of these patterns in our lives and relationships, as well as in the lives of future generations.

Fortunately, we also inherit *gifts* from our lineages—even if our living family and recent ancestors may not have expressed those gifts in recognizable ways. Ancestral blessings may include excellent health;

tendency toward prosperity, fertility, creativity, artistic talent, or intelligence; strong intuitive and dreaming abilities; strong values, good morals, or kindness; affinity for spiritual practice and healing arts; specific hands-on skills and talents; spontaneous happiness, humor, and psychological resilience; and gifts for connecting with plants and animals.

A teacher of mine shared the image of receiving both blessing and burden bundles from our ancestors. With the blessing bundles, we ideally open them, embody the gifts, and perhaps even add to them for future generations. With our burden bundles, in a worst-case scenario we open Pandora's box and, compelled by the momentum of lifetimes of suffering, unconsciously reinforce painful patterns and thereby add to burdens for future generations. A somewhat better approach is to keep the burden bundles closed and let the patterns gradually weaken and die out. This is the approach of "dry drunks" or people who end cycles of violence and abuse without transforming the inner wounds or impacts of previous pain. By any measure, this is *much* better than simply allowing the patterns to continue unchecked. It is often a necessary step on the path toward more complete healing. But in a best-case scenario, we will face our ancestral burdens with the support of ritual, community, or other means, transform the poisons at their root, and thereby eliminate the momentum of any negative karma or destructive patterns for present and future generations.

Understanding your personal gifts and challenges through the lens of your lineage ancestors supports you by:

- Creating a greater sense of connection and support from loving ancestors
- Transforming shame that often accompanies personal struggles
- Healing unrealistic expectations and harmful projections onto family

Gaining greater awareness of the inseparable link between our ancestors and the living family, no matter how estranged you may be from them at present, can relieve feelings of isolation or disconnection. Individuals from fragmented or conflicted family backgrounds may realize that, contrary to their assumptions, they stand at the center of the circle with their ancestors, that they are in fact the one upholding the gifts of the lineages, even if every other living family member lives in dysfunction and turmoil. Taking in the support of loving ancestors, irrespective of the actions of our living family, can radically improve our experience of family and sense of being welcome here on Earth.

Because modern Western cultures focus so much on the individual, we tend to experience our suffering as purely personal and private rather than as also being familial, communal, and intergenerational. When we believe that our core struggles in life live only inside ourselves and are not connected to family and culture, we may feel shame about our pain and feel more disconnected from others as a result. Like an infection, this secondary pain can grow to be more harmful than the original wound.

Ancestor work reveals that our gifts and burdens are legacies that we participate in and that connect rather than separate us from earlier and future generations, as well as to larger movements of culture and history. This realization can help lance and ultimately heal feelings of guilt and shame. Understanding family patterns also makes it easier to externalize or detach ourselves from any given pattern or legacy— and not take our own lives so personally. For example, if I know that my challenge to be more open-hearted and expressive is something my father, his father, and the recent generations before them all struggled with, I can see the pattern as its own kind of living thing or configuration of energy. It is no longer something of my essence, but rather a complicated habit in the house of my life, family, and culture. In this way, I can spend less time indulging in shame about it and more time working with family and friends to together transform our burdens.

As a psychotherapist and community leader, I have also observed the unrealistic psychological expectations people place on their parents and elders in the United States. Longing for our caregivers to embody the divine mother and father is entirely natural. But it's also unrealistic. Some cultures anticipate and address this problem in certain ways. First, children often have multiple parent figures (e.g., aunts, uncles, elder siblings, extended family), which can reduce the intensity of the divinity projection onto one's actual parents. Second, adolescent rites of passage encourage young initiates to forge direct relationships with the gods. When these rites are successful, they can soften expectations placed upon parental figures by facilitating direct, nourishing relationships with the sacred feminine and masculine and thus prevent a potentially devastating level of disappointment in family. Finally, traditions of ancestor reverence help people see parent figures in an intergenerational context and in this way shrink (or inflate) family back to a normal size—not too large, not too small.

If you can see your parents as regular-sized human beings, with all their beauty and imperfections, you can support your own healing, relieve them from godlike expectations, and move toward a more healthy, reciprocal, and realistic relationship.

Identify Not-Yet-Ancestors along the Lineage

In addition to tracking the flow of ancestral blessings and burdens from the life of the guides to the present, your diagnosis of the lineage should also include scanning for unelevated ancestors or ghosts who need attention. In this stage, you will first try to understand where along the lineage there needs to be specific work with not-yet-ancestors. This will help you approach this work with all the necessary preparations and precautions. As with exercise 4, gathering this information calls for maintaining clear energetic boundaries and resisting any temptation to get involved. If you are not able to do so, you are not ready to be doing ancestral repair work.

When you are tracking the lineage before remembered names, the dead may present themselves as a group consciousness, as individuals, or as individuals who speak on behalf of a group of ancestors. In the *Lord of the Rings* series, the dead in the mountain are a great example of a group of not-yet-ancestors represented by an individual leader. When the ghost king takes an opportunity for redemption with the living, he releases the entire group from their ghostly condition so they can finally join the ancestors.

Because of the lack of effective rituals for the dead, the souls of at least one or two deceased relatives of many individuals I meet are not-yet-ancestors—not yet woven into the vibrant web of older lineage and ancestral blessings. This typically becomes clear during the lineage diagnostic process, if not earlier (see exercise 4, page 91). During ancestor weekend trainings, participants have reported experiencing groupings of troubled dead along their lineage, such as women whose voices were silenced, those dead from war and murder, those who endured intense poverty and scarcity, and those persecuted for their beliefs. In cases where a chronic or collective wounding weighs on the lineage, the dead may speak with one unified voice, or many spirits may appear with a shared concern.

In addition to identifying individual not-yet-ancestors, the diagnostic process occasionally reveals problematic other-than-human energies that have become entangled with the human lineage. These can include ancestral curses, offended spirits of the natural world, and diverse types of low-vibration entities (see chapter 8, page 164 for more on this). Again, the focus at this stage is merely to understand the story and to get an overall feel for the repairs that will be necessary.

In conclusion, four indicators of health for any given ancestral lineage include:

- The lineage itself remains firmly anchored in ancient mythic time, and this source of blessings reaches the more recent ancestors.
- Lineage blessings predominate over burdens, and remaining burdens are in the process of being transformed.
- Relationships are intact with other-than-human powers or affinity spirits who support the health of the lineage (such as spirits of place, elemental powers, deities, and animal and plant spirits).

- Most or all individual ancestors along the lineage are clearly bright and elevated in spirit.

To restate this in the negative, four indicators of illness or potential trouble include:

- The lineage is unconscious of its mythic origins or sacred time, so this source of blessings does not reach the recent dead or the living.
- Lineage burdens predominate, and blessings have been distorted or forgotten.
- Relationships are not remembered or nourished with ancestral affinity spirits.
- Numerous recent dead are not-yet-ancestors, and there is no awareness of or attempt to resolve this problem among the living.

∞

EXERCISE SIX

GETTING TO KNOW THE LINEAGE

INTENT: Get to know the lineage between your ancestral guides and the present

WHAT YOU NEED: A quiet space and whatever helps you connect with your ancestors

For this exercise, you will again record your own reading of the following guided visualization and then play it back. Alternatively, you could ask a friend to read it aloud for you while you listen. Once you have recorded the visualization or found a friend to narrate, find a space conducive to ritual work. When you are there, do whatever helps you **establish sacred space and ritual intent** (e.g., light a candle, offer incense, make prayers). If possible, identify the cardinal directions and consider sitting near the center of the ritual space. Play back the recording, or ask your friend to begin to narrate.

1. (*Begin recording.*) Start by taking a few minutes to **get physically and emotionally centered**. This may include some meditation or breathing, personal centering prayer, unstructured movement, or just a pause to remember your intent for the ritual. Do what you need to do to calm your mind and connect with your heart. (*Pause for one minute.*)

2. When you feel centered, **call in the supportive ancestral guide along this lineage with whom you connected in exercise 5.** Confirm that this guide is both willing and able to guide the work (i.e., is an eight or above in the 1–10 scale). If there are recently deceased ancestors along this lineage who are also well and with whom you already work, you may invite them to join this process. Share with these guides about your intent to better understand this lineage as a whole. Confirm that you have their support before proceeding. (*Pause for one minute.*)

3. **Respectfully invite the guide to show you the condition of the lineage as a whole.** Seek to understand what has happened in the lineage, to learn where any repairs are needed between the life of the guide and the present, and to receive this information in a safe way. Perhaps the lineage appears as a thread, a river, a rope, a cord of light, a series of fires, or something else entirely. See the lineage as a collective energy. How does it look as a system? Notice the bright spots, the blockages, and where the energy has gotten tangled. Ask the guide to show you and to drive the process. Again, you are just here to observe; resist the urge to intervene, make contact with more ancestors along this lineage, or change anything at this time. (*Pause for three to four minutes.*)

4. **Once you have observed the lineage as a whole,** you may ask the guide to show you the stories of some defining individual lives along it. Looking at the line overall, ask the guide: Where are the individual lives that are *not* well (if any)? Also inquire about the recent dead along this bloodline. You can ask the guide about a particular ancestor (e.g., a great-grandparent, grandparent, or parent). Are they basically well? In between? Not so well? Again, be clear that your intent is only to understand, not to fix, heal, or change anything at this time. (*Pause for three to four minutes.*)

5. **Finally, inquire about the blessings and burdens of the lineage.**
(*This may also be done as a distinct visioning process.*) Ask your guide:
What are three blessings that come through this lineage? They might
take the form of gifts, medicines, natural talents, or positive attributes.
Identify three of them. (*Pause for one to two minutes.*) Next, ask the
guide: What are three burdens that come through this lineage? They
might take the form of challenges, addictions, health ailments, poisons,
or negative attributes. Identify these burdens. Again, remember that
you aren't trying to fix anything, just seeking to understand. (*Pause for
one to two minutes.*)

6. After you have some clarity on blessings and burdens, **visualize
stepping back from your focus on the lineage and returning
to the presence of your guides alone**. If needed, ask the guides
to help you clear your space and energy from any residual heaviness.
(*Brief pause.*) Invite any final communications before thanking your
ancestral guide and any others who accompanied you. When you are
done, return your attention to your physical body and surroundings.
(*Brief pause.*)

7. Before opening your eyes, gently scan your space and surroundings a
final time to **be sure that you are truly complete** and clear from
any ancestors or other heaviness you may have witnessed. (*Brief pause.*)
When you are ready, open your eyes and bring your attention fully back
to your physical body and your surroundings. If grief or other strong
feelings arise at any point while bearing witness to the lineage, honor
those feelings, but make sure to keep your personal energy clear and
your link intact with the ancestral guides overseeing the process. To
ensure that you recall all that you have been shown, often it's helpful to
make some notes immediately afterward. (*End recording.*)

With knowledge comes responsibility, and when you become more conscious
of the ancestral blessings and burdens along your bloodlines, you may consider
some type of ritual commitment to embodying inherited gifts. This could be as
simple as stating out loud to your ancestors how you understand specific gifts

to be part of their legacy and how you plan to carry on this positive legacy, or it could be a more elaborate ceremony where you feast the ancestors (see exercise 12, page 192) and invoke their support for major life transformations. Likewise, you may be moved to offer ritual with the intent to end the intergenerational transmission of specific ancestral burdens for yourself and your descendants. Of course the best fix is to live the desired changes in your life and relationships.

With respect to the transformation of burdens, I suggest first completing the repair cycle and then returning to ask the ancestral guides if they believe further ritual with this intent is helpful. If so, you may want to represent the burdens with something physical (e.g., a handful of seeds, a statement written on paper, a bundle of sticks) and ask your guides about how they wish to ritually transform them (e.g., burning, burial, release into a body of water).

Making Repairs with Older Lineage Ancestors

In this and the next stage, you will move into catalyzing healing and beneficial change for your ancestors and living family. Some may find this intention presumptuous, arrogant, unnecessary, a reversal of the natural order, or otherwise inappropriate, because it implies that we living humans can help our ancestors. These concerns are legitimate and worth exploring. Objections typically revolve around one of three assumptions: our ancestors are already well and do not need our help; intervention is only ethically appropriate when help is explicitly requested; and we are not in a position to usefully assist our ancestors even if the help is needed and requested. To some degree, I agree with all of these objections.

For one, the ancestors don't exactly need our help; it's those who are ghosts, not-yet-ancestors, or otherwise in a conflicted and unelevated condition who could use the support. So we are not exactly *helping* the ancestors, but rather inviting them to assist the dead in *becoming* ancestors. In this way, the repair cycle restores the natural order, in which ancestors are spiritual elders who actively and effectively support their descendants.

As for the second objection—the importance of not rushing in to heal or fix without invitation—if you follow the steps in the repair process, you first come into relationship with ancestral guides or guardians of the lineage and then, with their support and guidance, proceed to understand the lineage without changing anything. Only after coming into relationship with the true elders of the lineage do you even attempt to act in ways that benefit the dead. By this point, the work should be driven by the ancestral guides, not by your script for what ought to happen. If the guides say back off, you can try to understand their reasons, but you should still respect their counsel.

In regard to the third objection: the spiritual energy necessary to effect real change comes from a place beyond ego, conscious intent, and personal agenda. Ritual methods call for a dance between effort and surrender. In this way, *we* are not the ones who help the troubled dead; rather, we are catalysts and supplicants at the feet of larger forces, calling out from the heart for the older, well ancestors to catalyze personal, family, and cultural healing. As with so much of traditional healing, it's less about what you know and more about *whom* you know and how much love, beauty, sincerity, and passion you can muster for the greater good.

Although mystery and grace reside at the heart of transformation, I've noticed that some themes do seem to recur. They can be helpful to remember in ritual repair. Four key themes are explored in more depth below.

Medicine and Sickness Heal Each Other

A Zen teaching exchange between ninth-century master Yunmen Wenyan and one of his students reads:

> *Medicine and sickness heal each other.*
> *The whole world is medicine.*
> *What am I?*[2]

In other words, blessings and burdens often correspond to or mirror one another. Blessings of healthy warriorship, when lacking a relevant cause, can twist into dogmatism, senseless violence, and suicidal despair. Along one lineage, my ancestors were big drinkers and were not always the best with personal boundaries, but this burden points to the obscured blessing of a sensual and ecstatic appreciation for embodied life. Gifts of great spiritual vision with no support or place in the larger culture can manifest as grandiosity, psychosis, and psychological inflation. How do the blessings and burdens along your respective lineages relate? Through studying lineage poisons, corresponding medicines also become clear.

"Whoever Saves One Life Saves the World Entire"

Popularized by the film *Schindler's List,* this verse from the Hebrew scripture known as the Talmud[3] reminds us that care for one individual can have potent effects on the whole. For example, Carol, a participant in the weekend trainings, when working with her maternal grandmother's lineage, encountered a Japanese ancestor who lived about two centuries ago, at a time of transition when aspects of the larger culture were opening to outside influence. This ancestor felt torn between two realities, and as her story unfolded over the course of the training, it became clear that this ancestor's journey closely mirrored core challenges that Carol also struggled with of integrating and harmonizing different cultures and bloodlines. By the second day of the training, both Carol and her ancestor were weaving together previously disconnected and disparate strands into a coherent whole, and in this way raising the vibration of the entire lineage.

Carol's experience also illuminates the collaborative nature of the work. If she had simply viewed this ancestor as someone needing fixing and impatiently beamed her with white light, the richness and intimacy of the relationship would have been lost. This individual ancestor expressed the crux of the repair needed for the entire lineage. By taking the time to return again and again to her ancestor's story, Carol made important new connections in her life and embodied the patience and wisdom necessary for healing.

A Canoe Made of Our Tears

Indigenous elders emphasize the sacredness of grief, including when we are assisting the dead to become ancestors. Malidoma Somé wrote,

> The average western person is grieving about being isolated. Western men in particular are grieving about the dead they didn't grieve properly because they were told that men don't cry. In my work, I hear this everywhere. Grief is not only expressed in tears, but also in anger, rage, frustration, and sadness. An angry person is a person on the road to tears, the softer version of grief.[4]

Reflecting on his grandfather's funeral, Somé wrote of the importance of grief in the elevation of the dead: "The Dagara believe that the dead have a right to collect their share of tears. A spirit who is not passionately grieved feels anger and disappointment, as if their right to be completely dead has been stolen from them."[5] Time in the realm of spirit is not linear, and even if the ancestors lived on Earth centuries ago, their spirits still speak in the present moment, and living descendants may help to finally grieve them into the ancestral realms.

Although all emotions are inherently natural, in my experience not all expressions of grief are equally healing and helpful for the living or the dead. Grief is ideally held in a supportive and safe container, whether in community, with a trusted friend or ally, or even with the support of ancestral guides or other helpful forces. The energy of grief is potent, and if it is blocked or allowed to overwhelm for too long, it can injure the body and spirit. For me, a guideline is that "good grief" eventually helps me feel more connected to others, more healthy, and more human, whereas I feel more cautious about grief that leads me to feel more separate, consistently overwhelmed, or self-pitying. Sometimes simply calling into awareness loving guides and a memory of our fundamental connectedness is enough to shift the experience in a more healing and connective direction.

When departed loved ones are in limbo or still tied to the living, this can also complicate the grieving process for those who remain on Earth. Consider ghosts as people who haven't finished dying—souls still in the rite of passage that began with the death of the body, which will hopefully complete when they are welcomed as an ancestor. Even if the recent dead are not in your immediate vicinity, how can you mourn the loss of someone who hasn't fully departed this world? Expressed in this way, lineage repair work helps the dead to finish dying and to be born as ancestors. As the family dead settle into their new status as ancestors and the living get clear of any potentially disruptive influence from the spirits of the deceased, this supports both closure and new layers of emotional healing. This is not to imply that grief waits in some tidy way until the dead are fully well in spirit, but when the dead have truly finished with their time on Earth, the living can often more fully feel and accept their loss in ways that support healthy grieving. This can include not only grieving more deeply the loss of a loved one, but also feeling the end of dreams and longing for connection with the deceased that will never be met, at least not during the grieving person's time on this Earth. Remember, grief in itself isn't a bad thing; it is a sacred and necessary human emotion that can catalyze profound life changes, wash away old structures, and open pathways of heart and soul-level knowing.

As empathic creatures, we are also capable of feeling the grief of others, of spirit energies, and of the world in a larger sense. This can be profoundly healing and connective, as long as we respect our personal limits and remember that we have a say in how open we are to larger forces moving through us. Making ourselves available for repairs with our bloodlines sometimes calls for opening the floodgates of years, if not centuries, of stuck grief in ways that can be hard to predict. Sometimes deeply grieving past harms along a lineage is exactly the means by which we can transform those harms. If this type of emotional release wants to move through you, consider staying open to depth of feeling, both for your own healing and for your family and people. When the waters of grief are able to flow and reshape the landscape of our hearts, the spirit of forgiveness and reconciliation often arises naturally from the tender space of well-grieved losses.

Story Repair Is Lineage Repair

Our identities, our cultures, and our basic understanding of the world come from stories. When the narrative of our life is meaningful, we're happier and more able to metabolize the adversity that comes our way. When our sense of being a part of a larger story breaks down, we tend to feel more alone and to suffer. Lineage repair can remedy this sense of isolation by helping you understand and embody the specific blessings of your blood lineages in your life today. By claiming our place in the line, we affirm that the ancestors also live in our bones and in each cell of our bodies, and that we deeply affect one another. Ceremonial leader Hua Anwa says:

> I really believe in us having our ancestral memory in our bones, and being in sacred space will help birth that reconnection to your ancient self. You're an ancestor. You carry the line, right here. And so when we acknowledge that, it's kind of overwhelming, because we should have all these wisdoms inside of us; if we're the vessel for our ancestral lineage then it's all inside of us. It's not gone, it just needs to be reawakened and remembered. This ancestral connection is extremely important, and we're the vessel for it, so it's our job to remember it. And then pass it down, pass it forward.[6]

In ritual work, repairing the ancestral story sometimes looks like remembering and picking up the mantle of dormant lineage gifts, thereby completing a circuit of energy and meaning between the living and the older ancestors. When we relate directly to older, elevated ancestors, whatever needs healing along the lineage between us and them can start to seem more like an exception, a period of temporary amnesia now bracketed by awareness and ancestral memory. In visualizations or shamanic journeying practices, you and the ancestral guides may work with the lineage as a living energy or even as symbols rather than as individual spirits. For example, you and your guides may give care to the lineage by relighting a series of torches or signal fires (each a lifetime), clearing blockages in a river, combing out tangles from long hair, sending electrical charges back and forth along a wire, or otherwise nursing the line back to health with love, care, and remembering. Buried ancestral treasures hidden in the bones reawaken to transform fragmentation into a story of renewal, to enliven and affirm lineage, and to raise the vibration of the dead who lived between our life and the ancient guides.

⚭

EXERCISE SEVEN
Ritual to Assist Lineage Ancestors

INTENT: Offer ritual for the well-being, healing, and elevation of older lineage ancestors

WHAT YOU NEED: A quiet space and whatever helps you connect with your ancestors

In this exercise, the repair work on your chosen bloodline begins in earnest. There are two important points to remember as you are preparing for this ritual: (1) focus on repair work for one section of your lineage or an individual ancestor at a time, and don't try to take on too much at once; and (2) expect to repeat this ritual as many times as you need until it feels complete. You might focus on this ritual once a week or once monthly until the lineage feels bright and strong. Remember to read the entirety of part 2 before engaging in ritual, just to be sure you have sufficient context for the things you may encounter. Also, while I provide one structure for the ritual below, your work might appear quite different, depending on the guidance you receive from your ancestors. Trust your instinct and let the ancestral guides do their guiding.

As with the exercises that came before, you may record yourself reading the following progression for playback or ask a friend to read it aloud for you during your visioning. Once you have made the recording or found a friend to narrate, find a space conducive to ritual work. When you are there, do what helps you **establish sacred space and ritual intent**.

1. (*Begin recording.*) Take a few minutes to **get physically and emotionally centered**. This may include some meditation or breathing, personal centering prayer, unstructured movement, or just a pause to remember your intent for the ritual. (*Brief pause.*) When you feel centered, **call in any supportive guides** with whom you already enjoy a relationship. Be sure to connect with the ancestral guide you met with earlier along the specific lineage you are working in. Share with the guides your intent to support healing and repairs on behalf of your lineage ancestors. Confirm that you have their support before proceeding. (*Pause for one to two minutes.*)

2. You are now ready to do the ritual. Remembering your assessment of the lineage as a whole (see exercise 6), begin by focusing on the part of the lineage that is closest to the lifetime of the ancestral guide. (*Brief pause.*) Following the lead of the well ancestors, bring your attention to the generations directly following the guide. Look for areas in need of healing, and invite the guides to draw forward the healing to those places with the intent to welcome the ancestors there into the lineage. Remember to be patient and to focus the repairs on one span or point along the lineage at a time. This may be limited to a single lifetime, or it may include themes that arose along a span of several centuries. In either case, tend to one section or joint in the overall lineage. Go to that place now and, following the lead of the guides, make intent that healing love and care arrive for these ancestors in your bloodline. Continue to focus here until you feel some kind of movement or improvement in the energy. (*Pause for five minutes.*)

3. When the guides are complete for the time being with that spot in the lineage, **consolidate the repairs** up to that point so that the work itself

is likely to "stick." Picture a river of ancestral blessings from the elevated guides. You are widening the channel from the past to the present, making sure that all is well up to the spot you are working with. Once the current cycle of tending feels complete for the moment, ask your guides: "What is a simple way I can reinforce the healing?" This may include physical offerings, an action to be taken now in ritual space, or something to be done later. Be open to the guidance you receive and only commit to doing what you are certain to fulfill. (*Pause for one to two minutes.*)

4. Once you have consolidated your repairs, **double-check the lineage up to that point**. If something still feels troubled along the line up to the spot you are working with, stay with it until it shifts. If it feels complete, either move to the next area of healing focus along the lineage or complete the overall visioning for now. In any event, don't proceed to another area along the lineage until the span you've been working on is an eight or above on the 1–10 scale. Be patient with the work as you gradually move the new "well point" closer toward the present. Take a moment to assess whether or not you are ready to progress to another span of the lineage. (*Brief pause. If you are recording and you wish to allow for a second round of tending, go back to step 2. Begin with "Go to that place now . . ." and record through the end of step 4 again.*)

5. As you finish for now, **step back from the lineage repair work to focus only on the ancestral guides**. From this place ask them to help you **clear your space and energy from any residual heaviness you may have encountered during the repairs**. Be open to any final messages they have for you. (*Pause for one minute.*) When they indicate that the process complete and you're in the clear, thank them and return your attention fully to your physical body and surroundings. (*End recording.*)

You'll know you're complete with this stage of the repair work when you confirm with your guides that all the ancestors up to the threshold of remembered names are well in spirit and are integrated into the energy of the lineage as a whole. Using the metaphor of the Chinese dragon dancers, the head of the dragon will now be at the threshold of remembered names, with your most recently forgotten ancestor at the front of a healthy lineage stretching back to the mythic origins of your bloodline.

Getting the lineage back to this level of vitality almost always takes more than one ritual, and for many people the bulk of the repair work occurs at this stage. Be sure not to rush the process. As with the entire repair cycle, each step builds upon the previous work, and when your older lineage is glowing, this helps you tend to the recent dead with relative ease. Consider returning to the practice of "Pray with the Ancestors for the Lineage Between" shared at the end of chapter 6 (page 113). You may alternate between that gentler and more integrative practice and the more direct ritual intervention of exercise 7. Keep in mind that there's nothing about this work that requires you to connect with heavy energies; it's critical to let the guides drive the process. Finally, make plenty of space throughout the process for personal transformation, family healing, and new connections in your own life.

EIGHT

ASSISTING THE REMEMBERED DEAD

D eath touches us nowhere more closely than when we lose a beloved family member or friend. Learning to relate safely and effectively to the remembered dead can not only be healing in lineage repair work but also allow relationships with loved ones in spirit to continue naturally after their passing. In this chapter, you'll learn about the importance of emotional healing and completing unfinished business with recent ancestors—including ways to put this into practice with your own family and other beloved dead. You'll also learn the foundations of soul guidance and ancestralization practices that can be used to assist recent generations of family members to become ancestors. Finally, you'll learn ways to work with challenging situations that occasionally arise with the troubled dead (e.g., fragmented and nasty ghosts, family curses, unhelpful spirit entities). Upon completion of this fourth stage (of five total) in the lineage repair process, you will have assisted all recent ancestors in your lineage of focus to be welcomed by the guides into their rightful place in the lineage.

Emotional Healing, Forgiveness, and Unfinished Business

Just because someone we know dies, it doesn't mean we are instantly at peace with that person in spirit. Nor does it mean that that person is automatically a peaceful, loving ancestor. Upon the passing of close family and friends, feelings such as anger, resentment, and relief are common, even if they are not always openly expressed. Cultural or family censorship of unwelcome feelings can make emotional healing and grieving more complicated and can introduce an element of guilt or shame. Despite these challenges, it's ideal to give care and consideration in emotionally honest and vulnerable ways to any unresolved issues between ourselves and the deceased before we provide more involved ritual support. Not only is this healing for us, but it also supports the dead in completing their life on Earth, and helps us show up more effectively for any follow-up ritual work. For the recent dead, completing unfinished business may also include concerns that don't directly involve us but we may in a position to understand and assist in fulfilling.

Emotional Healing

In the United States, there is an epidemic of physical, sexual, and emotional abuse from parents and caregivers to children, within intimate partnerships, and within extended families. For some people, when a loved one dies, it may mean the death of an abuser—the end of a very real threat to their safety, even if the abuse itself ended years ago. If you or someone you know experienced this, you may feel relief or freedom after the abuser's death. Normal reactions can include an upwelling of suppressed anger that is now safer to express, guilt and shame about past abuse that was never addressed, and sadness at the failure to bridge differences during life. Death of a parent or spouse can also mean the end of secret hopes for reconciliation and validation of your past experiences, or hopes for being seen and loved for who you are. If you have not healed from past harms by family members, this can complicate the natural grieving process after a loved one's death. However, when hope for a different life dies and you accept your losses, deep grief and other repressed emotions can finally flow, and emotional healing can begin in earnest. If you are in the midst of this type of emotional intensity, I recommend seeking professional support when possible, combined with proactive self-care and leaning on trustworthy family and friends. Healing old emotional pain on whatever timeline is necessary is an excellent way to honor your ancestors; it encourages personal vitality and keeps alive the possibility of reconciling with the spirit of the deceased.

The death of a loved one also changes family relationships in ways that can be both irreversible and hard to predict. In psychotherapeutic terms, the family system must find a new equilibrium or homeostasis. Ideally, the time of transition following the death of a family member will lead to major positive change as healthier patterns become the new normal. But things will never truly return to the way they were before the loss; this is not a realistic expectation. A parent's death may heighten your own felt proximity to the ancestral realm as you become next in line, and the passing of a partner or child may leave you with a hole in your heart and psyche in the shape of their life.

The passing of loved ones can also give rise to a longing to follow them into the realm of the ancestors—a genuine risk. Grieving the accidental death of his four-year-old son in his famous song "Tears in Heaven," musician Eric Clapton asks, "Would you know my name / if I saw you in heaven?" After singing directly to the spirit of his son, Clapton ends the song with "I must be strong and carry on / 'cause I know I don't belong here in heaven." Literature and history acknowledge that couples may follow each other in death (e.g., Romeo and Juliet, Othello and Desdemona, Tristan and Iseult, Layla and Majnun, Mark Antony and Cleopatra). Local news stories occasionally report on elderly couples who follow each other into the ancestral realms, dying within days if not hours of one another. Those who don't die or kill themselves in response to their partner's deaths commonly report having to resist the temptation to do so. Either the living person, the spirit of the recently deceased, or both can pull for this scenario. This risk is yet another reason to encourage the recently deceased to make their transition soon after death to the ancestral realms. The better the spiritual condition of the deceased, the less risk that the living will be drawn to follow them in death, and the more free from interference the grieving process will be for those who remain.

Participants in weekend trainings sometimes ask whether unresolved issues between the living and the dead can prevent the dead from moving on to become ancestors. This is a good and nuanced question. The short answer is, "Only if the dead allow themselves to be held back." The longer answer requires recognizing that we are all intimately related, and that we can't help influencing those we love simply by our own state of health or disease.

If you are a newly deceased spirit, can the attitude of your living family affect your journey after death? Yes, absolutely. Let's say you are a loving, elderly mother of five who struggles with depression, but you are still basically kind to people. Let's say you have no spiritual tradition of your own, you feel no real connection to your ancestors, and you have just died. Under these circumstances, let's estimate that you have a 50/50 chance of spontaneously making it into the realm of the ancestors in the months after your death; things could go in either direction. In one scenario, your children and their families attend the funeral and openly weep for you, express how much your life mattered, and pray for you to be at peace. In a second scenario, the tears don't flow, as your family, feeling abandoned, is unwilling to let go. Absorbed in their own internal conflicts, they say they are not ready for you to leave them and beg you to stay. In this type of situation, how your living family responds to your death can tip the balance one way or another. The best prevention for this type of post-death inertia is to emotionally heal yourself and your relations with loved ones as much as possible during life.

Forgiveness

Research confirms that forgiveness is good for our health and happiness, even though the prospect of forgiving can feel threatening and can evoke strong feelings and opinions.[1] To clarify, forgiveness is *not* about forgetting, condoning, or minimizing past harms, nor is it about failing to protect self and others in the present. Although forgiveness is important for emotional resolution, I'm not aware of any benefit in intentionally seeking to forget the past. Nor does forgiveness call upon you to downplay past harm or to justify or rationalize the ways in which you feel hurt or wronged. In tough situations, personal healing with living family may include legal intervention, breaking off contact, or establishing clear boundaries. If you or someone you know is in a toxic or unsafe situation, the priority must be to get safe. Only later can emotional healing and forgiveness follow.

Forgiveness, for me, is about completing or resolving past experience, especially regarding real or perceived harms. Forgiveness becomes possible when you accept things as they are rather than as how you wish they were. Again, acceptance does not imply approval, nor does it keep you from working to prevent future harms, but it does require you to face what has occurred. Your efforts at repair may call for asking for forgiveness as well as extending it. As a practice, forgiveness may be largely internal and personal, or it can directly involve other people, living or deceased. Even if you'll never know certain relatives or are not in contact with them, you can still hold them in your heart, forgive them, and pray for their happiness. If you do invite others to be a part of your process, you can forgive people without having to invite them back into your life; similarly, others may forgive you even if they don't want much to do with you. In other words, forgiving people doesn't oblige you to bond with them in the present; it can even help end unhealthy attachments. If the people we seek forgiveness from are not willing or available to engage, we can still imagine receiving their forgiveness. Provided we have done everything in our power to make amends, this may at least enable us to forgive ourselves. In my experience, although we can't pretend to feel something we don't, we can engage in forgiveness practices with an open heart and mind, staying receptive to whatever arises.

In lineage repair work, the practice of forgiveness can support healing with older ancestors, the remembered dead, and the living family. Keep in mind that when you are working with each group, issues may arise that need resolving. When addressing older ancestors, for example, you might feel certain concerns, such as a disappointment in their choice to leave behind their homeland or traditional ways of life, judgment of their historical misuse of power, regret about their failure to resist or prevent oppression, frustration that they passed on rather than resolving ancestral burdens, or disappointment because they failed to live up to your expectations as elders.

When working on forgiveness with the remembered dead, you might feel the whole range of human complication and pain, such as feeling responsible in some way for their death, believing that your life is a disappointment to loved ones, feeling regret for not resolving differences during their lifetimes, or needing to release long-held family secrets or lies.

When addressing unresolved pain with living family, common challenges can include fears that forgiveness will open you to further harm; frustration at their lack of openness to dialogue; and pride, self-righteousness, and underlying shame that prevents you from owning up to your past mistakes. Ask yourself honestly: Do you feel guilty about any past actions with your family? Would any of your relatives benefit from hearing an apology from you? If so, what stops you from acknowledging and healing past harms with this family member? When you are personally able to maintain appropriate boundaries with living relatives and you've done some emotional healing, explore possibilities for making amends. By first focusing on your own role in past difficulties, rather than demanding an apology for real or imagined wrongs, you can often open up greater space for healthy dialogue and repairs. Under optimal conditions, you may be able to craft inclusive rituals of forgiveness that include humble and heartfelt communication with living family members. If conditions don't support directly engaging with the living, you can still privately forgive them and keep your heart open to their forgiveness. Staying open to working with any feelings that arise when seeking to forgive (and receive forgiveness from) your ancestors, your family, and yourself supports happier and more vital relationships with both the living and the dead.

EXERCISE EIGHT

Ancestral Forgiveness Practice

INTENT: Engage in mutual forgiveness work with recent and more distant family ancestors

WHAT YOU NEED: A quiet space and, ideally, a supportive friend or ally for partner practice

Forgiveness practices can encourage emotional completion and healthy relationships with the ancestors. For this practice, you can recruit a kind and supportive human ally who also respects your work with family ancestors. I've always done this as an exchange in which each person has the opportunity to speak, but one person can serve solely as a listener. The practice can also be modified to function solo. Any revisions or additions that encourage forgiveness and healing between you and your ancestors are great. Keep it authentic and heart-connected, and don't try to force yourself to feel any particular way.

1. **Open ritual space and invite the ancestors.** Begin by establishing a safe space that is free from disturbance. Call to your loving and supportive guides, including any ancestral teachers from the lineage of focus. When you feel the ancestors present, seek their support for this practice of forgiveness. If you're doing the practice as an exchange, determine who in the dyad will speak first before you continue.

2. **Speak directly to ancestors and family.** In this first portion of the exercise, the listener is silent and holds a compassionate, receptive, and stabilizing presence for the speaker. The listener is not asked in any way to embody the speaker's ancestors. If you wish to limit the duration of the exchange, the listener can serve as a timekeeper (I suggest about ten minutes here if you are timing the exercise); however, adherence to a set duration for this part of the exchange is entirely optional. If you are practicing solo, invite the ancestors themselves, perhaps at your ancestor shrine, to serve as listeners.

The speaker in the dyad directly addresses the lineage of ancestors, voicing whatever is most relevant and in need of expression. As the speaker, you are talking not to the listener but to the ancestors and perhaps to living family in this lineage. This is the time to say whatever you want to say to these ancestors as if they are present before you. Consider speaking first to the older lineage (before remembered names) and then to the known ancestors or living elders of this lineage. Most importantly, speak without censorship and follow the energy on a heart level, allowing for moments of silence, if needed, to stay connected to your inner truth and experience. When you feel complete (or when the time is complete, if you are timing the exchange), simply drop into silence for a moment before proceeding to step 3.

3. **Forgiveness practice.** If you're doing this exercise solo, you'll need to read (or memorize) the sentences below. If you work with a partner, I recommend that the listener maintain supportive silence while the speaker reads the part below. The speaker repeats each of the two sides of the forgiveness practice three times, with a pause between extending (first part) and receiving (second part) forgiveness. If you have a third participant, he or she could read the passage below and ask the speaker to repeat what has been said in short segments of call and response. This frees the speaker from needing to read from a page or memorize the passage. Explore what works well for you.

When the practice calls for the speaker to "say their name or names," you may shorten this to "my grandparent so-and-so's people on back through time," or you could name a specific ancestor. As the speaker, address your ancestors directly, this time with the established wording of the forgiveness practice. There is no need to track time here; begin when you are ready and follow your personal rhythm.

I (say your full name) *forgive you* (say their name or names) *for all the harms, both real and imagined, known and unknown, intentional and unintentional, that you have done to me from the beginning of time to the present. And I release you from all of these.* (Repeat three times, then pause.)

I accept your forgiveness of me, for all the harms, both real and imagined, known and unknown, intentional and unintentional, that I have done to you from the beginning of time to the present. And I accept your release of me from all of these.[2] (Repeat three times.)

When you have voiced your intent to both forgive and receive forgiveness from your ancestors, pause to invite the energy to settle, and then proceed at your own rhythm. Before you begin this stage, decide if you wish to include a third aspect of the practice that focuses on self-forgiveness for any ways in which you have failed to respect, honor, or live up to your own potential. If so, you can modify the wording to "I forgive myself for all the harms . . . that I have done to myself . . . and I release myself from all of these" or whatever wording works best for you.

4. **Speaker and listener change roles.** After the speaker is complete, speaker and listener should thank each other, stand, and in some way cleanse the space energetically. I often burn cedar or sage for this purpose, but you could also use cool water, fresh plants (e.g., rosemary, lavender), song, or centering prayer. If you're doing the practice solo or you are the only one who wishes to speak, proceed to step 5. If the listener also wishes to address the ancestors, switch roles, return to step 2, and proceed to completion.

5. **Cleansing and completion share.** When you have finished speaking, pause to honor and give thanks for all that was shared. Following your own rhythm and instincts, cleanse the overall space and inform any ancestors or guides present that you are now finishing the practice. Be open to any final messages from them before respectfully asking them to depart. Consider making notes about any areas that could benefit from further healing and forgiveness.

Completing Unfinished Business

If you died today, would you have any unfinished business, anything that would make it hard to say goodbye to your life? Would you have difficulty letting go of family, friends, or relations? Are your will and financial affairs in order? Are there any projects, possessions, or places you would find challenging to release?

It's easy to underestimate how we can stay tied to this world and this identity, especially if we die in confusing circumstances, such as war, accidents, homicides, suicides, or sudden illness. It's even harder to move on to ancestor status if those in the generations before you are not at peace themselves or are not there to receive you. Do you feel the tangible support of your loving ancestors waiting to receive you when you die? Why leave the familiar when you're not sure where you're headed in the first place? Nobody plans on becoming a troubled ghost; it simply happens to all sorts of otherwise good people who do not have sufficient spiritual momentum after death to carry them into the realm of the ancestors.

The previous section addressed emotional healing and forgiveness with the ancestors, especially the recent dead. Getting current with the dead can also include completing whatever you—or they—experience as unfinished business (e.g., sorting out inheritances, possessions, debts, and legal affairs; honoring last wishes and requests; arriving at clarity and justice in cases of unexpected death; conveying final goodbyes; spreading ashes after cremation). Any effort you can make to resolve unfinished business is an excellent way to honor your ancestors. When practical matters don't go the way we want surrounding the death of loved ones, emotional healing, forgiveness, and completing unfinished business can weave together in ways that are hard to predict. But know this: caring for these concerns, with support, *is* ancestor work and *is* honoring the dead. Even if final requests or unfinished business mattered more to the deceased than to you or the rest of your family, respecting these requests can help release the deceased person from life on Earth and move into the ancestral realms.

Psychopomp, Elevation of the Dead, and Ancestralization

In the midst of your grieving, you may ask whether or not the recent dead are at peace. How are they doing in their new existence? This is an appropriate concern. However, simply raising the question does not oblige you to personally enact rituals and practices to assist the dead. How do you know they need assistance in the first place? If you're sure you want to know whether or not they're at peace, exercises 4 and 6 present safe and structured ways to assess any specific ancestor and the lineage in which they are embedded. You might also consider your dreams, synchronicities, or waking intuitions, as well as any other ancestral contacts, to form an overall picture of the state of the recently deceased. When multiple sources, including your gut instinct, tell you that specific ancestors are at peace, they probably are. If you consistently get the sense they are not yet well, chances are they're not. The following section discusses several different ways to think about the post-death journey and to help the troubled dead in joining the well ancestors.

Psychopomps and Soul Guides

From the Greek (*psychē*: soul; *pompós*: guide), psychopomps or soul guides are individuals (human or otherwise) who help the recently deceased reach the realm of the ancestors. Most religious traditions have explicitly named and honored forces that assist human souls in the post-death journey. In Greek mythology, the goddess Hecate and the god Hermes both serve in this capacity, as does Charon, the ferryman who escorts the dead across the River Styx to the underworld. European and North African soul guides in the form of deities, angels, or related powers include Freyja, Odin, and the Valkyries (Norse); Manannán mac Lir, Ogmios, and the Morrigan (Celtic); the archangel Michael, the Holy Spirit, and Jesus (Christianity); and Anubis, Thoth, and Hathor (Egypt). Zen Buddhists sometimes call upon the support of Ksitigarbha or Jizo, an awakened bodhisattva and guide of the dead, especially for children who precede their parents in death. Among some Buryat Mongolian shamans, the lord of the lower world, Erleg Khan, works with gatekeeper Mongoldi Nagts, "Mongolian Uncle," to ensure that the souls of the deceased arrive and remain in their new home.[3] For practitioners of the Ifá/Òrìṣà tradition, the elevated ancestors themselves may serve as support for the transitioning dead, as do various forces of nature, deities, or *ọ̀rìṣà* (e.g., Èṣù, Ògún, Ọya). In some indigenous cultures, animal spirits such as Owl, Raven, Bear, Horse, Snake, Salmon, and Dog may be guides on the journey to the ancestral realms. Angels, elemental energies, spirits of place, ancestral guides, and other helpful spirit relations may also serve as soul guides.

Living human beings, too, can serve as psychopomps. As with many types of spiritual experience, this may be intentional or spontaneous. Hospice workers, hospital staff, first responders, clergy, and family surrounding the dying may occasionally find themselves, through inspired prayer, meditation, or waking vision, guiding the recently deceased to join the ancestors. Dream contact with the dead might include assisting them to join the ancestors or bearing witness to their transition. Traditional medicine people and shamans often learn, as part of their training, how to pacify and make repairs with the troubled dead, including situations where this transition should have occurred years ago but in the present has resulted in hauntings, spirit intrusions, or possessions. I first trained in psychopomp work through revival forms of shamanism founded by teachers Michael Harner and Sandra Ingerman, and I later encountered resonant concepts and practices in other traditions. In the approach to ancestral lineage healing presented here, the ancestral guides along the lineage of focus steward the psychopomp process, although you as the living practitioner may be quite involved as well.

The first thing to understand about psychopomp work is that it emphasizes spatial change—moving from one location or dimension of reality to another. This relocation of the deceased requires real guidance. Visioning may include passing through a doorway or series of thresholds, crossing a bridge or a large body of water, ascending toward the stars, or returning the souls of the dead into the Earth. I remember my Grandma Foor sharing a vivid dream of contact with her father, Ezra Elton Conner, in the years after his death. He was dressed in a light-blue suit for a special occasion and, surrounded in light, said goodbye to my grandmother before walking into a railroad tunnel in the side of a mountain. Popular culture surrounding psychics and mediums sometimes describes this as *stepping across the threshold of death* or *going into the light* (or, in my great-grandfather's case, stepping into the welcoming dark). However the details look, the heart of this process is getting from one place to another—going from Earth to heaven, from this world to the next, from the realm of the living to the realm of the ancestors. When this transition is successful, the spirit of the deceased is no longer among us, at least not in the same way.

Consequently, psychopomp work often relies on visual-spatial narrative and metaphor. In my experience, the work tends to proceed in three steps: (1) connecting with the troubled dead; (2) making any repairs needed to prepare them for transition; and (3) escorting them where they need to go, typically to the realm of the well ancestors. For example, when I learned to work as a psychopomp, I would first connect and make any needed repairs with the transitioning dead, and then I would travel in spirit with them upward, to a natural spring where Earth touches Sky and Sun. At this crossroads place, the dead would engage in any needed purification and relay messages for the living before stepping across a threshold of light to join their beloved dead.

To serve as an effective guide, the psychopomp needs to know the way (or at least one way) to the realm of the ancestors, as well as methods of assisting the troubled dead to make this journey. This calls for safely relating to spirits who may be in highly conflicted states. After making connection and any necessary repairs, the psychopomp seeks cooperation from the soul of the deceased to make the journey to the ancestral realms. When the dead are ready to go and the way is clear, the work typically proceeds with little trouble.

Elevating the Dead

In West African traditions now also practiced throughout the Americas (e.g., Vodun, Ifá/Òrìṣà), practitioners sometimes think slightly differently about the transitioning dead. Although the intent remains the same as in psychopomp work—to help the souls of the dead become happy ancestors—the language is often less spatial and more about the quality or spiritual condition of the not-yet-ancestors. Elevating the dead does not necessarily refer to moving them up spatially (e.g., up to heaven), but rather to elevating their consciousness or vibration. In general this change is from heavier states of fear, constriction, and confusion to more elevated states of love, expansion, and clarity. Rituals may focus on improving the internal or psychic state of the deceased rather than relocation of their spirit, and the measure of success is the ability of the new ancestor to stabilize in a more elevated or "higher" vibration.

So how can you actually elevate the spirit of a dead person? In my experience, it's not so different from work with the living, except that the stabilizing vessel of the physical body no longer restricts the dead. They are therefore able to change states more easily. Consider the living as ice (or perhaps slush on a good day), the recent dead as liquid, and the collective ancestors as steam; all are H_2O, but not all are equally flexible. Years of good therapy, in-depth personal healing, or a transformative month of awakening and growth can enable living humans to feel lighter and to have greater presence, whereas changes of this magnitude can occur over a period of days or in the course of a single ritual for the dead. As the dead are all energy body (rather than consciousness expressed through the body), calling on love, light, forgiveness, and other healing energies can bring about substantial changes in the state of the soul in transition. Ideally, this type of intervention is directed by ancestral guides, trusted deities, or other wise and helpful powers.

In the Lucumi branch of the Ifá/Òrìṣà tradition, as practiced in Cuba and other parts of the Americas, some practitioners hold a nine-day elevation ritual for the spirit of the deceased. Because this process does not require direct contact with not-yet-ancestors, it is a relatively safe practice to draw upon when you believe that a person has not yet joined the loving ancestors after death. This ritual includes heartfelt prayer for happiness of the deceased; symbolic elevation of the soul of the deceased by gradually raising their physical representation; work with elements (e.g., fire, water, food/earth, prayers/wind); and gentle cleansing of heavy energies.

Here's how it works: On your ancestor altar (see chapter 4) or on any other clean and supportive ritual space, place something to represent the ancestor in question (e.g., a photograph, an object from their life). Near this, place a glass of clean water, a white candle, food or drink you feel this ancestor may enjoy, and any other heartfelt offerings. For nine days, at least once a day, sit at your ancestor altar with the candle lit, and pray for at least a few minutes from the heart, aloud if you can, for this ancestor's happiness, healing, and elevation. In addition to spontaneous prayer, you may include liturgical prayers, such as chanted mantras, praying the rosary, or offering verses from the Qur'an for this ancestor's well-being. If you know prayers and practices from the Ifá/Òrìṣà tradition, then celebrate your *egúngún* (ancestors) however your training and *orí* (personal spirit and intuition) move you. Remember during your prayers and offerings that you're not really seeking to dialogue with or hold on to this departed loved one, but rather to feed and strengthen them in their new reality.

Before you begin your daily prayers for this ancestor, respectfully offer the water from the previous day to the Earth outside your home and intend that the new water will continue to support the cleansing of the deceased. Also at the start of each sitting, physically raise the height of whatever you use to represent your ancestor; you can, for example, stack small books or boards under the ancestor's symbolic presence on your shrine. By elevating their representation a little higher each day, you are making literal and concrete the corresponding inner shift in their condition. You may light the candle anew at the start of each daily sitting or, if it is safe and practical, find a way to keep a flame burning continuously for nine days. You can offer food or drink to this ancestor anytime throughout the process, and you might consider a larger spirit feast (see exercise 12, page 192) at the end of the nine days. Dedicate all positive energies to the elevation and happiness of this ancestor.

Although elevation is an ongoing process and not necessarily a single event, after nine days of ritual feeding and care, odds are your ancestor will be better off in spirit.

Ancestralization

The obscure English verb *ancestralize* was likely coined when anthropologists sought ways to describe traditional African practices of ancestor reverence. Popularized over the last twenty years by Malidoma Somé through his ancestralization trainings, the term literally means *to cause the soul of a deceased person to become an ancestor.* Ancestralization rituals enable souls to join the lineage or collective consciousness of the already well ancestors. In other words, *one becomes an ancestor by joining those who are already ancestors.*

Here's how ancestralization differs slightly from the work of the psychopomp and from elevation: Psychopomps help the soul arrive at and enter the ancestral realms, but they don't always guarantee that the soul will reunite with the other ancestors or undergo the transformations that presumably occur after arrival at the ancestral realms. Elevation shifts the deceased from states of conflict and low vibration to more peaceful states and higher vibrations, but it may not always emphasize the connection between the recently departed and the lineage before them. Ancestralization seems, to me, the most relational of these three ways of thinking and speaking about the process of becoming an ancestor after death. The older ancestors are a critical part of the process and can make or break its success. Also, the recently deceased must stay accountable and eventually learn to embody the collective wisdom and will of the lineage. Nonetheless, all three ways of assisting the dead are valid and good, and they often blend in ritual practice. For example, practitioners who regularly work to assist the departed may report, "We did a healing for so-and-so, brought him to the light, and he joined his loving ancestors." In this example all three elements are present: elevation, psychopomp, and ancestralization.

During ancestralization rituals, participants call upon their loving, wise, and elevated ancestors to receive the dead. The ritual's success hinges upon an effective invocation of the supportive ancestors, their willingness to welcome the recently deceased to their ranks, and the ability of the latter to loosen their hold on this world. This transition is a rite of passage for the spirit of the deceased, a change of status from a not-yet-ancestor to a newly arrived ancestor, and an initiation into collective ancestral consciousness.

Preparation for service as an ancestor may begin even before physical death. As Malidoma Somé has written, "The elder aims at becoming an ancestor. It is his or her next status. So there is some sense in which we can say that the elder is an ancestor in training."[4] An authentic life of heart and service is ultimately our best preparation for the new responsibilities we will meet in our transition to the ancestral realms.

The following exercise presents one way to assist the recent dead. It draws on elements found in psychopomp work, elevation of the dead, and ancestralization. It presupposes that you are actively working your inner process (e.g., emotional healing, forgiveness) and are giving attention to worldly completions related to your loved one (see earlier in this chapter). Ritual work with the recent dead builds on the previous stages of the lineage repair cycle; in other words, don't skip steps. This will help you honor the structural integrity of this progression and will increase your effectiveness and safety with the work. Also, the following exercise is the best fit when there is an average level of trouble and confusion among the recent dead.

Before putting this ritual into practice, please read the following section on work with difficult cases to find out what you *could* encounter. Finally, be patient and kind with yourself when learning any new skill—ritual or otherwise—especially when engaging in tender regions of the heart. This stage of repair is close to the bone and can be psychologically and spiritually intense. Again, proceed at your own rhythm and reach out for support from trusted allies, healers, and others who regularly work with the ancestors.

∞

EXERCISE NINE

Soul Guidance for the Remembered Dead

INTENT: Assist the soul of a deceased family member to join the ancestors

WHAT YOU NEED: A recording device, quiet space, offerings, and any other support for your visioning (e.g., drum, song, prayer)

First confirm that all of the ancestors are well in spirit along the span of the lineage between the guide and the most distant person remembered by name. When this is the case, the guides may give permission for you to approach the eldest named ancestor, but remember that soul guidance work is on an "as-needed" basis. If these types of repairs are called for along the lineage, address the remembered dead one at a time, from the more distant past toward the present. This may entail a separate process for each, making sure at each generation that the blessings of the entire lineage are flowing closer to you in the present. If you have a strong emotional attachment to the person you are attempting to help, consider first doing some form of exercise 8, involving forgiveness (page 145). If the recent, remembered ancestors are already well in spirit, modify the exercise below to focus on extending the blessings of the older guides and lineage to the recent ancestors. Envision the remembered dead as being well connected to the more ancient lineage. Remember to take it slow and reinforce shifts as you go.

As in previous exercises, you will first record your own voice (or a friend's) reading the following guided visualization, and then play it back. Or you could ask a friend to read it aloud for you while you listen. Once you have made these arrangements, find a space conducive to ritual work. When there, do whatever helps you to **establish sacred space and ritual intent** (e.g., light a candle, offer incense, make prayers). If possible, identify the cardinal directions and consider sitting near the center of the ritual space. Play back the recording, or ask your friend to begin to narrate.

1. (*Begin recording.*) Take time to **get physically and emotionally centered**. This may include some meditation or breathing, centering

prayer, unstructured movement, or just a pause to remember your intent for the ritual. You might let your eyes close or settle into a soft gaze. Bring your breath to your belly center. Feel your bones, and feel your heart and blood pumping. Let your soul's light fill and shine forth from your body. Set the intent to stay present in your body for the entire visualization. (*Pause for one to two minutes.*)

2. When you feel centered, **call in any supportive guides** with whom you already enjoy relationship. Connect with your ancestral guide in the specific lineage you are working in. Share your intent with any guides present: to help the soul of a more recent ancestor join the well lineage before them. Confirm that you have the support of the guides before proceeding. (*Brief pause.*) With the support of your guides, **scan the earlier lineage** up to the named individual you intend to help. Double- or even triple-check that the lineage up to this point is well and integrated. (If the answer is no, stop here and return to the lineage repair work in exercise 7, page 135). Confirm that you have the blessing of your guides and the entire lineage before the ancestor in focus before proceeding. (*Pause for two to three minutes.*)

3. If you secure the blessing to proceed, letting the guides lead the process, **start by addressing any heavy, difficult, or conflicting energy** in the space around the individual you intend to help. Let the ancestral guides do whatever is needed to disentangle the soul of this more recent ancestor from any problematic energies so that all that is left is the one you are intending to help. (*Pause for two to three minutes.*)

4. With the support of your guide, take some time to be in the presence of this deceased individual. If appropriate, introduce yourself and let the soul know why you're here, but don't be attached to direct involvement. Then, either by interacting with this individual or through holding presence while the guides take the lead, **help the one transitioning to gain a greater level of brightness, wholeness, and wellness** in their energy body. (There is no right or wrong way to do this, and it may be different each time you experience it. Again, let the guides drive this process.) Continue until you can rank this

one a six or above in terms of wellness, knowing that this is a process that may proceed in stages and may take some time. (*Pause for two to three minutes.*)

5. When you feel this soul has reached a six or above in wellness**, check with your guide to see if this individual is ready to be welcomed and received by the ancestors**. (*Pause for one minute.*) If not, ask your guide what else needs to happen. It's possible that the work may require multiple rounds of ritual engagement for the same individual. If so, respect that; stop for now and come back later to do a little at a time. It's also possible this ancestor-to-be has a certain request or wishes to communicate something to the living—something that needs to happen before he or she is ready to step across. If so, try to find out what this is. Listen and consider their request, without making any promises you can't keep. (*Pause for one minute.*)

6. When this soul is ready to join the ancestors, they will do it. Much like a drop of water dissolving into the ocean, the soul is absorbed into the collective energy. You may sense or see elements of this rite of passage—the death of a ghost, the birth of an ancestor—but there is little left for you to do at this time. **Take a moment to bear witness and to gently reinforce the new equilibrium.** See this individual welcomed into the ancestral realm. Don't follow them; simply observe from a distance and make sure they are finding their way. (*Pause for one to two minutes.*) You might ask your guides if there is **any simple action you can take to celebrate or acknowledge the change in status** of this new ancestor. (*Pause for one minute.*)

7. When you are complete, **shift focus away from the lineage as a whole and back to being in the presence of your guide alone**. With the support of the guide, clear any residual heavy energy from you or your space. (*Brief pause.*) Thank your guides and say goodbye for now. (*Brief pause.*)

8. Gently scan your space and surroundings a final time to **be sure you are truly complete** and clear of any unhelpful energy. (*Brief pause.*) When you are ready, open your eyes and turn your attention fully back to your

physical body and your surroundings. If it's helpful, you might make some notes about what you observed. (*End recording.*)

Remember to work in a steady, patient, and systematic way with the known ancestors, moving from the past toward the present. Only approach your grandfather in spirit when *his* father, your great-grandfather, has joined the well ancestors before him. Only approach your father in spirit when *his* father, your grandfather, is well and settled with the lineage before him. In this way you eventually arrive at a stage where all of those senior to you along any given bloodline have joined the elevated and bright ancestors.

When the direct lineage ancestors (parents, grandparents, great-grandparents) are all well in spirit, concern may arise for children, grandchildren, or even great-grandchildren who precede you in death. This raises two important considerations: how does dying when one's parents or grandparents are still alive affect the journey to the ancestors, and how does the post-death experience of young children differ, if at all, from that of adults?

From my experience, assisting younger generations to join the ancestors follows the same basic steps. Unless the loving ancestors advise otherwise, male children will join the ancestors of their father's lineage, and female children will go to be with their ancestral mothers. For example, if your daughter has passed and you wish to ensure that she is now with the ancestors, you may want to contact the healthy ancestors of her mother's maternal lineage. If this outreach feels daunting, consult with the wise and loving grandmothers from your own lineages about how to help; they may be willing to escort the spirits of children to the lineage that is best for them at this time. As is always the case when helping the spirits of departed family, tend to your own emotional wellness throughout and let the elder ancestors guide the process.

Remember that the ancestors are not always "old," and that they include the spirits of those who lived on Earth only as children. Typically these souls are ancestors returning to Earth and will not necessarily continue to appear as childlike after their death. In any case, the passing of young children warrants the same care and consideration given to adults and elders. This includes the spirits of those who complete their brief incarnation in stillbirth, miscarriage, or abortion. Again, there is no one right way to honor the spirits of young and not-yet-born children, but their contact with incarnate life should be honored in *some* way, and rituals to grieve and honor young ones will ideally include the loving and wise ancestors. If anything, those who die young seem to have an easier time returning to the ancestors than do adults, who form strong attachments and a complex sense of identity over many years of life on Earth. The greater challenge is often with living family, especially parents, who may find it difficult to fully release souls who depart young from this life. After children have truly settled into the lineage, they may at times appear as supportive guides, lineage elders who came to Earth only briefly yet continue strong and mature in spirit.

Ritual Assistance for Extended Family Ancestors

When all of the ancestors, both forward and backward in time, along any given lineage are well and at peace, this may be sufficient that you can proceed to the final stage of ancestral repair work (see chapter 9). The ancestral guides may, however, wish to also assist spirits who are not in the direct lineage but who are family nonetheless. These may include siblings, aunts and uncles, cousins, spouses, in-laws, and family members by adoption. Remember to ask the ancestral guides whether or not they want you to engage in this work at this time. The further your focus goes from the direct lineage, the more your ancestral work begins to fall under the jurisdiction of other lineages. This makes it critically important that any ritual assistance for extended family be supported by the ancestral guides rather than being driven only by personal desire and concern.

When the ancestors do endorse assisting extended family members, first make certain that all ancestors in the direct lineage are vibrant and at peace. The wellness of the direct lineage serves as the anchor and foundation from which to assist the spirits of extended family. Next, assess the degree of ancestral connection (high, medium, or low) between the individual you wish to assist and the ancestral lineage on which you have been focusing. For example, if you are working with your maternal grandmother's lineage, extended family who would be strongly linked with these ancestors include sisters of your grandmother, sisters of your mother (from the same mother), daughters of the sisters of your mother (some cousins), and your own sisters (provided they are daughters of your mother from this bloodline). In this example, all of these women share an intrinsic, cellular-level affinity with this maternal bloodline. Any ritual assistance should therefore flow naturally from your work with the lineage of focus. When the link is strong, simply follow the guides and refer to the basic progression from exercise 9, "Soul Guidance for the Remembered Dead."

Individuals who have some blood relatedness but who are not directly in the lineage of focus will have a medium level of connection with the ancestors. In your maternal grandmother's lineage, ancestors with a medium degree of affinity would include brothers of your grandmother, brothers of your mother (from the same mother), and your own brothers (provided they are also your mother's children). In these examples, your grandmother's father and his people ideally receive her brothers, your maternal grandfather and his people welcome your maternal uncles, and your father or paternal grandfather welcomes the spirit of your brothers. Usually the men join the men, and the women join the women.

Consider the case of a female cousin on your mother's side. If this cousin is the daughter of one of your mother's sisters, then the link would be strong with your maternal grandmother's lineage. If, however, she is the daughter of one of your mother's brothers, then the affinity with the lineage of focus would be moderate. This individual would have a stronger affinity with the lineage of her mother (your aunt by marriage) and her mother's mother back through time.

A low level of linkage characterizes individuals whom we view as family but who are not related by blood. This commonly includes spouses and in-laws, stepfamily, and other adoptive relations. If the link is moderate or low between your lineage of focus and the extended family you aim to assist, ask your ancestral guides how they wish to proceed.

They may simply want you to make beneficial prayers and offerings for the healing and happiness of the extended family member in question. Rather than having ancestors from other lineages arriving on the scene to gather their own, your ancestors may prefer to escort the spirit in need to his or her ancestors. The spirit of the deceased's ancestors may also step forward to help him or her to transition. If this happens, be sure that your own guides and teachers are strong with you and that you welcome only healthy and loving ancestors into your ritual working space. Over time, extended family ancestors who are well in spirit may also serve as ancestral allies and teachers, especially when they are at peace with the larger lineage.

Work with the Very Troubled Dead and Related Spirits

Popular culture is replete with tales of the frightening dead: hauntings, vampires, zombies, poltergeists, and other horrors, both gory and subtle. Although this may reflect the unresolved shadow side of our cultural psyche, the idea of aggressive, violent, or otherwise problematic dead people is also quite common among many cultures.

To give a few examples:

- Mongolian shaman Sarangerel Odigan described *chotgor* as hostile and jealous souls of people who died, often in sudden or conflicted ways, and wrote that "they are the main cause of human illness."[5]
- In Burkina Faso, West Africa, Malidoma Somé writes, "dissatisfied ancestors are believed to be the instigators of violent death."[6]
- Ifá/Òrìṣà practitioners in Yorùbá-speaking Nigeria and the African diaspora view the ancestors (egúngún) as sources of both blessings and danger. They are capable of both protecting life and bringing about premature death.

- Martín Prechtel details how in the T'zutujil Maya tradition, the soul of someone recently deceased who doesn't join the ancestors may turn back to this world, where "scared and invisible, it takes up residence in the body of the tenderest and most familiar person it can find." From that point, the ghost eats the life of that person. "Alcoholism, substance addiction, most depression, homicide, suicide, untimely deaths, accidents, and the addiction to argument were caused by the endless hunger of such ghosts."[7]
- Old Norse and Viking views of the *draugr* or ghostly dead are still known throughout Scandinavia and are recognized by contemporary practitioners of Norse traditions.
- In Judaism, the Yiddish word *dybbuk* refers to one among the restful or troubled dead who interferes with a living person.

Troubled ghosts pose a real risk to the health and happiness of the living. From my experience, I estimate that no more than two-thirds of the spirits of those who die in the United States make their way successfully into the larger circle of ancestors in the first year following their death. Of the third who fail to make this transition, about three-quarters of them will be relatively common cases of an unelevated dead person, common ghost, or not-yet-ancestor. In other words, they're not particularly mean-spirited or attached to staying in a ghost state; they just didn't make it across, and nobody has followed up with them. They're now lost to some degree, and, like low levels of radiation, they are more of a passive and slow-to-manifest problem for the living. About 2.5 million people die annually in the United States, so, running the math, we're talking about eight hundred thousand new "American ghosts" annually and, of those, two hundred thousand new troubled, problematic dead.[8] Even if you don't have any troubled ghosts among your recent ancestors, you're statistically likely to encounter them sooner or later in your everyday life.

In the lineage repair cycle, what's important to remember is that every nasty ghost who used to be incarnate in human form on Earth is also someone's child and possibly someone's parent. Murderers, rapists, sociopaths, slave owners, dictators, and other scary dead people have families and ancestors of their own, and there is some chance that an individual from your recent blood lineages fits this description. What is the best way to relate to these scorned lineage ancestors, especially when you determine that they are now in a similar or worse condition than in their life on Earth? Although some teachers encourage rejecting or ignoring these relatives outright, there are ways to safely assist even the most troubled dead and establish them as respected family ancestors. In my view, this is one of the most sacred and necessary acts of family and cultural repair we can undertake. If you determine that some of your ancestors remain in an especially troubled condition and you are willing to assist them, make sure you exercise greater caution in the ritual repair work.

Eight-Step Process for Assisting Especially Troubled Ghosts

This type of ritual work is the edgiest and riskiest material presented in this book, in part because there are so many different possible scenarios, each with its own parameters for treatment. In order to present a complex and potentially unsafe aspect of ritual to readers I may never meet, I offer below a checklist, or decision tree, for work with the especially troubled dead. As with any guidelines, take caution: conditions on the ground may vary, so please trust your ancestral guides, gut instinct, and personal limits. If you find yourself in a tough place, reach out for support from a living ally or mentor, ideally someone with experience in relating to the dead.

When approaching ritual repairs with troubled ghosts, I suggest the following process as a base from which to craft ritual:

1. Consolidate existing ancestral support.
2. Make preliminary prayers and offerings.
3. Resolve the involvement of unhelpful entities.

4. Resolve unhelpful attachments with the living.
5. Address ancestral burdens and curses.
6. Guide soul repairs and energetic healing.
7. Facilitate voluntary transition of the deceased.
8. Reinforce a new equilibrium.

In an especially challenging case, you may need to observe all stages of ritual repair listed above. Repeated rituals may also be necessary at any given stage to fully address each concern before proceeding to the next step. Be tenacious and patient, and you'll eventually arrive at a tipping point where the loving ancestors welcome the spirit of the deceased. As all ritual work in the repair cycle follows from strong relations with the ancestral guides, remember to follow their lead with respect to when and how to engage the troubled dead.

1. Consolidate Existing Ancestral Support

If the guides endorse your attempt to help the troubled dead, confirm that the lineage prior to the ghost is in excellent condition and prepared to receive this individual. If the lineage is not in this condition, focus there until the situation supports proceeding. For example, let's say that your father was an abusive person and took his own life. You find him to still be in a conflicted and mean-spirited state. Before a ritual, you would need to ensure that his father and the men before him and his mother and the women before her are all vibrant in spirit and ready to help. By calling upon existing ancestral support, and by being thorough about rebuilding the lineage infrastructure *before* you directly engage, you will do three things: help the desired shift to occur more quickly, reduce unnecessary risks, and encourage the dead person and overall lineage to stabilize in a healthy pattern afterward.

2. Make Preliminary Prayers and Offerings

After confirming the ancestors' support for the repair, I encourage you to make prayers and offerings on behalf of the troubled dead before any direct intervention. In the prayers, make clear your intent for personal, family, and ancestral healing, and set the repairs in motion on a spirit level. Present any offerings to the older guides with the intent that positive energies will benefit the deceased. Such prayers and offerings will clear the way for more involved ritual intervention and will establish pathways along which healing and energies can flow. I believe that most, if not all, necessary repairs can be accomplished through heartfelt prayers and offerings, with few of the risks of direct intervention. If you prefer this approach, you can visualize the deceased from a distance, surrounded by the bright and loving ancestors, and together with the elders of the lineage, you can hold a prayer in your heart for the happiness of the deceased.

3. Resolve the Involvement of Unhelpful Entities

In the culture of psychotherapy and recovery, there is a popular idea that someone struggling with addiction can't really dive into their inner work and healing until they first address the addictive behavior. This implies that any intoxicant is its own force or spirit, and that its presence prevents a new equilibrium from emerging. Imagine you are a doctor and a patient walks into your treatment office with a vampire bat stuck to his neck and a bullet lodged in his arm. You would naturally prioritize removal of the bat and the bullet before treating him. The idea is the same on the spirit level. Although there are few terms in English for the diverse types of unhelpful spirit entities, these entities are real and can keep a troubled ghost from joining the ancestors. These entities often feed off the energy of their surroundings and the ghost with whom they are associated much as ghosts can feed off the living. These beings may be weak in vibration and relatively unsophisticated (picture mosquitoes or barnacles), or they may be smart, potent, and nasty (picture kidnappers or a mother bear guarding her kill).

If problematic spirit entities are linked to the soul you wish to assist, let the guides make the call on what happens next. Relevant treatment and/or relocation will depend upon the nature of the spirit, and the guides are better positioned to handle this type of situation. Weak or inanimate energies can sometimes be composted, swept away, or directly cleared. Other ghosts connected in unhelpful ways to the ghost in focus may need to disconnect and make a transition themselves. More powerful spirits will likely require appeasement and skillful negotiation before releasing their attachment to the dead—and they will not likely appreciate bullying, or being bypassed if you try to directly transition the deceased. In most cases, I have found it best to convince the unhelpful spirit that it will be happier in some other specified location or condition. When addressing unhelpful entities, make sure that you—or those near you—do not become a new focus (i.e., food) for the unhelpful entity, and that you maintain clear energetic boundaries with the powers you are engaging. Once such entities have been cleared, cleanse any residual energy from you, the ritual space, and the ghost you are seeking to assist, much as you would disinfect a wound after extracting a foreign object. Again, ask for assistance from living teachers or guides if you feel you are out of your comfort zone.

4. Resolve Unhelpful Attachments with the Living

Sometimes the recent dead remain bonded to this dimension through a living family member in ways that, to put it politely, are not helpful. Ghosts tend to seek out close relatives, children, or anyone in the family who is most susceptible. Although full possession by a troubled ghost is possible, more commonly the not-yet-ancestor travels with a living family member or resides in their shared home, without being fully incorporated in the body of the living. If you find that a recent family ancestor needs to release an attachment to a living relative, you will have to face important ethical questions about intervening in others' lives without their consent. Consider this theoretical example:

You have a thirty-year-old daughter who struggles with alcohol and lives on the other side of the country. She is a single mother with a history of depression and a young child in the home, and you're worried about possible neglect. Your daughter is not speaking to you right now, and she has made it clear that she's not interested in any weird rituals or prayers for her and that she doesn't need you to save her. From your work with the ancestors, you realize that your deceased mother is also unwell and has been attached to your daughter for years. The lineage before your mother is well in spirit, and those guides encourage you to disentangle your mother's spirit from your daughter and help your mother finally transition. But you are worried that this would be invasive or destabilizing for your daughter and may also endanger your grandchild. The guides confirm that this is a possibility, because if your mother leaves to join the ancestors, your daughter's psyche will remain a fragmented mess, and she will need soul repair. They say that you should only do the work for your mother if you're also willing to do some kind of soul repair work for your daughter. They add that they can do a version of this work well enough from a distance without contacting your daughter in person. But they also say that there is risk either way, and that the choice is yours on how to proceed.

Can you justify doing soul retrieval or repair on another living human without her consent—especially when she has explicitly asked you *not* to get involved? If you do choose to intervene in a situation like this and there are harmful consequences, are you then responsible? If you choose not to intervene, are you responsible in a different way? These are tricky questions, with more than one right answer. I personally have seen only a handful of cases like this over the years. Provided the ancestral guides support the work, I tend to encourage the living practitioner to intervene with prayers and the support of the guides to untangle and transition the recent ancestor, and to clean things up afterward if necessary with the living.

5. Address Ancestral Burdens and Curses

Another complicating factor is curses. They are relatively rare, at least in my experience of American culture. Much like computer viruses, they are foreign energies that can appear to be integrated with the host energy, and they can be either unintentional or directly placed. A curse can appear as a configuration of subtle energy or as an animate spirit in someone's aura or energy body. Unintentional or self-generated curses can include unwise but powerful vows, self-hexing, and self-defeating beliefs passed down over generations. For example, a person might vow, "If you just let my wife live, I swear I will dedicate my life to God and attend church every Sunday." When the wife recovers but her husband does not fulfill his agreement with Spirit, it can create a debt with powerful consequences. These types of agreements can sometimes be made with forces, deities, or spiritual powers that later come to collect. One verse (*Ìrosùn Òfún*) from the Ifá/Òrìsà tradition tells of a woman, Olúróunbí, who so strongly longed to experience motherhood that she made an agreement with the spirit of a sacred *ìrókò* tree that she would eventually return her child to ìrókò.[9] When the child, a son, grew to be a teenager, the spirit of the ìrókò came to retrieve his life. Olúróunbí ran terrified to Òrúnmìlà, the chief diviner, who made a difficult intervention with the ìrókò to save her son's life. Because the woman remembered her original agreement, she, with the help of the diviner, could renegotiate these old debts in a conscious way. But without this knowledge and the diviner's skills, Olúróunbí's son would likely have died young. These types of self-generated unintentional curses can continue to play out over generations until they are unraveled at the source and the powers involved are sufficiently honored and pacified.

Intentional curses typically come from someone who has both the knowledge and willingness to put their hostility into action in a focused, ritualized way. Untangling old-school curses is beyond the scope of this book. If you choose to wade into this terrain, again, consult with your guides throughout and attempt to work at the root of the problem. Honestly, I haven't encountered many intentional curses here in the United States, but I know that some colleagues see "curses" where I see intergenerational patterns and entrenched unhelpful beliefs. If you actually encounter a well-crafted traditional curse, work closely with your guides, treat the whole situation with appropriate caution, and consider asking someone with relevant training for support.

6. Guide Soul Repairs and Energetic Healing

Once you are confident that the spirit of the deceased is relatively free from problematic influences, assess their temperament and energetic condition and consider how you will approach the next phase of repair. Are they receptive but still weak and fragmented? Are they strong and intact in spirit? Are they friendly, confused, or belligerent? Do they know you are there and, if so, who you are? The goal at this stage is to prepare the dead to join their loving and supportive ancestors. Ideally they are already in a condition to make this transition, but if not, you may need to work with the guides to prepare them. Imagine getting a ship seaworthy for a long ocean voyage, or preparing a space shuttle to safely leave the atmosphere.

This first of two stages of repair is to make sure that the soul you're trying to help is fully intact and present. Consider asking if there is anything *not* present in their soul essence that needs to be. When I supported my paternal grandfather in transitioning in 1999, he first appeared to me as missing the section of his abdomen where he had shot himself. His energy body or aura was gray; he just wasn't all there. The guides went to retrieve the part of his spirit that had been fragmented from the whole. When they returned this soul light to him, he was brighter, more whole, and more able to recognize me as well as his condition. This type of repair is similar to methods of soul retrieval popularized by Sandra Ingerman and others, only in this case the client is no longer physically incarnate.[10]

Once enough of the deceased's energy body is present and accounted for, you may need to do some energy work and balancing to get them into optimal condition before the transition. This final stage reinforces and confirms the new status of the soon-to-be-ancestor as an intact soul free from harmful external influences. In practice this can look a thousand different ways, and it may include seeing the deceased surrounded in love and healing light to the degree that they are able to take in this new energy. The goal here is not necessarily to facilitate a radical transformation of consciousness, but merely to make sure that the soul of the deceased is coherent and intact enough to understand that they are dead and to agree to the journey ahead.

7. Facilitate Voluntary Transition of the Deceased

In many cases the ancestral guides will ask you to simply witness their work of repair with confused, belligerent, or dangerous ghosts. If they call for this, obviously follow their lead and be glad that you don't need to be overly involved.

On the other hand, they may place you in the role of the ancestrally supported diplomat—either for your own training, or because the repairs will be most effective if you are the one who is negotiating. In this situation, with your guides surrounding you and your personal protection intact, first establish some kind of dialogue with the spirit of the deceased. If there is a high level of negativity or threat, you may picture a protective energetic shield as a transparent barrier between you and the ghost.

If you haven't done so already, introduce yourself and state with humility your relation to the deceased as well as your intentions. Determine early on if the not-yet-ancestor understands that they are now dead. If not, you may need to tactfully explain this, including the importance of joining the ancestors after death. Try to understand and address any residual attachments to this dimension. Overly protective ghosts may need to understand that by releasing themselves into the arms of the loving ancestors, they will be able to support and protect the living more effectively. Facing the authority and presence of the older ancestors can be scary for some who have yet to make their transition, so be compassionate. You may also be in a position to relay messages to the living; just be sure not to promise anything you can't follow through on. Be patient with negotiations, and remember to let the guides drive the work.

Once the soul of the deceased is ready to make the transition, guide them to the realm of the wise and loving ancestors. As we saw with psychopomp work, destinations may include into the Earth, across the waters, up to the celestial realms, or into the light. Go to wherever the dead who are well in spirit go in your tradition. If possible, make sure that ancestors receive the one you are assisting on the other side.

8. Reinforce a New Equilibrium

After this transition, inquire occasionally about the recently assisted dead to make sure they are adjusting well. Heartfelt offerings to celebrate this new ancestor are one great way to reinforce the shift. Making positive changes in relationships with living family members also helps the dead settle into their new role. For them, knowing someone is looking after things among the living can be comforting. Spontaneous communications through synchronicities, waking intuitions, and dreams may give a sense of how they're doing. You can also ask your ancestral guides directly about them in later rituals. If called for, offer follow-up ritual and prayer to support the full embrace of this new ancestor by the lineage.

NINE

INTEGRATION AND WORK WITH LIVING FAMILY

You will know that the previous stages of your lineage repair work are complete when all of your ancestors, both distant and recent, along your bloodline of focus are well in spirit and have joined the loving and supportive dead. This fifth and final stage of the lineage repair method grounds ancestor work in healthy and empowered relationships with living family members. You'll be introduced to ways the ancestors can speak through living humans (e.g., embodiment, mediumship, possession) and learn practices you can do with your ancestors for the well-being of living family and relatives. As the end of part 2, this chapter concludes with information that will help you take your ancestor work beyond the lineage repair cycle.

Prayer for Self, Family, and Descendants

At this final stage, I suggest praying with the guides and lineage ancestors for the well-being of the family and any descendants. The example below offers one starting point for spoken prayer. With a nod to the universality of ancestor veneration, I have included translations of this English prayer in the five other official languages of the United Nations (Arabic, Chinese, French, Russian, and Spanish).[1] If you speak another language, explore how prayer with your ancestors feels to you in that tongue. Consider incorporating elements of meditation, offerings, song, movement, or whatever supports your connection with the ancestors.

Regular heartfelt prayer is one great practice to help bring the ancestral lineage into a healed and whole condition. Through this practice, you can also anchor ancestral blessings here on Earth in the present, both in your personal life and in the lives of your family. Remember to periodically include siblings, children, and future generations in devotions, either implicitly or by name, and to let love guide your practice.

PRAYER FOR FAMILY HEALING

May all my ancestors be happy and at peace.
May my living family be happy and at peace.
May I be happy and at peace.
May all future generations of my family receive only blessings
 and love from our ancestors.
May my ancestors guide me on my path of destiny and purpose,
 and may I embody their love and wisdom for the benefit of
 all my relations.
May all my ancestors and all my family be happy and at peace.

دعاء لشفاء العائلة

أسأل الله أن يكون أجدادي سعداء وأن يكونوا بسلام

أسأل أن تعيش عائلتي بسعادة و سلام

أسأل أن أعيش بسعادة وسلام

أسأل أن تتلقى جميع الأجيال القادمة من عائلتي البركات و السّلام و الحبّ من أجدادنا

أسأل أن يرشدني أجدادي في حياتي ، و أسأل أن أجسّد حبّهم و حكمتهم لخير جميع الكائنات

أسأل أن يكون أجدادي و كلّ أقاربي و عائلتي سعداء و أن يكونوا بخير و سلام.

緬懷祖先

祈求祖先平安喜樂
祈求家人平安喜樂
祈求我心平安喜樂
祈求世代子孫承襲先人之福祉及庇蔭
祈求祖先引領我人生的道路及歸宿
闡揚先人福祉及智慧以造福人群
祈求祖先及家人都平安喜樂

Prière pour l'apaisement au sein de la famille

Je prie que tous mes ancêtres soient heureux et en paix.

Que ma famille soit heureuse et en paix.

Que je sois, moi-même, heureux et en paix.

*Que toutes nos générations futures ne reçoivent qu'amour et
bénédictions de nos ancêtres.*

*Que mes ancêtres guident mes pas, vers ma destinée et ma raison
d'être, et que je puisse personnifier leur amour et leur sagesse,
et en faire bénéficier tous mes proches.*

*Je prie que tous mes ancêtres et toute ma famille soient heureux et
en paix.*

Молитва о благополучии семьи

Пусть все мои предки будут счастливы и пребывают в мире
и спокойствии.

Пусть моя семья живет в мире и согласии.

Пусть я буду счастлив и спокоен.

Пусть все будущие поколения моей семьи получат только
благословение и любовь от наших предков.

Пусть мои предки ведут меня по моей судьбе к исполнению
жизненной цели, чтобы я мог обратить их любовь и
мудрость во благо всех окружающих меня.

Пусть все мои предки и вся моя семья пребудут в мире и согласии.

Oración de Sanacion para la Familia

Oro para que todos mis ancestros estén felices y en paz.
Oro para que toda mi familia en vida este feliz y en paz.
Oro para que yo este feliz y en paz.
Oro para que todas la generaciones futuras de mi familia reciban bendiciones y amor de los ancestros.
Para que los ancestros guíen mi camino, destino y propósito en esta vida, y para que yo pueda vivir su amor y sabiduría por el beneficio de todos los seres.
Que todos mis ancestros y familia estén felices y en paz. Que así sea!

Embodiment, Channeling, and Mediumship

Many traditions include ways in which living family may embody or merge with the spirits of loving and wise ancestors. To embody, incarnate, or incorporate the ancestors literally means that they are *en/in* our *caro* (flesh) and *corpus* (body). The spirits of the ancestors are in flesh, inside the physical body. Practices that call for intentional embodiment of the ancestors usually occur in ritual or ceremonial space and have a clear start and end—meaning that the practitioner does not stay merged with the spirits indefinitely.

To temporarily embody the spirits of your ancestors doesn't mean losing your sense of choice or memory about what happened when they shared your body. Such a displacement of consciousness is possible in stronger states of possession; however, as I see it, even when people go into such states, they are still accountable for their actions. I suspect this is one reason that full possession tends to occur in a communal context: ceremonial leaders and supporters share responsibility for the well-being of the participants and can hopefully bring them back if needed.

Below I highlight three related terms—*embodiment, channeling,* and *mediumship,* each a way to think and talk about our capacity to embody the spirits of our ancestors. Notice as you read what language most resonates for you. I also highlight three traditions—Mongolian, Norse, and Ifá/Òrìsà, each with established practices for ancestral communion. If you already have a similar practice, notice how these examples compare with your training and experience.

Embodying the Ancestors

According to Buryat Mongol shaman Sarangerel Odigan, "One of the things that distinguish Mongolian and Siberian shamanism from some (but not all) other shamanic traditions is the idea that the shaman actually embodies the spirits in many of the rituals he performs." Sarangerel described this state of embodiment as *ongon orood:* "having the *ongon* spirits inside the body" and "the shamanic state of having one or more shamanic helper spirits in possession of the shaman's body."[2] These helpers may include ancestral guides, the lineage as a collective energy, and other spirits connected to our human bloodlines (see chapter 6 for details on crafting an ongon). Sarangerel believed that among Western practices, channeling is the closest analog to embodying the spirits, and she wrote, "Most trance channelers learn to cultivate a receptive state of mind that allows the channeled spirits to speak through them." When in a condition of ongon orood, Sarangerel advised to "not think too much about what the spirits are doing. It is as if you are a passenger in your own car, allowing someone else to drive you to a place you do not know. You are watching but not controlling." She described embodying the spirits as "the most important breakthrough in becoming a shaman."[3] In her tradition, shamans often carry out ritual work while embodying the spirits.

Almost anyone with sincere intent can embody the spirits of their ancestors. Most of my experience with this practice has been through shamanic journeywork or through ritual in the Ifá/Òrìsà tradition. I've also felt merged with the ancestors on occasion during dreams, meditation, and solo wilderness time, always with my personal choice and continuity of memory intact. During trainings I have invited participants to access states of partial embodiment in ways that are grounded and not too overwhelming. Often they are then able to access this direct connection in their own ancestor practice.

Speaking for the Dead

The thirteenth-century *Saga of Eric the Red,* set in Greenland, describes at some length a ritual involving a seeress or oracle (Norse: *spákona*) who served her community as a mouthpiece for the ancestors. In the record, the spákona (Old Norse *spahen,* cognate with the English *see* + Old Norse *kona:* "woman" or "wife") or "seeing woman" assumed her place on an elevated seat before the community. She then entered into a state of direct contact with the ancestors and proceeded to answer questions from the audience. Inspired by this seven-hundred-year-old account, some practitioners of northern European Earth-honoring paths (e.g., Heathenry, Asatru, Norse Paganism) have revived and adapted this ritual under the name of oracular *seidh,* high-seat seidh, or *spae*-working.[4] For example, respected author and teacher of Norse tradition Diana Paxson wrote, "In the early nineties, I began exploring ways to reconstruct oracular seidh as a native Northern European magical practice that could serve the pagan community."[5] In the times I've participated in oracular seidh rituals with Paxson and her community, a facilitator guided a seated group visioning with song, prayer, and guided group visualization down and around the World Tree (Old Norse: *Yggdrasil*) to the gates of Hela's realm, the dwelling place of the dead. All participants remained outside the threshold between the living and the dead except the spákona, who was seated on an elevated chair facing those assembled. After the seeress entered the realm of the dead and found her bearings, a mediator then helped participants address questions to the spákona and by extension to the ancestors and gods.

During seidh rituals, I have heard the medium both respond in the first person (e.g., "This is your grandmother speaking and you should do X") and convey messages from the dead in the third person (e.g., "Your grandmother is telling me to tell you to do X"). In both instances, the seeress serves as an intermediary with the ancestors. When they speak through her directly, she may be guided to serve as a medium for ancestors who are connected to other ritual participants, most of whom she has never met and will not likely talk with after the ritual. The medium may be called upon to contact different types of spirits in addition to human ancestors. This trance work takes place over the course of several hours, unbroken, sometimes in service to over a hundred participants.

In the seidh ritual, the seeress travels in spirit or a state of light trance to the realm of the ancestors and from there works on behalf of a larger community. In a much less demanding practice, you can vision and pray, either alone or in supportive small group settings, with your ancestors and guides for the well-being of your family. When working with ancestors with whom you have already made some relationship, there is no need to leave your body to connect. In fact, you may feel them present while you are in an ordinary state of awareness. Once you have done whatever helps you invoke their felt presence, you can harmonize their intentions with your own through prayer, meditation, song, or other devotions. This may include praying for the health of living relatives, visualizing your family surrounded by the love and blessings of ancestors, and allowing the ancestors to share some of the responsibility you may feel for the care of your family. By joining forces with your ancestors to intend wellness for the living—possibly to the point of partially incorporating or embodying them in spirit—you complete a circuit between our world and theirs and serve as a channel for ancestral blessings here on Earth.

Ancestral Mediumship

Practitioners of diverse lineages of Ifá/Òrìṣà tradition in both Nigeria and the African diaspora know that one way to invoke and celebrate the ancestors is through ancestral (egúngún) masquerade. Egúngún mediums are understood to be in a state of intentionally invoked and ritually supported embodiment or possession with helpful ancestors. These initiates ritually embody the ancestors, often through highly expressive spontaneous dance, during communal ceremonies while wearing colorful, consecrated costumes that cover their bodies from head to toe (see plates 6 and 7). Ritual supporters help invoke and sustain varying degrees of possession for the masqueraders and follow the medium (and the ancestors they embody) throughout the ritual—herding the masqueraders along, possibly making note of spoken messages from the ancestors, and generally tending to the ancestors in their temporarily incarnate forms.

In mainstream American culture, *possession* is a loaded word. Images from Hollywood horror films come to mind of involuntary, troubled, and complete possession by unfriendly ghosts or spirits (e.g., *The Exorcist, The Shining*). Although ghosts can, in rare cases, overpower a person's sense of self and bodily control, the focus here is on voluntary possession by one's loving and supportive ancestors. In these cases, the human medium, typically after an involved period of training, consciously invites the ancestors fully into their body, and the resulting state of incorporation or possession (partial to complete) is desirable, temporary, and supported by community. Full or complete possession refers to the flooding or displacement of the ego or personal self, and it may be accompanied by loss of personal choice and memory of events while possessed. One is taken over, "ridden," and subject to the whims of the possessing spirit or force.

These more complete states of possession ideally happen under the supervision of trained elders. Experienced ritual leaders can bring the medium back, if needed, and can help regulate the situation if the ancestors come through in ways that are unrestrained or too "hot." I have limited personal experience with complete possession that includes loss of memory, although I've been a supporter and participant in rituals with mediums in those types of states. In my experiences of embodying the ancestors, even when I have allowed them to speak with my voice in a community ritual, I have always felt that I could put myself back in the driver's seat if necessary and that I was aware of what was happening around me.

Plate I. *Tumuli* or burial mounds, such as those at the Viking sacred site of Uppsala in Sweden, are one ancient form of monument to the dead and can be found throughout Europe, the Americas, Asia, and parts of Africa.

Plate 2. The despacho is a ceremonial form shared by
Quechua-speaking peoples of the Andes that can be adapted for various
ritual intentions. This ancestor-focused despacho made in Nederland, Colorado,
made use of aspen for *kintus* (leaves used to carry participants' prayers).

Plate 3. This despacho to feed the ancestors was crafted in Asheville, North Carolina, by participants in an ancestral healing practitioner training. The entire offering bundle is typically burned in a sacred fire as a ritual completion.

Plate 4. Despacho ceremonies for the ancestors may include local plants, offerings familiar to the lineages being honored, and traditional ingredients from the ritual's homeland in the Andes. At this ancestors training in Berkeley, California, some participants of diverse East Asian lineages were moved to include offerings of citrus and joss paper.

Plate 5. Jewish traditions of ancestor reverence include ritualized grieving, reciting Kaddish, lighting a *yahrzeit* memorial candle, and pilgrimage to the graves of beloved dead. This offering and prayer used only ingredients known to Jewish traditions.

Plate 6. Known as *egúngún* in Yorùbá-speaking West Africa and neighboring cultures, ancestor mediums must be covered from head to toe. They provide one way for the dead to continue to relate in the affairs of the living.

Plate 7 (right). Egúngún ancestral mediums in Òdè Rẹ́mọ, Nigeri

Plate 8. Grave visits, such as this one at a Chinese cemetery in Ratchaburi, Thailand, may include offerings, heartfelt dialogue, and quality time with the ancestors

Plate 9. Ancestor offerings at Da Jiu Festival in Shek O, Hong Kong.

Plate 10. The tomb of Muhammad, located in Medina, Saudi Arabia, is part of the larger Mosque of the Prophet (al-Masjid an-Nabawi) and one of the holiest sites for the world's 1.6 billion Muslims.

Plate 11. The Tomb of the Unknown Soldier at Arlington National Cemetery near Washington, D.C., uses the remains of several unidentified soldiers as a focal point to memorialize thousands of unknown ancestors of war. Tomb Guards preside over this sacred site twenty-four hours a day, seven days a week.

Plate 12. The Mexican holiday of Día de los Muertos or Day of the Dead combines pre-Christian traditions of ancestor reverence with the Catholic holiday of All Saint's Day and may include establishing an ancestor altar, making offerings, and visiting the graves of loved ones.

Plate 13. Over eight hundred thousand Rwandans were killed in a one-hundred-day period in 1994. The Ntarama Catholic Church was the site of the massacre of five thousand people.

Plate 14. During the Balinese cremation ceremony (Ngaben), the deceased is placed inside a sarcophagus, typically shaped like a buffalo or temple, before being burned.

Plate 15. The Merry Cemetery in Sapanta, Romania, illustrates one way that beauty and artistry can play a role in memorializing the dead.

Plate 16. Many cultures identify certain trees as places of heightened connection with the spirit world and the ancestors. This sacred tree stands near the shores of Lake Baikal, Siberia.

Plate 17. During the midsummer Mitama Festival at the Yasukuni Shrine in Tokyo over thirty thousand lanterns are lit to honor the ancestors. Over two million kami (spirits or deities in Shinto tradition) are enshrined at Yasukuni, including the nearly four thousand kamikaze pilots who died during World War II. (Photo by Takashi Ueki via Wikimedia Commons.)

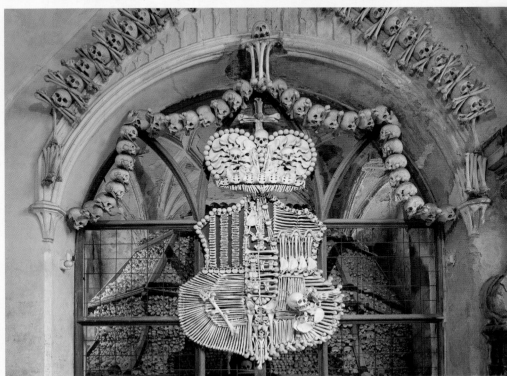

Plates 18 and 19. Sedlec Ossuary near the town of Kutná Hora, Czech Republic, houses the remains of forty thousand to seventy thousand people. Common where burial places are scarce, some ossuaries were established in Europe to address the many thousands of unidentified dead on the battlefields of World War I.

States of partial possession are more common. To me they seem very similar to states of embodiment and channeling.

Unless you have prior training and strong communal support for full possession work, I recommend first getting comfortable working with states of light or partial embodiment or merging with your loving ancestors. Exercise 10 below invites you to explore partial merging with the ancestral guides and, when merged, to pray for your living relatives and descendants. Embodiment of elevated lineage ancestors can also be done with the bloodline of focus earlier in the progression—that is, before getting to know your more recent family ancestors. Just be sure that whatever you're embodying of the ancestors is bright, loving, and positive energy.

⌇

EXERCISE TEN

EMBODY THE LINEAGE AND OFFER PRAYER FOR THE LIVING

INTENT: Embody guides and lineage ancestors while praying for the living

WHAT YOU NEED: A recording device, quiet space, offerings, and any other support for your visioning (e.g., drum, song, prayer)

At this point, all the ancestors along the lineage should be well in spirit. If you have any doubt that this the case, return to exercises 7 through 9 and tend the lineage patiently, until all the dead are clearly settled as bright and healthy ancestors.

As in previous exercises, you will first record your own voice (or a friend's) reading the following guided visualization, and then play it back. Or you could ask a friend to read it aloud for you while you listen. Once you have made these arrangements, find a space conducive to ritual work. When there, do whatever helps you to **establish sacred space and ritual intent** (e.g., light a candle, offer incense, make prayers). If possible, identify the cardinal directions and consider sitting near the center of the ritual space. Play back the recording, or ask your friend to begin to narrate.

1. (*Begin recording.*) Take a few minutes to **get physically and emotionally centered**. This may include some meditation or breathing, personal centering prayer, unstructured movement, or just a pause to remember your intent for the ritual. You might let your eyes close or settle into a soft gaze. Bring your breath down to your belly center. Feel your bones, and feel your heart and blood pumping. Let your soul's light fill and shine forth from your body. Set the intent to stay present in your body for the entire visualization. (*Pause for two to three minutes.*)

2. When you feel centered, **call in any supportive guides** with whom you already enjoy relationship. Connect with the bright ancestral guide in the lineage you are working in. Share with any guides present your intent to gently embody this lineage of ancestors while praying for the living family members. Confirm that you have their support before proceeding. (*Pause for one to two minutes.*)

3. **Call in the experience and awareness—outside your body—of the overall lineage** you are working with, including the most recent ancestor (likely a parent or a grandparent). Take a moment to confirm that everyone along that lineage is truly well in spirit. (*Pause for one minute.*) If you find that this is not the case, shift your focus for this ritual to making repairs wherever they are needed.

4. If the lineage *is* well in spirit, **invite partial embodiment of the lineage**. First, notice the concentrated light or presence near to you but still outside your body. (*Brief pause.*) When you are ready, allow this energy to gently share the space of your physical body— to merge with you on literal and spiritual levels. In doing so, you are personally embodying the light and blessings from this ancestral lineage, further assuming your place in the line. (*Brief pause.*) Only invite this merging as much as is right for you, and allow time to sink into the experience. (*Brief pause.*) Notice how it feels to incorporate these ancestors and to know that you are part of this lineage. (*Pause for one to two minutes.*)

5. Once you are merged with the lineage and ancestral guides, **hold a prayer with them for the living family**. You might begin with a

prayer for living elders—parents, grandparents, aunts or uncles, elder siblings, and any others who are older than you and connected by blood to these ancestors. (*Pause for two minutes.*) Next, offer a prayer for yourself and for anyone in your generation—siblings and cousins. Envision those relatives taking in a blessing of health and happiness from these ancestors. (*Pause for two minutes.*) Finally, extend a prayer to younger generations who are alive right now—your children, nephews, nieces, and grandchildren. Try to maintain a state of being lightly merged with the lineage, allowing their blessings for the living to flow through you. (*Pause for two minutes.*)

6. Notice your energy level and see if you still feel comfortably merged with the lineage. (*Brief pause.*) If you are, **proceed to make prayers for all future descendants of the family lineages**—all of those who are not yet born. See these ones who are to come being blessed by the ancestors. (*Pause for two minutes.*)

7. When you have completed these prayers, **visualize your personal energy gently separating from the greater presence of the lineage and ancestral guides.** (*Brief pause.*) Now that they are outside your physical body, affirm that you commit to embodying their blessings in your life—that you will let in their support and that you want to embody what is good from them. (*Brief pause.*) Inquire if there is anything else that they want you to know. (*Pause for one minute.*)

8. Before finishing, pause to **be sure the ancestors and guides are relatively distinct from your personal energy and space** (with respect for the unbreakable ancestral link that also exists). (*Brief pause.*) **Thank your ancestral guides** and any others who accompanied you, and say goodbye for now. (*Brief pause.*)

9. Gently scan your space and surroundings a final time to **be sure you are truly complete** and clear from any residual energy. (*Brief pause.*) When you are ready, open your eyes and bring your attention fully back to your surroundings. If it's helpful, make some notes about what you experienced or were shown. (*End recording.*)

Completing the Lineage Repair Cycle

When both recent and older ancestors are well and prayers for the living family are clear and heartfelt, ask the guides if you're complete with the lineage repair work on that side of the family. If they respond in the affirmative, assume that you have restored the foundation of healthy relationship with them. If they respond in the negative, ask them which actions can help bring this lineage to a state of health. For those who have living family, the guides may want you to make repairs or other changes with extended family members (see "Ritual Assistance for Extended Family Ancestors," page 160).

When the guides have confirmed that things are well, return to start of the cycle and repeat stages one to five (chapter 5 through 9) with the other three sides of the family in turn. To recapitulate, here is a list of the five stages of lineage repair.

The Five Stages of Lineage Repair

1. Gather information about your ancestors from the living family members and genealogy research. Decide which quarter of your blood ancestry you will start with in the lineage repair process and establish boundaries as needed with those who are not yet at peace.

2. Connect with wise and loving ancestral guides, and access their blessings and gifts.

3. Understand lineage burdens and blessings, and restore the line to a state of health up to the time of the remembered dead.

4. Assist all recent ancestors in being welcomed by the guides and the lineage.

5. Ground ancestor work in healthy and empowered relationships with living family members.

If you're unsure about which lineage to focus on next, return to exercise 4, "Attuning to Your Four Primary Bloodlines," page 91. Notice the bright energy on the side of the family that you've been working with, and consult with the ancestors about where to focus next. For each of the four cycles of repair work, allow at least a month or two to really embody the shift. Invite the restored and enlivened lineage ancestors to get to know one another along the way.

After the repairs along any given lineage are complete or when all four primary lineages are in a vibrant condition, you may also wish to include a simple ritual to extend blessings and ritual care to the physical remains of your ancestors. This is typically done at a distance; however, if you have access to the final resting place of your ancestors, you may opt to weave this intention into a visit to their graves (see chapter 10, exercise 13, page 207). In brief, many traditions hold the view that the physical remains of the dead continue to reflect the energy or state of the deceased at their time of passing. Christian reliquaries, Sufi saints' tombs, Tibetan ritual items made of bone, and many other traditions involve intentional association with the remains of exemplary ancestors to receive a blessing. This same principle suggests that the remains of the troubled dead will carry or emanate a less well quality of energy. If this is the case, what happens when those ancestors go through a process of healing and elevation? Does this automatically mean that their remains now reflect a new, more beneficial energy? Although I don't presume to have definitive answers to these esoteric questions, consider asking your now bright and healed ancestors to extend their blessings to the physical remains of the dead along any given lineage. You may envision this as a process of asking that the gravesite, bones, and ashes (in cases of cremation) reflect the new vibrant energy of your lineages in a way that is also harmonized with the Earth and spirits of place. Simply raise the question with your ancestral guides and let them show you what may be useful.

When you complete the repair work with all four of your primary lineages, the final step of the repair work is to ritually harmonize them with one another and in your direct, embodied experience of your ancestors. Even as you complete a cycle of healing and repair, the relationship with the ancestors is ongoing, and opportunities to engage both the ancestors and living relatives will often arise in surprising ways.

Harmonize the Ancestral Lineages

When the recent dead have all joined the ancestors, it's natural to be curious about the interplay of your four primary lineages both as distinct energies and as a singular family or ancestral soul. One way to visually render this interplay of unity and diversity is to revisit the ancestral mandala (see figure 9.1).

If you have the names of your four grandparents and eight great-grandparents, add them to the mandala or sacred wheel (provided they have passed). Forming these associations can help integrate ancestor work into your existing practices and structurally implies equal respect for the different bloodlines. If you haven't already organized the names in this way, ask your ancestors if they want to be honored by being placed in a certain direction. Invite associations between your four primary lineages, the cardinal directions, and other forces of nature, deities, places, colors, ancestral gifts, and so on. For example, as a resident of the northern hemisphere, I associate the direction of the south with elemental fire, the color red, and the season of summer. My Grandma Howell was a strong-willed, loving, and assertive Aries woman, and this is also how she presents herself to me as an ancestor. My grandmother and her people seem happy to be associated with elemental fire and the south in my mandala.

If the graphic shown in figure 9.1 feels too confining, work with a larger surface (e.g., canvas, poster board) or with whatever artistic media speak to you. Have fun and follow your creative instincts!

You could also imagine the interplay of individual ancestors, lineages, and bloodlines as an orchestra, with percussion, woodwind, brass, and strings sections. When the individual souls in each lineage are healthy and sounding clearly, that quarter of the ancestral orchestra comes into tune with itself. As all four sections come into tune with themselves, the harmonized sound of the entire orchestra begins to

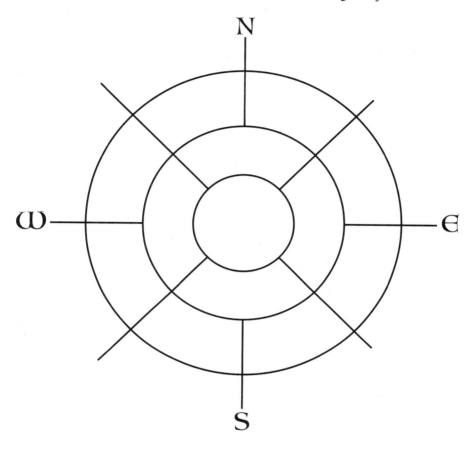

Figure 9.1. Ancestral mandala

emerge, and you may experience your bright and loving family ancestors as a single sound, energy, or consciousness. I highly recommend this
collective way of relating with the ancestors, and it may inform your
experience of them beyond lineage repair work.

⌀⌀⌀

EXERCISE ELEVEN

Harmonizing Your Four Primary Lineages

INTENT: Offer ritual seeking a more integrated experience of the four
primary ancestral bloodlines

WHAT YOU NEED: A recording device, quiet space, offerings, and any other support for your visioning (e.g., drum, song, prayer)

What follows is really three rituals presented as one: experience of your mother's people, your father's people, and then both lineages as a harmonized collective. Err on the side of going slow and being thorough. Over time you may consider combining elements of ancestral embodiment as presented in exercise 10 with the experience of them as a harmonized collective.

As in previous exercises, you will first record your own voice (or a friend's) reading the following guided visualization, and then play it back. Or you could ask a friend to read it aloud for you while you listen. Once you have made these arrangements, find a space conducive to ritual work. When there, do whatever helps you to **establish sacred space and ritual intent** (e.g., light a candle, offer incense, make prayers). If possible, identify the cardinal directions and consider sitting near the center of the ritual space. Play back the recording, or ask your friend to begin to narrate.

1. (*Begin recording.*) Take a few minutes to **get physically and emotionally centered**. This may include some meditation, personal centering prayer, unstructured movement, or a pause to remember your intent for the ritual. You might let your eyes close or settle into a soft gaze. Bring your breath to your belly center. Feel your bones, and feel your heart and blood pumping. Let your soul's light fill your body. Set the intent to stay present in your body for the entire visualization. (*Pause for two to three minutes.*)

2. When you feel centered, **call in any supportive guides** with whom you already enjoy a relationship. Connect with the bright ancestral guides in the four lineages you have been working with. Confirm along each of these four lineages that the ancestors are well and at peace. If you have the impression that further work is needed with any lineage, shift the ritual focus to address that. Share with the guides your intent to harmonize your four primary lineages, and seek their blessing before proceeding. (*Pause for two to three minutes.*)

3. **On your mother's side, invite the lineages of your maternal**

and paternal grandparents to blend and weave into a single river or current of ancestral consciousness. If there are any obstacles to this merger, seek to understand and address them. See these two lineages become one in a way that flows through the spirit of your mother (especially if she is an ancestor) or both around and through her (if she is still alive). As some traditions say, you might sense that the mother's side is on the left side of your body. See which side feels right to you. (*Pause for two to three minutes.*)

4. **On your father's side, invite the lineages of your maternal and paternal grandparents to blend and weave into a single river or current of ancestral consciousness.** If there are any obstacles to this merger, seek to understand and address them. See these two lineages become one in a way that flows through the spirit of your father (especially if he is an ancestor) or both around and through him (if he is still alive). The traditions I have studied associate the right side of the body with ancestors on the father's side. See what feels right to you. (*Pause for two to three minutes.*)

5. **Once the four primary lineages appear as two integrated lineages, notice how these two currents of energy feel outside your body**—your father's combined lineage on your right side, and your mother's combined lineage on your left. Notice and appreciate these two complex and vibrant sources of ancestral energy, and practice feeling the support of both lineages at your back and sides. (*Pause for two to three minutes.*)

6. Confirm with your guides and your own instinct that you are ready to go to the next step. What you've done may be enough for now. If so, move toward completion. (*Brief pause.*) If you get a yes to proceed, **invite the two ancestral rivers from your father and mother's side to blend and weave *outside your body*** into a single energetic current, signature, or vibration. You may visualize or feel this in front of your physical body as a blended light or energy. Notice the distinct quality and character of this blend of ancestral and family consciousness. (*Pause for two to three minutes.*)

7. Once you perceive the harmonized light of your blood ancestors

outside your body, **gently invite at least some of this ancestral light into your core**—your heart or belly center. (*Brief pause.*) Keep this practice grounded and manageable, rather than entering deeply into states of trance and embodiment. Invite their light, which is also *your* light, to gently infuse your cells and physical form with ancestral love, healing, and blessings. Only take in as much as is comfortable. Rest in this condition for as long as you are comfortable. (*Pause for five minutes.*)

8. **Before finishing, notice this same ancestral light in your siblings, and as one part of the ancestral fingerprint of any children or grandchildren.** See how these ancestors express themselves in similar or different ways through the lives of other relatives. Notice if you see this light in any living relatives with the same bloodlines as you. Perhaps offer a prayer with the ancestors for the happiness and well-being of these other living family members. (*Pause for two to three minutes.*)

9. **Ask if there is ongoing work to be done or anything your ancestors want you to know before you finish**. (*Brief pause.*)

10. **When you are ready, thank the ancestors, and return focus to your personal center.** Ask that the intensity of ancestral consciousness diminish enough for you to function normally. If you need to, you can formally separate from the ancestral light; however, this light is also you, and any disengagement is more a question of regulating intensity than of full separation. (*Pause for one minute.*)

11. Gently scan your space and surroundings a final time to **be sure you are truly complete** and clear from any residual energy. (*Brief pause.*) When you are ready, open your eyes and bring your attention fully back to your physical body and your surroundings. If it's helpful, you might make some notes about what happened. (*End recording.*)

In the hours and days after this kind of integration practice, periodically return to notice the ancestral light both inside your body and as a dance of energetic and spiritual support in your surrounding space or aura. See if you can get used to holding the ancestors' light and support in the background of your everyday awareness, much as you occasionally notice the automatic body process of breath or heartbeat.

Feasting and Celebrating the Ancestors

When the recent dead and each respective lineage are well and the four primary lineages are harmonized with one another, it's good to celebrate! At this stage, you've established the groundwork for maintaining relationships and have restored the foundation of your ancestral house. If moved, you may extend the repair work to include the additional lineages of your other four great-grandparents (eight total lineages); however, I've come to think of healing your four primary bloodlines as a kind of ancestral proficiency or reasonable goal for the lineage repair work. Although relationships with the ancestors are ongoing, and in this sense ancestor work is never "done," the emphasis on making repairs can and should eventually yield to a different kind of relationship with your ancestors as guides and allies in your everyday life. Malidoma Somé wrote, "You know that the ancestors are healed when things begin to change dramatically for the better around you."[6]

Ritual feasts to honor ancestors are common in many traditions. In one example, the Celtic holidays of Halloween and Samhain, some people traditionally set out extra places and food at the table for those ancestors who choose to return. This is sometimes known as a "Dumb Supper" because participants sometimes enjoy the shared meal in silence with their loved ones. Although Halloween is one potent time for this ritual, you can do it at any time to honor and enliven your connection with the ancestors. I recommend a shared meal once a year after you have completed the full cycle of lineage repair. As with any party, it should take into account the style and preferences of the guests of honor—in this case, your ancestors. The spirit feast is also a great practice for celebrating the positive shift after each cycle of healing and repair with the four primary lineages or as a completion of healing work with all four lineages.

⊗⊗⊘

EXERCISE TWELVE

RITUAL TO FEAST YOUR FAMILY ANCESTORS

INTENT: Offer a spirit feast, including offerings of food and drink, for your ancestors

WHAT YOU NEED: An ancestor altar or shrine (even if temporary) and offerings of food and drink

This ritual feast is one way to celebrate the transition from a focus on repair and healing to one based on mutual support and regular tending. A shared meal can also be a regular time of communion with your ancestors and guides and a staple ritual for ongoing ancestor work. There are two parts to this ritual—preparations and the actual feast.

⊗⊗⊘ RITUAL PREPARATIONS ⊗⊗⊘

1. Sit in meditation with your ancestors. **Ask what kind of offerings they would enjoy**—for example, food, drink, smoke (tobacco or incense), flowers, fire (candles), music, or colorful cloth. Ask them how they want you to celebrate the cycle of lineage repair work. What kind of feast would please them? You might also ask if there are certain days or times when they would like the celebration to occur. Many people favor nighttime for ancestor ritual, but stay open to the guidance you receive.

2. **Set aside some time to prepare and hold the feast.** Consider it a formal date as with anyone you love and respect and for whom you want to make a good impression.

3. **On the day or night of the feast, prepare yourself physically.** You might ritually bathe or shower to transition into the space. Dress intentionally. Some people wear all white, but you may wear any other clothing that helps you feel ritually connected to your ancestors.

4. **Prepare the offerings.** If you don't have an ancestor altar, establish a place temporarily where you will honor them (see chapter 4, page 60, for suggestions on ways to establish an ancestor altar).

∞ Holding the Ritual Feast ∞

1. At the time of the ritual, **bring your offerings to your ancestor altar** or designated space. Prepare the plate of food, drink, and other offerings as you would for a respected guest at a dinner party.

2. After taking a moment to center and ground yourself, **invoke your ancestors**; call them to be present. Open your voice in some way— song, chant, or spontaneous toning. When moved, invite your ancestors by name: "I welcome you (name). I welcome you (name)." You might call out the names from the present toward the past. Trust your instincts. Unless your intuition or tradition guides you differently, men can start with their father's father's side, and women with their mother's mother's side. Stay with this welcoming invocation until you feel them present.

3. **Share with them what you've brought and why.** Present the spirit feast as if you were presenting a gift to someone. Once presented, tune in with the ancestors for a moment to **ask if your offering is well received**. Is there anything else they need to be satisfied? Trust your instincts here, and stick with the process until they are satisfied with your offering.

4. At this point, traditions vary, and **there are at least three ways to proceed**. One is to completely step away and let the ancestors enjoy their feast without interruption. A second is to sit in silence and enjoy a meal as well. A third approach is to continue talking aloud and interacting with them, as if sharing a meal with living family members. Decide how this will go before you begin the ritual. If you choose one of the two latter options, eat from your own food and drink rather than what you've presented to the ancestors. When you feel complete, thank them, and if possible let the offerings and shrine rest in silence.

5. **Leave the offering with the ancestors for a certain period of time**—usually at least one night, but not longer than a few days. Check in and trust your instincts about when to remove the offering. If possible, return the offerings to the earth in an ecologically sensitive way.

6. **After the ritual, check back in with your ancestors** in the days and weeks that follow. Sit in meditation or prayer, and make some time to enjoy the connection you've energized through the ritual feast.

Ancestor Work
beyond the Lineage Repair Cycle

The ancestors were with you before your birth, and before you had words with which to communicate with them. They were present before your contact with ancestor reverence, and they will continue to be part of your life whether or not you engage in these practices. And when your soul and body finally part ways, representatives from the realm of the ancestors will welcome you back. If you've completed the lineage repair cycle in this book, you have restored a part of your psychic infrastructure to such a degree that you can not only relate well with living relatives and family ancestors but also comfortably embody ancestral blessings and support in your everyday life. You have also implicitly prepared for your own death. So what now?

Some reasons to call on family ancestors beyond the lineage repair cycle include guidance and support for daily challenges; celebration and renewal of relationship; prayers and support for living family; clarification of life path and destiny; and ritual tending related to family responsibilities to the degree that you choose to take them on. The ancestors may support you as the embodiment of the family spirit, and they may help optimize your physical and mental health and the health of your relationships. They may also have insight and skills related to your vocation or the work of those around you. For example, if you serve others in a healing capacity, your ancestors may want to play an active role in helping your work; similarly, if you are an artist, they may inspire your creative process (see chapter 11).

Below I will consider two possible directions for family ancestor work beyond the lineage repair cycle. In addition, you may also seek to harmonize the blessings of family ancestors with other types of ancestors (see part 3) and with other-than-human forces (e.g., deities, elemental powers, spirits of place), but this is an involved topic that is largely beyond the scope of this book.

Inviting Ancestors to Clarify Your Destiny and Life Path

When healthy, your relationship with family ancestors can help you remember your life's calling, your destiny and sense of purpose. Different traditions approach this topic in different ways, but the basic sense is that we each have certain gifts, talents, and contributions we bring to the world. These gifts are blessings that may connect to your vocation, or they may be more about your relationships and your personal embodiment of love, kindness, or other redeeming human qualities. Many indigenous cultures believe that we are morally obligated to at least *attempt* to remember and fulfill our unique calling—and that one function of community is to help individuals realize their calling in service. In simple terms, I'm talking about living a sane and meaningful life that brings your specific flavor of goodness into the world.

Asking the ancestors how they see your life calling is not always as straightforward as it may sound. By consciously participating in any lineage, biological or cultural, you receive increased support but also increased demands. If you feel like the black sheep in your family or in the world in general, the ancestors may ask you to sacrifice some of this outsider status in exchange for greater belonging and communal responsibility. Especially if you were not raised with healthy respect for recent ancestors, this sense of being part of a larger human family may take some getting used to. One of the founding fathers of psychology, Carl Jung, spoke to the sense of belonging and purpose that can emerge when working with the ancestors:

> The individual's life is elevated into a type, indeed it becomes the archetype of the woman's fate in general. This leads to restoration or *apocatastasis* of the lives of her ancestors, who now, through the bridge of the momentary individual, pass down into the generations of the future. An experience of this kind gives the individual a place and a meaning in the life of the generations, so that all unnecessary obstacles are cleared out of the way of the life stream that is to flow

through her. At the same time the individual is rescued from her isolation and restored to wholeness. All ritual preoccupation with the archetypes ultimately has this aim and this result.[7]

Asking the ancestors to help clarify your life calling can start with a review of the blessings and burdens you have inherited. Are there ancestral blessings that already contribute to a meaningful and inspired life for you? Are there burdens that you have already worked to transform as part of your service to current and future generations? In reviewing the lineage repair cycle, ask yourself whether there are specific bloodlines that more strongly inform your sense of self and calling. Some cultures believe that we are more aligned in spirit with one side of the family or another, and that we may even be ancestors reborn from a specific bloodline. Noticing how you resonate with certain lines can give you clues to whose work you are carrying forward and which ancestral blessings shine most brightly in your life today.

You can bring the question of life calling and path directly to the ancestors, but with a topic of such magnitude, your conscious mind can often be your greatest obstacle to hearing the guidance. Asking for messages through dreams can minimize distortions from your own preconceived idea. In practice, the task of aligning with destiny often feels like a game of "hotter, colder," whereby you make incremental changes that bring you into a greater sense of alignment. As you feel more aligned, you will likely find that the ancestors are a vital source of support for walking your path and facing challenges that naturally arise.

Taking on the Mantle of Family Ancestor Person

In my own journey of guiding others in ancestral repairs, I have come to understand an important difference between getting things to a healthy place with one's ancestors—or what I would call ancestral proficiency— and following a soul-level calling to specialize in ancestor work.

In my case, relations with the ancestors happen to be a prominent part of my overall destiny. I am called not only to engage with my own ancestors in active, ongoing ways but also to focus on this aspect of the spiritual path in ways that are useful to others.

Most people who walk a spiritual path will *not* be called to specialize in ancestor work. Although everyone ideally embodies a basic level of alignment with their ancestors, after making necessary repairs, most people will revert to a relationship of maintenance with their ancestors as they return to their work in the world. This is normal, natural, and to be expected, as human ancestors are just one type of mystery or force in the larger ecology of the sacred. But if you feel called to more specialized work with your ancestors, trust that they will reveal to you the nature of that calling, including if, when, and how you can support others to also work with their ancestors.

This calling can also take the form of a lifelong vow to serve as your family's diplomatic link or ritual representative with the ancestors. Drawing on his experience with Dagara culture, Malidoma Somé wrote that almost every family has "at least one person who functions as the receptacle of energies from the Other World, one family member who has the sensitivity to be aware of, and respond to, the deeper spiritual and sometimes physical needs of the family across generations. Sometimes these people are recognized as caretakers of the family." He describes these individuals as "the shamans, the shrine keepers, and the healers of the family tree," and he cautions that this is not necessarily an easy or glamorous role, as these individuals may be called upon for thankless, difficult, and at times dangerous service.[8]

After years of witnessing individuals gravitate toward the role of ancestral caretaker, I began to offer a formal dedication ceremony for those moved to pick up this mantle. A key component involves making vows in ritual space before the ancestors and living community. I've developed a list of responsibilities as a starting point for the "job description" of family ancestor specialist. If you do choose to commit to this lifelong work, remember to be creative about how it will look in the context of your own life and family. The suggestions below are merely a starting point.

1. Establish clear and ongoing lines of communication with the elevated ancestors, and do what is needed to keep your relationship with them healthy.

2. Ensure that all blood lineage ancestors are in an elevated and sound condition.

3. Lift up the spirits of the living family in prayer and regularly feed the spirits of the ancestors on their behalf.

4. Coordinate efforts in humble and constructive ways with any relatives who show an interest in getting to know and honor the ancestors.

5. Compile existing information on family history, and consider engaging in further research to establish names and stories for the past seven generations, and beyond if possible.

6. Make information on family history accessible to the living family in ways that are useful and culturally sensitive.

7. Assist family members in becoming ancestors (rather than ghosts) upon their death.

8. Actively work for the health of relationships between family members, including, when appropriate, resolving family conflicts and healing family burdens or toxins.

9. Maintain family graves or tend to other remains. This task may be coordinated with other family members.

10. Support births of new family members and other important rites of passage (e.g., adolescent rites of passage, marriages) in culturally sensitive ways.

Part Three

HONORING
OTHER TYPES
OF
ANCESTORS

Part 3 explores ways of relating with human ancestors who are not necessarily related by blood. In this part you will learn:

- Different ways of relating with the body and elements after death
- One framework for multiple souls and different types of ancestors
- Cemetery practice and ritual to honor ancestors of place
- How to call on ancestral support for success in your vocation
- Ways to offer support at funerals and to offer ritual for the recently deceased

Like part 1, the final third of this book is an experiential guidebook for relating to different types of ancestors. These may include adoptive family, ancestors of tradition, deceased friends and mentors, and ancestors of place. I strongly encourage first being grounded in work with your blood ancestors before focusing too much on these. In the final chapter you'll be invited to reflect on your own death, practices to encourage conscious dying, preferred funerary customs and the post-death journey, and beliefs about consciousness after death.

TEN

Ancestors and Place

When you die, will you still remember the land of your childhood? How about your current home or favorite places on Earth? If your loved ones visit your grave or hold your ashes, will this make it easier for you to speak to them? One way the human dead speak in this dimension is through the mediation of specific places, both in the world shaped by humans and in wilder environments. In this chapter you'll learn about the relationship of the ancestors to places such as cemeteries, public monuments, and more natural settings. You'll learn basic guidelines for navigating these different types of locations safely and respectfully. This chapter also includes practices for honoring family ancestors when visiting a cemetery, as well as a ritual to greet the ancestors of place near your home.

Home Is Where the Bones Are

If you're like many people in the United States, you may not live especially close to places where recent generations of your ancestors were born, died, and are buried. Compared to many cultures, modern Americans tend to have high rates of mobility, and this informs how we think and feel about place. My life happens to fit this pattern and can illustrate the situation of many people. At least the last five generations of my blood ancestors are mostly buried in Ohio and Pennsylvania and, before this, in centuries-old graves unknown to me in Ireland, England, Germany, Holland, and Austria. Like most people in the western hemisphere with some European blood, I have not spent significant time in the lands of these earlier ancestors. Even if I had the income to hire a professional genealogist and dedicate a season in northern Europe to intensive ancestor-focused travel and ritual, this still would not make me English, Irish, or German. The fact that I do not have the means for such a pilgrimage makes me like the majority of modern Americans who are not wealthy, are not ancestrally from what is now the United States, and have no means or strong desire to relocate to ancestral homelands. I suspect such an international undertaking would be enjoyable and spiritually potent, but traveling to far-off lands or chasing an idealized past isn't needed for connecting with the ancestors. After at least five generations of life and death along every family bloodline, my home, as well as the remains of my recent generations of ancestors, is now in the United States.

In contrast to this pattern of mobility, the terms *indigenous* and *native* imply "of a place." When applied to human culture, *indigenous* usually refers to people who have enduring relationships with specific places and active connections to traditional, tribal ways of life. For example, in 2010 I had the opportunity to be a support at a multiday Bear Dance ceremony in the Bayview–Hunter's Point neighborhood of San Francisco. Ceremonial leaders of the Costanoan Rumsen Ohlone tribe chose this location in part because of its proximity to known burial and village sites of Ohlone peoples. Urban development without regard for the legal requirements or for Native protocols on disrupting human remains continues to threaten many sacred sites throughout California and beyond. What stood out from the ceremony was the specific type of empowered, natural pride that seemed to radiate from some of the Ohlone bear dancers. This quality seemed to say without words, "I am home here. This is my place."

Living and worshipping directly over the ash and bone of centuries, if not thousands of years, of family ancestors carries a psychological and spiritual significance that is often overlooked in modern culture. In her seminal work on the relationship of California Indian peoples to the land, M. Kat Anderson wrote:

> Living in the same place as one's ancestors establishes a multidimensional bond to that place. It is tremendously important for California Indians' connection to a place to have depth of time, for them to be able to point to a particular harvesting patch, shrub, tree, living site, or sacred spot and know that many generations before them used the same plants, walked the same path, tended the same land. To many California Indians, a gathering site is consecrated by gatherings carried on over long periods. Each generation honors the ancestors, honors the customs, and honors the plants by using and tending them. The tremendous pool of intergenerational knowledge from which to draw is a blessing and a gift. In general, each of us is deeply dependent on the trials and accomplishments of many generations of humans before us.[1]

The same could be said for most living indigenous cultures, as well as for most communities throughout history. When groups pass down through generations their knowledge of how to live and thrive in a particular location, this continuity contributes not only to community survival but also to a greater sense of intimacy and place.

This is not to say that tribal peoples have always stayed put in one location; all human beings were new arrivals at some point in the past, even if it was thousands of years ago, and some peoples have remained seminomadic until recent times. Similarly, some modern urban Europeans may be living within a day's walk of their blood ancestors from the last several thousand years or more. Here's the important part: the older your ancestral claim is to a place and the more generations of your people who have lived and died there, the more likely you are to feel that you belong in that place. If you're one of the rare persons whose recent ancestors lived near where you live now, then you're probably aware that relocation would have an impact, because you would then be outside the immediate field of energy and blessings that accompany your ancestral homeland. For all non-Native peoples in the Americas, even if you live in the same area as your recent ancestors, there are still other human communities, often with living representatives, who have an even older ancestral presence on the lands we currently call home. This makes achieving the experience of "I am at home here; this is my place" complicated. But it is certainly possible.

Before continuing, take a moment to reflect on the following questions:

- Do you have family ancestors buried in the Earth near your current home? If your current home is not where you grew up, did you have family ancestors near your childhood home? If you answered yes to either question, do you notice that this history helps you feel more at home in these places?
- If you are not an indigenous person living in your traditional homeland, have you spent time with any people who are indigenous to your current place of residence? If so, did you notice anything about how their relationship with place differs from yours?
- Where on Earth have your experienced the greatest sense of "home"? Did ancestral ties to that place play any role in this felt sense of belonging?
- Do you know where you would like your remains to return to the Earth? Is this a new or familiar burial place for your ancestral lineages?

What is it about our ancestors' remains that so powerfully informs our sense of home and place? One way to think about bones, ash, and other types of human remains is as intrinsic points of contact with the deceased. In chapter 6, you learned how to craft and energize an ongon or spirit house for your ancestral guides. Think of remains, including cremation urns, as already energized spirit houses. Just as a hawk feather is already a consecrated magical link with Hawk and sunlight inevitably corresponds to the Sun, so are human bones the reverberating letters of the verb that was an incarnate soul. Human remains are an extension of the spirit of the deceased, or at least an aspect of the shell that retains connection with the living soul. This can be helpful to know if you end up caring for the bones of a deceased loved one or, more commonly, their ashes. In general, I recommend treating any human remains as consecrated materials worthy of the respect and consideration that you would give the original owner if they were still present in the flesh. I do not, however, personally work with human remains in my practice. Like most practitioners of ancestor reverence worldwide, I do not believe that direct contact with human remains is necessary or even inherently helpful, aside from conscious rituals of completion with the body after death (see chapter 12). If you are in doubt, bring the topic of how to best care for the remains of a loved one to a trusted and nonjudgmental spiritual guide or elder for advice.

Two principles for handling human remains are common across cultures: first, the desire for a proper or meaningful funerary service, and, second, the right to freedom from disturbance for human remains when at all possible. In Sophocles's tragedy *Antigone,* from the fifth century BCE, Antigone advocates for the right of her brother Polynices to a proper burial, even though he has been a traitor. Tiresias, the prophet and visionary of Thebes, supports her efforts on behalf of the gods. Last rites and reverential care for the body after death were implicitly important for the symbolically adorned cadavers at our oldest known archaeological sites, and such care is no less important for the vast majority of people on Earth today. "In the United States alone, there are more than 22,000 funeral homes, approximately 115,000 cemeteries, 1,155 crematories, and an estimated 300 casket sellers. The total U.S. death-care industry is $11 billion. Enough embalming fluid is buried every year to fill eight Olympic-size pools; more steel (in caskets alone) than was used to build the Golden Gate Bridge; and enough reinforced concrete to construct a two-lane highway from New York to Detroit."[2]

As is true nearly everywhere else in the world, law and popular culture in the United States forbid the desecration of human remains. For most people, this is an obvious and well-established taboo: you don't mess with dead bodies. Why not? Of course, the living family may experience distress if they learn that the graves of their ancestors have been desecrated, but what other beliefs reinforce this as a cultural given? One is the belief that the bones retain a link with the spirit of the deceased. The "mummy's curse" refers to popular accounts of archaeologists in Egypt who died because they disturbed ancient mummies. If you ask people on the street what brought doom to the archaeologists, many would point to the spirit of the mummy, awakened by the desecration. In the same way, grave robbers and people who use human remains in unethical ways risk incurring the hostility of the spirits who inhabited those remains. If, several months after your death, someone dug up your grave and stole your bones to be used in harmful practices, imagine how you would react on a soul level.

Because of this inherent link between human remains and souls, the location of the remains (cemeteries, ossuaries, catacombs, the bottom of the sea) can support heightened contact with the spirits of specific ancestors and with the ancestors in general. Most people instinctively understand this and tend to treat cemeteries and places like them with reverence and respect. When entering a cemetery or other consecrated burial grounds, I recommend first making a simple, ecologically sensible offering to the gatekeeper and the guardian spirits of place. If local traditions or your own faith provide guidance on the topic, follow that. If not, consider that there may be a particular type of deity or collective force that cares for the spirits in the Earth at places of concentrated human burials. By leaving a pinch of cornmeal or tobacco, natural incense, local flowers, or simply a heartfelt prayer of greeting, you enter the space with a gesture of respect for any local inhabitants, seen or unseen. Even if you do not have loved ones buried within, carry out at least one tangible gesture of respect and goodwill during your visit. This could include removing trash, cleaning off a covered headstone, straightening a fallen grave marker, or leaving an offering at a grave that could use the extra love and care. Spontaneous prayer and songs of appreciation and respect can convey positive energy. The following exercise presents one way to relate to the graves of family ancestors.

∞

EXERCISE THIRTEEN

CEMETERY PRACTICE WITH FAMILY ANCESTORS

INTENT: Safely and respectfully commune with your ancestors at a cemetery or other burial place

WHAT YOU NEED: Offerings (e.g., flowers, incense, a stone, natural items, food and drink your ancestors might enjoy) and any other support for your visioning (e.g., drum, rattle, songs)

Cemeteries or any burial grounds are places between worlds. Intentional communication between the living and dead can be heightened in these places. This exercise will help you engage in ritual to honor and commune with your ancestors where they are buried. When you come to a cemetery to greet the spirits of the dead, observe basic precautions to prepare and protect yourself, as described below.

1. Before you go to the site, find a quiet, supportive space, and ask yourself and your guides: What ancestors do you wish to visit? What do you know of them, and why do you want to visit them at this time? Are they ones you've worked with in the past? What's your sense of the state they are in now? (See chapter 5.) Note: It's okay if you don't have a sense that these ancestors are at peace; it just changes the ritual approach you will take during the visit. If your ancestors are not well in spirit, the cemetery may not be the best place to work out your grief and sadness, because it increases the likelihood of direct connection. Ask your intuition, guides, and elders if it's a good idea for you to visit your ancestors' burial place at this time. Be open to hearing "no" or "not yet." Assuming you hear a "yes," continue with the following steps.

2. **Prepare for the visit.** There are a few things to consider before going to a cemetery.

Specific days and time of day. Does your tradition recognize certain days of the week or cycles of the moon as auspicious for honoring the ancestors? Anniversaries of birth and death or holidays such as the Day of the Dead or Halloween? Time of day may also be significant. Some traditions see the world of the living as ascendant as the sun rises, so a morning visit could serve to temper the intensity of the ancestral contact. Visiting near sunset can amplify the felt presence of the dead. I suggest visiting while there is daylight unless you are sure that a night ritual is both legal and wise.

Are you better served going alone or with a family member or friend? There are benefits to each. Solitude allows you the freedom to follow your own rhythm, but traveling with an ally can offer extra support. If you go with someone, be sure they know your intent and understand that you may need to stay at the gravesite for some time without interruption.

What kinds of offerings are good to bring to the gravesite? Offerings might include food or drink you imagine your ancestors would enjoy, flowers, stones, other natural offerings (e.g., tobacco, cornmeal, incense), songs, music, and prayers. In addition to offerings for your ancestors, consider bringing an offering for the spirits of place—the cemetery itself, or the spirits or powers there. Some traditions believe that a deity looks after the cemetery; others believe in giving offerings to the collective dead that are there. Use your instinct or trust your guides to inform your choice.

What else should you bring—or not bring? Obviously, you want to bring what you need to care for yourself and your personal needs. However, decide whether to bring along personal food and drink. Some traditions discourage eating while communing with the dead, while others encourage it. If you do feel right about bringing food or drink along on your visit, consider sharing, before you eat, a small portion of whatever you're having with the resident dead and other local spirits.

What should you wear? Some traditions dress in light colors or all in white, which offers a protective quality, while others associate black clothing with a state of mourning. Whatever you choose to wear, dress with purpose as a sign of your respect.

3. **Enter the space with intent.** Remember as you approach the cemetery that, although there is nothing to fear, you are crossing a threshold into a different space. Either immediately across the threshold or just before, pause to acknowledge the land and spirits of place with prayer or offerings. If your beliefs support the practice, after entering you may directly address the guardian or gatekeeper spirit of the cemetery.

4. **Proceed to the gravesite.** Upon arriving, find a comfortable, quiet position and settle in. Notice what kind of spiritual condition these ancestors seem to be in. Their state will determine your next steps.

   If you know that the ones you're honoring are *not* well in spirit, enter in a state of protection. You are there not to invoke them but to honor and remember them. Without asking them to be present, respectfully make your offerings as a gift and leave it at that. Ask that the offerings have a healing and beneficial intent for the deceased.

   If you know the ones you're honoring *are* well, invite them to be present.

5. **Invoke the presence of those ancestors who are well in spirit.** You might make a small offering first and then invoke their presence, saving your main offering for after the invocation. The invocation doesn't have to be fancy or formal—just speak to them from the heart, as in, "Hey, it's me, I've come to see you." Then you might talk with them, sing, or pray. Stay with it until you feel an echo back.

6. **Present your offerings.** Tell them what you brought for them and why you brought it. Give it to them, and then sit and listen. Trust your instincts on what, if anything, needs to happen next. Are there certain things you need to say? Do they need to say something to you? After listening with patience and an open heart, voice any concerns and express yourself as needed. Be willing to sit there for as long as it takes to allow the connection to happen. Stay in this receptive space until you feel complete.

7. **Leave the cemetery.** When you are ready, say your goodbyes and move away from the grave(s). Once you walk away, scan your energy to make sure you aren't pulling any heavy energy with you. Set the intention and request that whatever is not *you* will stay *there*—and that your energy body is clear.

As you are leaving, make a final offering and prayer to release any troubling energy. You might confirm: "I have come in peace; I apologize for any unintended disrespect, and ask that death remain here. May the spirits of this place be at peace." Do a second cleansing scan of your energy at the place where you make this last offering, then leave the grounds.

When you return home, before you do anything else, do a third and final check to make sure your energy body is clear. You might need to change your clothes, shower, or do some ritual of cleansing to make certain you're not carrying any heavy energy with you. Trust your instincts and do as much or as little as needed.

Public Memorials and Monuments

We memorialize the dead in many locations other than family shrines and cemeteries. This section considers some of these other ways to honor the ancestors. Such considerations include:

- Are human remains present at the site of the memorial? If so, to what degree?
- Is the memorial located at the place of death?
- What was the means of death (e.g., human violence, illness, accidents, natural disasters)?
- Are the names of the dead known and included in the memorial?
- Is the memorial intentionally harmonized with the land, elements, or other forces?
- To what degree do these ancestors symbolize something important in the larger culture?
- How much time has passed since the death of those memorialized?

Sensitivity to these factors can increase your understanding of how a culture understands the relationship between the living and the dead. It can also support you in engaging with the ancestors at diverse types of memorials. Generally speaking, the more factors above that are considered at a memorial site, the more potent it becomes in connecting with those memorialized there. In this next section, we will explore different types of memorials, from less to more potent.

Near the United States Capitol in Washington, D.C., stands a forty-four-foot-tall white marble statue known as the Peace Monument. It commemorates those who died at sea during the American Civil War (1861–65). The monument is close to memorial statues for presidents Grant and Garfield. None of the individuals memorialized died at these locations, nor are their remains on-site. In each case the dead crossed from this world over a century past, and visitors are less likely to feel the same depth of emotional charge that they would at monuments for the more recently deceased. The Peace Monument incorporates certain deities such as Mars and Neptune, but they are not gods with whom most Americans have a personal relationship. All of the monuments are, however, harmonized to some degree with other spirits of place insofar as they are part of the spiritual and psychic ecology of the site. In this way the memorialized dead presidents and the naval war dead continue to hold vigil at the western perimeter of the Capitol.

Heading west past the Washington Monument to the base of the Lincoln Memorial (neither of which is a burial place), one arrives at the Vietnam Veterans Memorial. None of the 58,195 service members named at "The Wall" are interred on-site, and most died more than eight thousand miles away in Southeast Asia; however, especially for some veterans and their families, the monument undoubtedly functions as a point of heightened contact with the spirits of those named. The monument is often ranked among America's favorite architectural structures, and ritually it "works." Why? The Wall memorializes those who have died much more recently, which also means that these individuals live directly in the hearts and memories of many of the living visitors. Thus the amount of grief is greater than at most of the surrounding memorials. Because places of intense grieving for the dead are natural sites of communion with the ancestors, the collective grief associated with them can facilitate contact with and healing for the dead. As a result of their relatively recent deaths, those named at the Wall are more likely to retain connection to their recent incarnations (either because they have not yet joined the ancestors or simply out of love for the living), and this also makes them more likely than the deceased Civil War sailors to connect with visitors. The Wall is also part of the energy matrix of the Capitol, another factor that contributes to its potency.

One of the most powerful and direct ways to invoke ancestors is by name. Writing the names encourages speaking them aloud, a kind of ongoing invocation at these types of monuments. The sound of the name can function as a kind of auditory link for connecting with the deceased who responded to it over a lifetime. The names of the deceased are certainly one part of the magic of the Vietnam Memorial. When I visited the Wall at age ten, my father in Ohio asked me to locate the name of a fellow naval officer who was killed in combat. When I found it, I paused for a moment and made a point of touching the inscription. I spoke the name aloud for the first time that night on the phone with my dad. This fulfilled his wish to pay his respects to this friend in spirit, and I suspect that it also reverberated in a positive way for his friend.

A mile west across the Potomac River, in Arlington National Cemetery, the Tomb of the Unknown Soldier highlights some of the sacredness, symbolism, and ritual potency of human remains (see plate 11). More than forty nations maintain monuments to the unknown dead, and all of them typically contain the body of one individual who died in a war. At Arlington the tomb has been overseen twenty-four hours a day through all weather conditions by a rotation of Tomb Guards, an elite unit of the U.S. Army's Third Infantry Regiment. In the crypt itself rest the bodies of three unidentified soldiers who were killed in World War I, World War II, and the Korean War. The anonymity of the soldiers in the crypt is an essential part of the function of the memorial. A fourth soldier held the role for the unnamed war dead of Vietnam from 1984 to 1998, but Air Force First Lieutenant Michael Joseph Blassie was later exhumed after his identity was confirmed through DNA testing. Blassie's remains were returned to his family, and he was reburied at Jefferson Barracks National Cemetery in Saint Louis, Missouri. The Vietnam portion of the monument has since been replaced with a dedication committing the Armed Forces to attempt to account for all missing service members.*

What are the implications of an entire nation using the remains of one unnamed solider to represent a much greater number of deceased soldiers? In rituals to elevate family ancestors, Malidoma Somé sometimes guides participants to first symbolically represent a specific deceased male or female family elder and then to use this ancestor as a focal point for the larger work of helping the souls of *all* one's lineage dead to join the loving ancestors. In this case, traditional African ways and the practices of modern nations are structurally similar.

Even in cases where the body is cremated or buried elsewhere, the location of death may itself become a place of memorial. Of the fifteen leading causes of death in the United States, three are relatively sudden: accidents, suicides, and homicides. According to the National Highway Traffic Safety Administration, about thirty-three thousand people die in car accidents each year in the United States.[3] Suicide numbers are higher, at forty-one thousand,[4] while homicides number sixteen thousand.[5] Roadside memorials with flowers, crosses, and images of the deceased mark the sites of many fatal accidents, and similar monuments sometimes honor the places of death for homicides or

---

*Before interment in the crypt, the four unknowns were posthumously awarded the Congressional Medal of Honor. In 2013, I spoke with the Congressional Medal of Honor Society, who confirmed that the medals were awarded *not* for service during these soldiers' lives, but as a symbolic action for the unknowns as a collective. When the body of Lieutenant Blassie was identified and transferred in 1998, his family's requests that he keep the medal were denied. The Medal of Honor for the Vietnam unknowns remains in the chamber beneath the crypt. It is the only Medal of Honor that is not linked with a specific human being, living or deceased.

even suicides. A more recent tradition of "ghost bikes" involves placing a bicycle painted all in white, typically in urban areas, at locations where bicyclists were killed by motor vehicles. In addition to alerting drivers to dangerous locations and raising awareness about violent crimes, these shrines provide ways to communally honor and grieve the deceased. Such memorials, tended by family and friends, also affirm a connection between the deceased and specific locations; the dead become part of the story of these places.

The most potent type of ancestral memorials typically (1) include large numbers of human remains; (2) incorporate the names of the deceased; (3) are located at the location of death; (4) honor relatively recent deaths; and (5) mark a place of profound human-to-human violence. Examples of twentieth-century genocide memorials that fit these criteria include the Auschwitz-Birkenau Memorial and Museum in Poland, the Kigali Genocide Memorial in Rwanda, and the Tuol Sleng Genocide Museum in Phnom Penh, Cambodia. In each case, thousands if not hundreds of thousands of violent deaths took place at the memorial site as part of a larger genocide. These locations are not only mass graves or crematoriums but also places of mass murder. Battlefields throughout the world often fit these criteria. The Douaumont Ossuary in northeastern France houses the bones of at least 130,000 unidentified French and German combatants from World War I, a fraction of the over 900,000 total estimated casualties in the 1916 Battle of Verdun. In Pennsylvania, the Gettysburg National Military Park memorializes the greatest single loss of life in a battle on American soil, with more than 50,000 casualties in three days of fighting in July 1863. Genocide and large-scale human violence leave an imprint on the land, creating a connection between those ancestors and the place that endures through cultural memory (and potentially on other levels) long beyond the killing. Well-crafted memorials are one way to start to transform fear and suffering into healing for the living, for the dead, and for the land that holds both.

Except for several natural disasters in the first half of the twentieth century, the September 11, 2001, attacks on the World Trade

Center in New York City account for the greatest loss of life on any one day and place in the United States since the end of the Civil War. That Tuesday morning in lower Manhattan, more than twenty-five hundred human beings died in a span of two hours, many in a state of fear and confusion. Fewer than three hundred whole bodies were recovered after the attacks, and in the subsequent decade, bone fragments have been positively identified for just over half of the victims. As of 2013, new remains were still being found in site debris, and the remains repository at the World Trade Center site continues to analyze the more than ten thousand fragments of bone still to be identified. As at most such sites, challenges in identifying the human remains can compound trauma for the living and may be a source of disturbance for the dead as well.

If you were charged with creating the memorial at Ground Zero, what principles would you consider? The final design of the National September 11 Memorial and Museum draws heavily on the tempering energies of trees and water in the form of large reflecting pools and waterfalls. By harmonizing the memorial with natural energies as much as possible in a highly urban setting, the designers invited the vegetative worlds and the restorative qualities of water to participate in the healing needed at this location. Also, by including the remains repository as part of the memorial, the designers have acknowledged the sacred process of tending to the human remains. When people spend millions of public dollars on building and maintaining memorials and on identifying human remains, we affirm on some instinctual level that these things matter.

Ancestors and the Natural World

Certain places on Earth support heightened connectivity with the ancestors. First and foremost, our ancestors speak through our blood and bones. Like it or not, we are walking, breathing ancestor shrines.

The ancestors may also speak through specific locations in the natural world. The subject of how living humans, ancestral spirits, and material culture relate to specific places in nature and with the larger matrix of other-than-human consciousness is beyond the scope of this book. This is in part because the rest of nature has tremendous complexity and diversity even before we take into account human meaning and modification. Some wild places and powers may be healing and friendly toward humans, some may be neutral or wary, and some may be hostile. Thorough and respectful consideration of such sites should therefore take into account the perspectives of their other-than-human inhabitants.

With a nod to the depth of this subject, I briefly explore below three ways in which human ancestral spirits may retain connection, both from their own side and in the psyche of the living, with places in the natural world:

1. Living humans, using their cultural teachings, may automatically associate specific types of living beings (e.g., certain plants or animals) and natural formations (e.g., caves, waterfalls) with the ancestors.
2. Places may serve as anchors in cultural memory for meaningful past events at those locations.
3. Natural formations may be consecrated in ways that focalize ancestral consciousness.

When we view specific animals or plants as linked with the human ancestors, their appearance can function as a trigger or portal for direct ancestral connection. Moreover, their dwelling places may also be portals to the ancestors' realm. For example, many cultures on Earth associate certain trees with the dead. In this way, the landscape of everyday life is populated with antennae or points of linkage from which the ancestors could connect with us (or vice versa) at any moment. Among the Celts, the apple tree is associated with Avalon, the otherworld, and with the ancestor-focused holiday of Samhain. In Roman culture, willows were sometimes planted over graves, and ancient Greeks associated the willow with Hecate, patron of witches and guide for the souls of the dead. Yew, juniper, and other evergreens are often associated with death and the ancestors in European lore, as in the Grimm fairy tale "The Juniper Tree." Are there specific animals or plants that, when they appear, cause you to think of the ancestors? If these life forms dwell in certain areas (e.g., a bear in the nearby mountains, a willow along a certain stream), do you also think of their homes as places of heightened ancestral contact?

In his book *Wisdom Sits in Places*, Keith Basso explores the Western Apache practice of anchoring a certain type of teaching story in specific locations. These stories involve historic events and narratives that include the ancestors, and they also emphasize the places where the original events took place. "Placeless events are an impossibility; everything that happens must happen somewhere,"[6] he notes. For individuals who learn the stories, the landscape comes alive over time with different ancestral wisdoms, each residing in its respective place, and each waiting to be activated when needed in response to life challenges. Places and the wisdoms rooted therein may be invoked as medicine, whether or not the place is nearby. Basso writes:

Travel in your mind to a point from which to view the place whose name has just been spoken. Imagine standing there, as if in the tracks of your ancestors, and recall stories of events that occurred at that place long ago. Picture these events in your mind and appreciate, as if the ancestors were speaking to you directly, the knowledge the stories contain. Bring this knowledge to bear on your own disturbing situation. Allow the past to inform your understanding of the present. You will feel better if you do.[7]

In modern Western cultures, having the ancestors speak through places is far less common than in many other societies, but it does occur. Place names may be invoked in ways that, because of events that took place there, convey a condensed set of meanings that can then apply to other situations. For example, *Waterloo* is both the name of a historic battle in Belgium that was a crushing defeat for Napoleon and a word that may signify impending disaster and serve as an admonition to avoid walking into one's demise.

Can you think of a place that, because of a past event in your life, conveys some life wisdom or lesson? If you paused to call into your awareness "The Place Where X Happened" or even visited that place in person, could you reconnect with the wisdom expressed by the event? If others remembered this connection and passed it down after your death, we can see how ancestral wisdom may come to be anchored in a specific location.

Practitioners of ancestor reverence may also choose to establish a shrine in the natural world that supports heightened contact with the dead. For example, if you want to regularly honor and commune with the ancestors connected to a specific sacred mountain, you may ask them to guide you to a place on that mountain conducive to dialogue (e.g., a particular tree, grove, or rock). By returning, sharing offerings, and communing with them there, you are consecrating a space in nature for ancestor work. This space doesn't need to look any different to a passerby. Some of the most high-energy ancestor shrines on the planet are shared on a need-to-know basis and would be unrecognizable to outsiders. I can think of a handful of consecrated shrines in the San Francisco Bay Area that others almost certainly pass by, as well as several mountains that I associate with the human dead. Are there places in the natural world that you already associate with the ancestors? What about these places helps you connect?

At the northern gateway to San Francisco, the Golden Gate Bridge has one of the highest incidences of suicide of any place on Earth. Of the thousands who have taken their lives since the bridge's completion in 1937, the few who survive the initial impact typically drown. To honor and support these ancestors of place, in 2008 I guided a ritual to consecrate a peace tree (*barisaa*) at Kirby Cove, a public park near the base of the bridge. This Mongolian-style ritual invites a living tree to serve as a beacon and healing place for the local dead. Establishing this shrine at this specific place incorporates all three elements explored above. The Monterey cypress, like its relatives (cedar, juniper), is often associated with the ancestors and with continuity of consciousness after death. Although I was drawn to this type of tree due in part to the association between evergreens and the ancestors, I still checked with this specific tree directly to find out if it wanted to serve as a peace tree. Second, as we see from Basso's writings on Western Apache culture, our ritual intent embraced and was shaped around the human history at that specific place. By focusing on the spirits of those who died there from suicide since 1937, we read the wisdom of this particular place as transforming emotional pain and isolation into healing and love. There are of course other wisdoms at this place; one could focus on the military history and abandoned bunkers, the fateful entry of Juan de Ayala through the Golden Gate in 1775, or earlier Coast Miwok ancestors of place. Finally, the choice to consecrate that specific cypress tree as an ancestor shrine was pragmatic; that natural feature at the cove was one of our closest ritual focal points for an ecologically stable shrine to honor the local ancestors. If you feel drawn to consecrate a peace tree to honor the ancestors of place, please refer to the instructions in Sarangerel Odigan's book *Riding Windhorses*.[8]

Nine Suggestions for Honoring Ancestors of Place

If you are interested in honoring the elevated ancestral spirits who dwell near your home, the first step is to ask them what they want from you and to go with that (provided it's not contrary to good sense). Rather than guess, just ask how you can communicate respect and goodwill. Admittedly, unless you are fairly intuitive, this type of inquiry is not always so straightforward, and there may be conflicting voices and groups of ancestors who speak up. The following suggestions will help you on your way to a conscious, uplifting, and mutually satisfying relationship with the ancestors of place either near to you or in places you visit. Respect your personal limits if you encounter conflicted energies or any other potentially harmful or negative forces.

1. Learn the Human History of the Land

If I were to ask you to connect with the spirit of the kudu and you have no idea that it is a type of South African antelope, you are at a serious disadvantage in your intuitive work. If you want to get to know the human ancestors of place and you don't have a basic outline of their history, you are facing an uphill battle and are at risk of making things up. Thanks to the Internet, a few hours of research can vastly improve your literacy about the history of your place of residence. Consider learning the human history of the land well enough that you could devise an interesting five- to ten-minute narrative for someone new to the area. Start to move beyond facts into what is distinct, beautiful, terrible, and moving for you about the history of the place. Weave in the story of your own ancestors and family who moved here. How did you come to live here? What were your motivations, or theirs, for coming? See if you can find a friend willing to supportively listen to your tale.

2. Learn the Ecological History of the Land

Nearly all ecosystems on Earth have undergone radical changes over the past several centuries due to colonialism, human migrations, and increased travel. These changes in flora and fauna often parallel and give fresh insight into the human history of the land. One way to approach ecological literacy is to become educated enough about the land you call home to be able to picture the landscape fifty, a hundred, or five hundred years ago. How did humans live there in those times? What were their primary sources of food and the rhythms of everyday life and the seasons?

By coming into relationship with the local spirits of plants and animals, you make friends with the friends of the ancestors. This may be on a species level (e.g., the living red-shafted flickers in the San Francisco Bay Area are descended from flickers who related to traditional Ohlone communities before Spanish contact) or may be connected to a single organism (e.g., some oaks and redwoods in that area were certainly alive during precolonial times). Direct communion with these other-than-human relations may be another way to approach the local ancestors. What does Flicker know of traditional ways? What do the oaks remember? Speaking with the stones in any given location is another common way to get more perspective on the long arc of human history.

3. Ensure That Your Home and Any Properties in Your Care Are Vibrant

If you own or even rent property, you will ideally relate to it as a sacred trust that calls for stewardship. On a physical level, you may need to address any trash, contamination, or other environmental hazards. Keeping the insides of living spaces clean, vibrant, and well loved also promotes a positive energy that ripples out to surrounding areas. Consider the ecological impact of any plants and animals on your properties, and strive to be an overall positive influence on your human neighbors, local ecosystems, and the spiritual ecology of place. Without first tending to our own homes in a quite literal way, reaching out to the local powers risks skipping steps. As a guideline that can apply to a one-week visit or a lifetime of habitation, attempt to leave any place in better condition than when you arrived.

4. Understand and, When Possible, Honor Older Protocols for Inhabiting the Land

The land itself is a living, breathing convergence of many different elder powers, some of whom appear to modern ways of thinking as mountains, rivers, forests, stones, and so on. The ecological convergence of the biosphere is the dancing of the gods. Many cultures have traditionally maintained active, conscious relationships with these forces. As a result, these forces are able to guide the humans on how to live in conscious and reciprocal relationship with them over time. This includes etiquette for people who are new to the area. For example, if you travel to a traditional village near a sacred mountain, it may be customary to make offerings not only to the ancestors of your host family but also to the spirit of the mountain. Are any customs and protocols still known for relating consciously with the land where you live? If so, consider learning about them and determining if it would be beneficial and respectful to observe them.

5. Introduce Your Ancestors to the Ancestors of Place

During a conference on spirits of place, the audience asked Ohlone artist and educator Catherine Herrera how non-Native people can convey respect to the Native ancestors of the San Francisco Bay Area when doing ritual work on the land there. Herrera suggested, "Introduce *your* ancestors to the ancestors here."[9] This of course hinges upon knowing your own ancestors. In other words, working with your blood ancestors positions you to relate more deeply with ancestors of place. When individuals have come to a place of clarity with their blood ancestors, I have witnessed the impact it has when they ritually introduce them to the ancestors of place. In some cases, the local ancestors offer a more heartfelt welcome once you know and love your own ancestors. Consider bringing an offering of peace and goodwill, something simple and biodegradable, from you and your people to the local ancestors. Find a place in nature to leave the offering, and take a moment there to share some good words with the ones you wish to honor.

6. Identify Areas of Ancestral Vitality and Disturbance and Tend One of Each

In most areas with any substantial history of human habitation, there are spaces that are linked with the ancestors in relatively peaceful ways and others that carry a heavy imprint. For me, the mountains around San Francisco Bay are one place where I have sensed the older ancestors in uplifting ways. For others, cemeteries, places of worship, or historic sites can be places of tranquillity and contemplation. Identify a place that helps you attune to the local ancestors. On the less peaceful end of the spectrum, areas of disturbance may include locations of past murder, war, oppression, or human suffering, as well as sacred spaces that have been desecrated. Cemeteries, in my experience, tend to be peaceful, but if they are physically disturbed or not well harmonized with the other local energies, they can create some mild disturbance. In more conflicted spaces, basic rituals may be used to gently and gradually transform heavy, stuck energies into expressions more compatible for human life. Tending one or more troubled locations in your area can help you feel more connected to the full spectrum of local ancestral consciousness and can bring you the satisfaction of useful service. In any case, respect your personal limits and keep clear energetic boundaries, especially when relating with the troubled dead. Becoming unwell because have you gotten in over your head is not a useful act of service.

7. Incorporate Ways to Honor the Ancestors of Place into Your Existing Practices

If you have a ritual practice, do you ever honor or call upon the local ancestors? Do the teachers or traditions with whom you practice ever acknowledge human ancestors as part of the spiritual ecology of place? Even if these ancestors have not been a part of your devotions to date, experiment with weaving in a simple prayer of acknowledgment to the dead who reside near where you engage in ritual. This does not necessarily mean calling them to be an active part of your practice (although they may choose to participate whether or not you invite them); however, the simple gesture of respect can open new pathways of energy and connectivity. You may also consider making regular offerings to the local ancestors at the start or end of ritual. Try honoring them in a humble way, without asking anything of them, and notice the echo back over time.

8. Advocate for the Tangible Needs of Local Human and Other-Than-Human Neighbors

In the United States alone, there are more than twelve hundred species of both plants and animals identified as endangered. Some of them are popular animal totems or "shamanic allies." If Wolf, Bison, or Condor appears to you as a spirit friend or guide, one powerful form of reciprocity is to support organizations that work for these species' survival. Likewise, if you attune to local spirits of place and you come into contact with human ancestral spirits who are not of your blood, educate yourself about the concerns of their living descendants. Ask yourself if there are ways to be a conscious, helpful ally. Any actions of useful service will become reflected in your energy body and will support ongoing relationships.

9. Ask the Ancestors of Place How You Can Honor Them

At the risk of stating the obvious, once you have a clear line of connection with the local ancestors of any given place, you can simply ask them what would be a welcome way to honor them. Be certain never to promise them (or any other beings) something that you're not able to deliver. You also don't want to do anything illegal, contrary to good ecological sense, or too unusual by local standards. Stay open to unexpected guidance and directives from the local ancestors, and be sure to run anything that is too involved by your own gut check and your established guides. If you do implement such a message, notice the ripple effect that follows, and in the days and weeks after tune in and see if the gesture was well received. As in any relationship, you'll ultimately get out what you decide to put in over time.

This chapter ends with a basic ritual that can be used to initiate contact with the spiritually well and more or less receptive human ancestral spirits local to your home. This exercise assumes that some (if not most) of the human ancestors who have lived and died near your home are outside of your extended blood family and may in fact be of different ethnic and cultural roots. Again, the more you have worked with your own blood and family ancestors, the more you will be able to respectfully engage local ancestors outside of your family or ethnicity. Remember that if you do experience beneficial contact with ancestors of place who are not of your personal heritage, this does not give you sanction to speak for those communities whose ancestors you have contacted. Finally, please honor that ancestors of place, just like living humans, may run the full spectrum from highly conscious and helpful to troubled and harmful. Be discerning.

∽

EXERCISE FOURTEEN

RITUAL TO GREET THE ANCESTORS OF A PLACE

INTENT: Offer a ritual to acknowledge and honor the ancestors of a specific place (typically the place where you live)

WHAT YOU NEED: To be outside in nature, natural offerings, and a knowledge or the history of the land if possible

I. **Before you do this exercise**, check with your own intuition and spiritual guidance to determine if it's a good idea to offer a ritual to honor the ancestors of a particular place. Consider these questions:

- Is it a good idea for me personally to do this? Is now the right time?
- If yes, which ancestors of place will I focus on (e.g., indigenous ancestors, early settlers, all previous inhabitants)? Or will I offer a ritual to honor them all collectively?
- Where will I do the ritual? (It helps to choose a place that you already know and where you won't be disturbed.)
- Is it better to offer this honoring ritual individually or in a small group? If a group, whom will I invite to join me?

Note: If you know that other communities of worship already conduct rituals in a place or hold that place to be sacred, choose a different location unless you have explicit permission from those groups.

2. **Once you are clear about the questions above, prepare for the ritual.**

- Educate yourself about the human history of the land.
- Walk the land and scout out where you'll offer ritual. Confirm that your intentions are welcome, and be open to hearing "no."

- If others will accompany you, harmonize the plan with them to minimize confusion.
- Determine the offerings you'll bring by asking the ancestors of land what they want. These may or may not be traditional foods. Only bring natural, biodegradable offerings that are welcome in that space.
- On the day of the ritual, bring whatever you need to be comfortable on the land and in the elements without needing to rush.

3. **On the day of the ritual**, know that everything you do as you set off and arrive is potentially part of the ritual itself. When you arrive at the overall location, make a basic offering and prayer as you begin to walk the land. In the prayer, state who you are, who your ancestors are, and why you've come.

4. **Settle into your ritual location, and begin with an invocation.** (Refer back to chapter 6, page 100, for a description of these basic ritual steps.)

- Invite your guides and teachers, including your ancestors, to be with you and support this ritual. Stay with this intent until you feel that they are present and that it's good to proceed.
- Make a basic offering to the local ancestors. Save the bulk of your offering for later, but give something that invites the ones who wish to be honored to join you. You might say something like, "If there are ancestors of this place who wish to step forward to be honored, I welcome you now."
- Once you sense a response from them, introduce yourself again by way of your ancestors. Let them know who you are, why you've come, and that you are open to listening to them. An example: "My name is *(your name)*, child of *(parents' names)*, and grandchild of *(grandparents' names)*; our people are from *(overall places of deeper ancestry)*. I've come to pay respect, to listen, and to make offerings with the intent of being in a good way with you."
- Present them with your offerings as your gesture of honor and

respect. Be clear throughout that you only wish to relate to the healthy spirits of the place.

5. **Just listen.** Sit in silent, receptive meditation. If you or others present are used to visioning with the spirits by using instruments or song, now is the time to drop into that space. Do what helps you tune in. The intent is to commune with the ancestors present. Some questions you might hold in your awareness include:

- What would you like me to know and understand about this land and the ancestors here?
- Is there anything I can do or not do to honor you? Is there any gesture of respect that would be welcome here?

Note: Know that their messages may not feel warm and fuzzy. They may want you to see things that are difficult. Honor your limits, and if it feels like too much, respectfully convey this.

6. **You may hear certain requests from the ancestors of place.** Stay open, but at the same time, don't agree to anything you can't fulfill (e.g., "I'll come back once a month" or "I'll bring these specific offerings" and then not do it). Remember, you are in a stage of building trust. Be honest with yourself and them regarding what you can do; it is best to undercommit and overdeliver than the other way around. If you are in a group, make sure no one is overcommitting, because that will affect everyone.

7. **Complete the time of direct communion.** Ask if there is anything else the ancestors want you to see or understand. Stay with it until you feel a natural completion.

8. **Thank the ancestors of that place as well as your own guides and supporters.** Close the ritual by asking that any unhelpful or heavy energies remain there. Stay in ritual awareness as you walk out of the space.

9. **When you leave the overall space, make a final offering** for all beings there and ask forgiveness for any disrespect or oversights.

10. **Consider a return visit for integration on a different day.** If you return, reflect on how you now experience the land there in your heart and intuition. Notice the space that the ancestors occupy so that your picture of the land includes them. See the human ancestors as part of the ecology of place, a living force of the land.

Note: This type of ritual acknowledgment could lead to ongoing relationship with the ancestors of place. If so, remember to be culturally sensitive about the topic, and don't claim to speak for ancestors who are not your own (see chapter 11 on reincarnation and past lives).

ELEVEN

AFFINITY ANCESTORS, MULTIPLE SOULS, AND REINCARNATION

Many of the most inspiring and influential human ancestors are neither connected to us by blood nor by the places we call home. One catchall term for these others is *ancestors of affinity*. They can include extended family, friends, teachers and cultural heroes, ancestors of spiritual tradition, and trailblazers in your chosen vocation. In this chapter you'll learn ways to think about and call on the support of affinity ancestors. The chapter will also provide one framework for dealing with multiple souls, reincarnation, and past lives. The chapter concludes with an exercise for harmonizing your experience of all three categories of ancestors explored in this book: blood/family, place, and affinity.

Ancestors of Affinity

The following section explores four types of affinity ancestors: friends, teachers and cultural heroes, ancestors of spiritual tradition, and ancestors of vocation. As you read, notice if there are ancestors from these categories with whom you already feel a connection. Are there other types of affinity ancestors that are important for you?

Beloved Friends

As mentioned in previous chapters, the ancestors of any given lineage may come to accept as family select individuals who are not related by blood. This may happen naturally over time, or it may be accelerated by adoptions, marriages, and similar rituals. In these cases, friends become family and they essentially have two (or more) sets of ancestors—a kind of dual citizenship in the otherworld, with all the privileges and responsibilities entailed. Other friends are not family per se; they are simply beloved personal friends of one type or another who happen to precede us in death.

If you are relating to one of these ancestors, I encourage the same basic precautions as when relating with any who are recently deceased. Most importantly, you want to be sure that they are bright in spirit and, ideally, as well as or better off than you. If friends who have passed visit you in spirit and they do not seem well, I encourage making prayers, offerings, and possibly rituals of repair on their behalf until they have clearly joined their own ancestors. Should you choose to assist friends in this way, be certain that you have permission from your own guides to do so, that the spirit of the deceased desires your support, and that you respect your own limits and the sensibilities of the living family.

On occasion, individuals ask about ongoing relationships with deceased friends as ancestral guides. Assuming the individual in question is truly vibrant rather than maintaining an unhelpful bond to avoid transition, I see nothing problematic about this, although I personally prefer to relate to lineages of ancestors. If you wish to maintain a relationship with the spirit of a deceased friend (or believe they wish to remain in such a relationship with you), I suggest the following steps:

- Be absolutely certain that they have joined with their own beloved ancestors and guides and that they are vibrant in spirit. This often includes giving space for at least a few months, if not more, after death.

- Once you are sure that they are well in spirit, be certain that neither you nor your deceased friend wish to maintain the connection primarily to avoid the pain of loss. Grieving is normal and healthy.

- If they are well in spirit, you are both emotionally current, and you still have the impression of mutual desire to relate in a regular way, introduce the spirit of your deceased friend to your family ancestors and other guides and teachers. Be open to what your guides have to say, and determine whether they believe that this relationship would be beneficial for you. Be open to hearing that it's best to gain closure or only interact on occasion with the spirit of this friend.

- If deceased friends are the only type of spirit guide you relate with, consider seeking additional types of guides dedicated to your personal awakening and path.

These suggestions are not intended to discourage you from communing with the spirits of friends. However, from my training and experience, I have learned that most often the spirits of deceased friends are best related to on occasion, with honoring and love, but not necessarily as regular guides who are then integrated into one's spirit family. In addition to remaining open to the occasional contact through dreams or waking visions, remember that you can always praise and honor the spirits of friends during annual ancestor festivals or communal spirit feasts.

Teachers, Mentors, and Cultural Heroes

Another important type of affinity ancestor includes inspiring mentors, teachers, and cultural heroes. These may simply be figures who, during their human lifetime, showed us great love and care in ways that changed the course of our lives for the better. They also include political leaders, artists, and other inspiring public figures. For example, in my late teens, I was nourished by the poetry of Allen Ginsberg and had the chance to hear him speak in person twice before his death. Through his connection with Walt Whitman, Ginsberg modeled for me the possibility of communing with an ancestral artist in one's chosen craft. I clearly remember the day I received news of Ginsberg's death. I had the feeling that his spirit was being poured as a kind of tangible, magical substance into each of his words and actions, the joining of soul and legacy. Although I don't invoke Allen Ginsberg or Walt Whitman by name at my ancestor shrine, for me they are cultural heroes and are among the mighty dead—ancestors whose courage and creativity opened doors in my life and the lives of countless others.

Which teachers and guides, both personal and public, have enriched your life and are now among the ancestors? If you have never done so, consider making a list of those who have deeply touched you and offering a simple ritual or heartfelt prayer of gratitude to them.

Ancestors of Spiritual Tradition and Lineage

Nearly all spiritual traditions revere their human founders and other important figures, even if these traditions discourage overt practices of ancestor reverence or dialogue with the dead. For example, the *silsila,* or chain of transmission, found in many Islamic Sufi orders affirms the importance of placing oneself in a lineage of devout and exemplary ancestors. Zen practice commonly includes chanting the names of one's dharma lineage or succession of enlightened teachers back to the historical Buddha or important lineage founders. Christian congregations draw inspiration and solace from biblical stories of patriarchs, prophets, and saints. Anyone who is represented or invoked as part of one's religious practice can constitute an example of ancestor reverence. Who are the revered ancestors of your faith? In what ways did you learn to affirm and renew your relationships with them?

Even if it is not an element of your tradition, you can still apply the principles of ancestor reverence to deepen your personal practice. When you feel stuck or discouraged, what would the ancestors of your faith do? How do you imagine they might advise and uplift you? Zen

Roshi Joan Halifax wrote, "The veneration of the ancestors confirms the continuity of existence in time and space or place. The world is brought back into balance through the renewal of ceremonial life that confirms that continuity."[1] As Roshi Halifax suggested to participants in a retreat I attended with her, "The practices themselves are the body of the ancestors." Notice the ways in which you connect with lineage ancestors through shared words and practices. When you feel you are in a place of balance and inspiration, how might the ancestors of spiritual lineage already be guiding and supporting you?

Ancestors of Vocation

In many traditional cultures, the divisions between sacred and secular are less pronounced: potters venerate gods who shape human bodies from clay, fishermen and fisherwomen make offerings to the goddesses of river and sea, and smiths align with the lords of fire and metal. Work is not separate from life, and everyone participates in transforming the raw elemental powers into food, shelter, and offerings for both the human community and the gods. Assuming that you have a vocation or trade, have you ever stopped to consider its ancestors and sacred roots? Some contemporary professions (e.g., office manager, truck driver, computer programmer) may seem less obviously connected to older ones; however, upon closer examination, these too have roots in the sacred. A contemporary office manager often calls upon skills familiar to early generations of scribes and record keepers, traders and merchants, and the project leaders employed by any ancient city-state with large population centers to feed, house, and defend. Drivers are as old as wheels, carts, and beasts of burden, and they share the solitude of long-distance travel and the requisite knowledge of the paths between places. Modern information technology, like phone and computer systems, rests upon innovative blends of refined metals (elemental earth) and electricity (elemental fire), often with an element of data transmission or storage. In this way, depending on the specific type of IT work, these vocations could be viewed as a collaboration between the gods of the forge, the spirits of lightning and electrical fire, and the deities of communication and the crossroads. What are the specific forces of nature and ancient analogues of your chosen occupation? The exercise below presents one way to apply core principles of ancestor reverence to the ancestors associated with your vocation.

ᏙᏖ

EXERCISE FIFTEEN

CELEBRATING ANCESTORS OF VOCATION

INTENT: Seek out ancestors who can support your specific destiny and vocation

WHAT YOU NEED: A quiet space and any other support for visioning (e.g., drum, offerings)

What's at the heart of what you do for work? Who are the sacred founders of your vocation? This exercise will help you connect with vocation ancestors who came before you and who can help you value and understand the sacred roots of your work. As with any ritual, before you begin, consult your intuition and guidance to see if this is beneficial work for you at this time. If you get a yes, follow the ritual progression below, and tailor the details according to your preference.

I. **Before the ritual**, reflect on what vocation you will focus on. This may or may not be the vocation that provides your income (i.e., you may love painting without making a living as a painter). Once you've chosen, ask yourself what you already know about the historical roots of that vocation.

   • Try to see your vocation in its most essential form (e.g., a truck driver may be a messenger, a pathfinder who knows the ways between things, and someone with an affinity for solitude). If your work involves creating something physical, consider the elements involved (e.g., cooks work closely with fire and the fruits of earth, and surgeons with metal, healing arts, and the mysteries of the body). Investigate the different names that have been used through-out time to describe that vocation and what they reveal about its sacred origins.

- Ask which people throughout history stand out as exemplary models of your vocation. Even if you have no names for them, what about them impresses you?
- Tune in to ask what kind of offering you can bring to these ancestors—one that they would appreciate and enjoy.

2. **Establish ritual space.** As you enter into ritual, call to your supportive guides and the teachers and ancestors you already know. Ask them for their blessing and protection going into the ritual. Once you have the okay from them, ask for the ancestors of your vocation to present themselves to you in a way that is safe and appropriate. Be sure you're only calling in well or bright energies.

- Introduce yourself to them by way of your ancestors and by way of your vocation. Let them know that you've come for learning and possibly support.
- Once you feel their presence, present any offerings to them at this time. You can present them either to one ancestor or to the whole group.

3. **Spend time in ritual communion** with these ancient colleagues. After some open-ended listening, you might ask them:

- What was it like for them to engage in the kind of work they did? Assuming you share a similar experience, you might talk shop a little bit and share about the work you do.
- How do they see their work? Were there other spirits or powers with which they interacted? If so, which of these would be helpful for you to recognize?

Notice what they are inviting you to see as sacred and how it can help you bring out your soul-level gifts to do what you do even more effectively.

This may include extending a blessing of protection if your occupation is dangerous.

4. **When you feel ready, complete the ritual.** Give thanks to these ancestors for what was shared. Be sure to note any invitations for further engagement or "to-do's." Shift your attention back, and make some notes if that's helpful.

Multiple Souls

Two questions about the nature of the soul and the post-death journey are likely to inform your approach to relationships with ancestors. One is this: *Is your soul singular or are your souls multiple?* From my experience, most people in the West have never considered the possibility that their soul or spirit could be anything other than a singular force or presence. But established traditions of ancestor reverence address the topic of multiple souls in diverse ways, and sustained ancestor work does not hinge on any specific stance on this topic.

A more common question is: *After you die, is your soul (or are your different souls) reborn in human or other form? Will you reincarnate (and have you already done so before)?* A follow-up: Assuming you *do* undergo some kind of reincarnation, do you retain any connection to your past lives?

I tend to sidestep involved questions about reincarnation and the nature of the soul. My instinctual answer to theoretical questions about these topics is often some combination of "I don't know," "doesn't really matter," and "go with whatever feels more magical and inclusive." Instead I favor a pragmatic approach to the ancestors. I do not give much attention to past lives, nor have I heard my teachers and elders in Pagan traditions, Mongolian shamanism, Native American ways, or Ifá/Òrìṣà give much attention to the topic. This doesn't mean that I (or they) dismiss the possibility of past-life experiences; I am just not motivated to focus on it. Yet I know with the popularity of focusing on past-life experiences and therapies in the West that I can't fully dodge questions about reincarnation and past lives in a book on ancestors.

Let's first examine the question of multiple souls. With the exception of nuanced esoteric teachings emphasized by relatively smaller groups within each faith, Judaism, Christianity, and Islam tend to more or less explicitly teach that humans have a single soul or spirit. This is not surprising, as we tend to see the outer world around us as mirrored on the inner or subjective level. These traditions emphasize the oneness or singularity of God, so this assumption of underlying unity can easily extend to the human soul, especially if we are "created in the likeness of God." This one God/one soul assumption is neither good nor bad, but human belief is tremendously diverse. Not all cultures emphasize the oneness of God or of the human soul.

In fact, many societies and religions understand the human spirit as multiple—as a convergence of different forces or souls that come together at the beginning of life and may go in different directions after death. Examples of such traditions include Celtic and Norse traditions, Ifá/Òrìṣà ways, ancient Egyptian religion, some lineages of Buddhism, Andean cosmologies, and Lakota ways of life. These traditions may or may not recognize an underlying coherence, God, or Creator; the two perspectives are by no means mutually exclusive.

Certainly there are elements of truth in both views, just as there are profoundly awake mystics, seers, and medicine people within any tradition. If you are new to the idea of multiple souls, please feel your way into this perspective and notice how it may resonate with, or differ from, your experience. To illustrate some concepts of a multiple-soul perspective, here is a snapshot from one tradition.

In 1999 and then again from 2003 until her passing in 2006, I learned from the Buryat Mongolian shaman Sarangerel Odigan about how her culture views multiple souls and ancestors. Below is a brief sketch of this framework for understanding multiple souls. Consider it as one example of the many possible ways to understand your relationship with the ancestors. According to some traditional Mongolians, what we might think of as the soul (singular) is more accurately described as an aggregate of three souls, all of whom function in different ways to animate and maintain the physical body. They are known in Mongolian as the *suld,* the *ami,* and the *suns;* in English I think of them respectively as our *bone, blood,* and *star* souls. These three souls begin to converge around the time of conception, give rise to our sense of self during life, and typically part ways after death. Our baseline "I am" consciousness is a composite of the moment-to-moment awareness of these three souls. Such views often imply (or state) that most or all of these of souls continue on their journey after an individual's death. As a result, different types of human ancestors emerge, each of whom calls for specific protocols or approaches, and each of whom corresponds to certain aspects of our consciousness. Let's explore each of the three souls in the Buryat Mongol model shared by Sarangerel.

The Bone and Body Soul (Suld)

The dominant soul in the human personality is the suld, the bone or body soul. The suld is distinct from our other two souls in some important ways. For one, it is unique to human beings, whereas animals possess the other two souls. In a personal conversation, Sarangerel speculated that suld souls arrived on Earth about 150,000 years ago, around the time when humans began diverge in pronounced ways from other animals. Unlike the other two, the suld stays firmly rooted inside the physical body. "Just as the body is unique to this lifetime, so is the suld, and the two are closely associated until the body dies, at which time the suld settles into nature. If the suld leaves the body, the body dies almost immediately."[2] When Buryat shamans guide ritual to locate and reintegrate the wandering soul of a client, they may seek out either of the other two souls, but not the suld soul.

Sarangerel taught that, of the three souls, the suld has the greatest impact on our personalities and sense of self. Unlike the other two, the suld takes human birth only once. This implies that experiences from this lifetime, including those with living family, often have the most impact in forming the human personality. After death, as the other two souls (ideally) transition from this dimension and prepare eventually for rebirth, the suld settles into the natural world, either near the place of death or at a place known to the recently deceased. Many suld souls become *ezen,* or guardian spirits, of natural formations such as stones, trees, and bodies of water. Like other types of nature spirits, suld souls can be helpful, troubled, or uninterested in the affairs of humans. They continue to change after death, but they incarnate as humans only once.

From this model, where in the natural world do you imagine your suld would settle after death? Where is your place of greatest soul-level resonance with nature?

The ancestral spirits who were previously incarnate suld souls are also among the most sought-after type of ancestral guide for Mongolian shamans. This is in part because suld souls remain within the matrix of consciousness that is nature. In other words, they're still around. For example, Sarangerel taught that many suld souls from First Nations or Native American ancestors have become integrated with the natural world in what is now the United States over the last few thousand years. She saw this as one reason that so many non-Native inhabitants of North America report being contacted by Native ancestors in dreams and waking visions.

According to this understanding, who are the likely suld souls or ancestors of place in your local area?

Sarangerel also taught that suld souls sometimes cause disturbance for the living, especially in places of historic trauma and violent death. In a conversation in early 2003, we discussed the 9/11 attacks, and I shared the view, held by several teachers I knew at the time, that because of global prayers and the outpouring of care, the souls of the 9/11 dead enjoyed tremendous support in their journey to join the ancestors. Sarangerel agreed that the suns (star) souls had transitioned, but she felt that no ritual had been done for the suld souls. She shared that, while she was leading a peace tree ceremony (see chapter 10, page 218) near Ground Zero in early 2003, the suld souls of the dead appeared to her as a "full stadium," thousands in need of care, and that she slept for a full day after the ceremony.

The Blood and Breath Soul (Ami)

If the suld or bone soul closely corresponds to ancestors of place (chapter 10), then the ami, the blood and breath soul, relates to family ancestors and the lineage repair cycle (chapters 5 to 9), although family healing work also draws heavily upon this-life (suld) experiences. Sarangerel characterized the ami as the least dominant of the three souls in shaping the human personality; the order of influence is suld, suns, and ami, respectively. Of the two souls that reincarnate, the ami tends to follow the bloodlines; hence the tendency in many cultures to view newborns as ancestors returning. In addition to the blood association, in Mongolian the word *ami* is related to the words for *life* and *breath,* and the ami is often associated with birds and flight.

Prior to conception, the ami travels from its nest in the branches of the World Tree down the spirit river Dolbor, descending from the realm of the mother goddess Umai and the upper world to enter the gateway of birth and bless the newborn with its first breath. Especially during childhood or in cases of trauma, the ami can take flight from the physical body. If the frightened ami does not return spontaneously, ritual interventions may be required to locate and return the ami soul to the body. According to Sarangerel, the most common type of soul retrieval performed by Mongolian shamans is to recover and return a wayward ami soul. In some parts of Siberia, bird tattoos are used to secure the ami inside the body. After physical death, the ami returns as a bird along the river Dolbor to its home in the sky realms.

Remember that humans aren't the only ones with ami souls. For example, hunting protocols demand reverence for the hunted, and these codes of respect rest in part on the understanding that the ami souls of hunted animals, after death, will report back to the collective ami of the species of that locality who are waiting to take birth. When hunters behave respectfully toward the animals they kill, it improves the reputation of that human community among that animal spirit community. (Conversely, disrespect diminishes a hunter's reputation.) This reputation in turn informs where future animals decide to be born.

Hunters honoring the souls of animal kin directly affect population levels of local game, which in turn supports the survival of the human community.

The ami carries what we might think of as body instinct, genetic memory, or past-life memory associated with our biological ancestors. It also links us with breath and blood mysteries: wind and water.

By this understanding, are there relatives who died before your birth whose ami may now be helping to animate your body? Have you seen in waking visions or dreams what type of bird form your ami will take when returning home to the Great Mother after your death?

The Star and Ghost Soul (Suns)

The third of the three souls that converge to create human consciousness is the suns. Like the ami, the suns reincarnates, although not necessarily along the bloodlines, making the suns our primary source of past-life memories from different cultures and affinities with other times and places. In this way the suns soul corresponds to affinity ancestors (those linked by neither blood nor geography). Arising into human form before birth and flowing down the spirit river Dolbor into the depths of the Earth after death, suns souls are often visualized as traveling through water when outside the body. Between incarnations, suns souls dwell in the lower world and are overseen by Erleg Khan, lord of the underworld. Sarangerel also spoke of the suns as being linked with the stars and the cosmic self.

Of our three souls, the suns is the most likely to become a source of disturbance, illness, and hauntings. The title of the popular 1990 film *Ghost*, with Patrick Swayze, was translated into Mongolian as *Suns*. Shamanic practices for resolving hauntings or spirit possessions may include escorting wayward or not-yet-transitioned suns souls to their proper dwelling place with Erleg Khan in the lower world. Sarangerel saw wayward suns souls as a common factor in physical and mental illness. Suns souls are also associated in Buryat Mongol tradition with the ability to shapeshift into forms such as animals. They may temporarily inhabit the physical form of animals or other human beings (consider the tendency to associate deceased loved ones with unusual animal appearances or specific animals over time).

Chapter 8 presented ways to partner with loving and bright ancestral guides to assist the troubled dead when you are working with family ancestors, but these same wayward ghosts can cause trouble for people who are not in your family. In other words, every troubled dead person is somebody's relative. Let's say that the spirit of my tormented great-grandfather still lives in my house, and a friend visits from out of town. If this friend is kept awake all night or has an unexplained nasty spill down the stairs, my friend is not being affected by one of his own troubled ancestors; rather it is the equivalent of encountering an unhappy stranger in the street. Ghosts or wayward suns souls tend to attach to people or places, with the former being more common in my experience. Suns souls who remain here after death and who focus on living people are often continuing a bond established during life (e.g., the spirit of a deceased parent, child, or spouse). Those who are more attached to places typically frequented those places during life, died nearby, or simply find it easy to connect with living humans there (e.g., bar ghosts).

When diagnosing a ghost problem or haunting, try to be sure that you're not just being paranoid or delusional. Some people who believe they have a ghost problem have more systemic mental health problems, some are pretty balanced people who really do have "guests," and some need both psychological care and help with the ghosts. Get second and third opinions on this assessment from trustworthy sources when at all possible. If you do conclude that a troubled human ghost has in some way linked his or herself to you or inhabits your home, consider contacting a ghost care specialist (also see the appendix). In a pinch, heartfelt prayers and generous offerings can help, and many elements of chapter 8's section "Work with the Very Troubled Dead and Related Spirits" (page 162) also apply when engaging unfamiliar ghosts or suns souls.

Thus, from a Buryat perspective, human consciousness is a composite of three souls or discrete forces that converge around birth and travel in separate directions after death. Yes, there *is* reincarnation (ami and suns souls), and no, there is *not* reincarnation (suld souls). Yes, reincarnating souls take birth along the same bloodline (ami soul), and no, they don't follow the bloodlines (suns soul). This model of multiple souls allows for many different types of experiences to coexist. It also implies that individuals raised by their biological families can expect, on average, about two-thirds of their sense of self (the suld and ami) to be mirrored by the world around them. Those raised by adoptive parents or with no connection to their biological family can expect about one-third of their soul-level identity (the suld) to correspond to their family of origin. Everyone is likely to have about a third of their soul energy (the suns) that is not necessarily mirrored by their culture of origin, although it is also possible that the suns chooses to reincarnate in the same culture, community, or family.

This way of understanding the soul also suggests that we have different types of ancestors, and upon death, the different souls that comprise us become different types of ancestors. In other words, we may experience continuity of consciousness after death in several different directions. By extension, a sense of self or identity may exist in multiple places at the same moment (this is also true during life). After death, you—meaning all three of you—may in the same moment be spreading your wings and going "into the light," making your way back into the dark womb of Earth, and simply walking out the door into the nearby woods. If you have a question that begins with, "Is it possible that . . . ?," chances are the answer here would be yes, as the model makes no attempt to reconcile plurality in any final way or to make all the pieces fit neatly. According to this model—a common one in indigenous cultures—each of us is a dynamic convergence of multiple forces that include not only human consciousness but the earth, the elements, and the stars.

Reincarnation and Past Lives

Almost every time I have heard people discuss reincarnation and past lives as they relate to the ancestors, they assume a single soul model. This gives rise to questions like, "How can I relate to my ancestors if they've already reincarnated?" My intent in exploring the subject of multiple souls has been to make the topic of past lives more open-ended and spacious, less certain and linear. For example, if two of the three souls animating you now were previously incarnate on Earth, this would mean that people still alive on the Earth today may be making offerings to you or even invoking one or two of "your" souls right now as one of their ancestors. I am not personally aware of anyone invoking my previous incarnations as an ancestor, and I don't experience being other people's ancestors, but I also don't rule out the possibility, as time is not linear and I am only conscious of a small fraction of my soul-level experience at any given time. This may be part of the reason that in the Buryat system, ancestral guides tend to be suld souls (who only incarnate once).

If you have a practice of honoring your ancestors by name, it stands to reason that you may be calling out to souls who, after death, have subsequently reincarnated as you, the one invoking. This raises a common question: "How can I distinguish relating with an ancestral spirit from past-life memory?" Although she taught and wrote about Buryat views of reincarnation and multiple souls, I never heard Sarangerel speak in any real way about past-life memories, encourage students to seek past-life memories, or bring up this topic in healing sessions. Ultimately, belief in partial or total reincarnation does not require that we focus on past lives in this lifetime, and it's not a subject that I emphasize. To be transparent about my reservations, below I will discuss three risks when emphasizing past lives: cultural insensitivity, ego inflation, and interpretive reduction of relationship with the ancestors.

Past Lives and Cultural Insensitivity

I can't count how many times in the last decade people with little to no recent indigenous ancestry have told me that they were Native Americans or Africans or African-Americans in a past life. I could, however, count on one hand or probably one finger the number of times I have heard Native or African-American people make claims in community space about past lives (of any kind). Why the difference? I think it's quite common for human souls to take birth in totally different cultures from those of their previous incarnations. I'm not disputing the spiritual reality of rebirth, but rather drawing attention to how these claims may function culturally and socially in a world with considerable racism, sexism, and inequality. For example, if as a privileged European-American male I tell a group of African-American women that in a past life I was a female slave in South Carolina in the early 1800s, I can hope for, at best, a cold shoulder for being rude and ignorant. I am making (at least) three claims to understand realms of experience that I have never and will never experience in this lifetime: being of African ancestry, being a woman, and being of a different socioeconomic status (in this case being related with as property by other human beings). Claims like this are often insulting because they can easily minimize the profound ways in which race, gender, class, religion, and similar factors shape experience in *this* lifetime.

I have also heard people imply that either they should have quicker access to status or that they should not have to undergo the same spiritual training and discipline as others because of their past-life claims. Doing years of meditation in a past life may confer benefits in this lifetime, but it does not give you a pass in your meditation practice today. Imagine getting on an airplane and being informed midflight that your pilot never went to flight school but has strong past-life memories of flying planes in World War II. The most high-profile reincarnating person on Earth, His Holiness the Fourteenth Dalai Lama, spends several hours each day in meditation and study of Buddhist teachings. The fact that he passed tests to confirm that he is the reincarnation of the

Thirteenth Dalai Lama (and his twelve predecessors) did not give him a "get out of discipline free" card.

If you believe that you are experiencing past-life memories from a culture other than your own, I suggest using this as a catalyst to become more educated about the living peoples to whom you feel attraction or aversion. If you do relate directly with such individuals in this lifetime, know that your claims to be from that culture in a previous incarnation entitle you to nothing and are usually best kept to yourself. If your affinity is sincere and your engagement is respectful, it *may* be possible over time to become known and respected among other cultural groups—but for the person you are in this life and for how you show up in the present. If you avoid making off-putting past-life claims, your personal past-life memories may even help you have greater empathy for the historical suffering of a community or individual. If you were a Native chief in a past life, then the necessary humility and ethic of service should come naturally to you, so begin by modeling this with all people in your life. If you were a slave in the southern United States, then your soul-level longing for justice and equality should help you identify current issues that call for greater social justice and correction. In a nutshell: be true to yourself in this lifetime and expect others to see you for that as well. Honoring your own ancestors and culture(s) of origin is a great foundation from which to begin a respectful dialogue with individuals from different backgrounds.

Past Lives and Ego Inflation

The value-neutral term *ego* refers here to one's sense of personal self. Part of spiritual and psychological maturation includes cultivating a healthy, resilient, and just-the-right-size ego or sense of self. Thinking we are better or worse than others is a form of egotism or inflation (thinking we are worse than others has been described as *negative ego inflation*). In both cases it's all about us—meaning too much focus on the personal self. So how can past lives play into this problem? Claims of past-life memories sometimes reinforce unhelpful stories about who and how we are. For example, if I am deeply insecure and therefore wish to be seen as important by others, I may claim to have been an important leader in a past life. If I seek to counterbalance or contain my inflated sense of self (and this process is often unconscious), I may make claims to have been a victimized person in a past life (e.g., victim of the Holocaust, witch burned at the stake, Native American killed defending his people). This second type of claim is a more subtle kind of egotism, as it implies that the person making the claim is humble, persecuted, or even victimized, although they have not gone through such experiences in this lifetime, at least not in the form they are claiming. In both examples, there is oscillation between positive and negative forms of ego inflation. I am not saying that the souls of pharaohs and burned witches don't take rebirth, but it's important to bring awareness and critical reflection to how these claims of past-life memory function psychologically and socially.

Past-life memories, worked with in self-reflective ways, may be catalysts for ego integration and personal healing. If you have chronically low esteem, past-life memories of being an important leader may help you activate leadership qualities in your present life. If you have trouble accessing personal pain from this lifetime, work with past-life experience as a victim may help you begin to grieve. Working with past-life memories as one would a dream or waking vision may also encourage a more flexible sense of identity and an increased ability to access different perspectives. I offer two guidelines for working with past-life memories: First, be willing to ask yourself, "What is my motivation for sharing this with others?" *before* doing so. Perhaps the intent of sharing during a psychotherapy session is to give voice to otherwise difficult-to-access insights in your healing journey. It is relatively common for individuals with a trauma history to recount memories of past-life trauma rather than speaking of more overwhelming or preverbal trauma in this life. In another situation, sharing a past life in a spiritual circle may be motivated by a desire for greater acceptance or validation from other members of the circle. This strategy may backfire. The goal may be better achieved by saying something more direct and honest like, "I really value all of you, and it makes me feel vulnerable to know right now how much your opinion of me matters. Would you be willing to share something you appreciate about me (in this lifetime)?" Second, the point of working with past-life material is not to reinforce old stories but to resolve previous experiences in ways that lead to greater integration in the present life. Here the question could be something like, "What is this past-life memory asking me to embody in this life, and how can I live this lesson today, once and for all?" In this way, work with past-life memories supports balanced ego integration in the present. It also avoids the risks of ego inflation and of getting lost in a labyrinth of stories about previous incarnations.

Past Lives as Barrier to Ancestral Contact

I have met many individuals who have a rich and involved practice of working with past-life memories but who have no interest in relating to the ancestors. All images, feelings, and impressions that cannot be traced to this-life experience are assumed to be from past lives. Assuming two coexisting truths—that reincarnation does occur and that the ancestors are "real" as a force beyond the personal self—how do you tell the difference? How do you know if your experience of the ancestors is actual contact with a force outside yourself or if it's a case of accessing a past-life memory?

Before trying to answer this question, I need to clarify why it's so important. In past-life experience, there is no self-other relationship; it's all self. It's not that different from past-day or past-year experience. If you see other beings merely as an aspect of self, these other beings may feel disrespected and unseen in the relationship, and you may try to integrate them into your sense of self in ways that can be problematic. This often happens when people seek to resolve attachments with harmful ghosts or spirit intrusions through psychological integration of shadow material alone. *Some things are not you,* and the failure to recognize that fundamental truth can contribute to ego inflation, psychological fragmentation, or physical illness. On the other hand, if you externalize aspects of self, including those that come from previous incarnations, then you may spend some time essentially talking to yourself. But the consequences of this are usually not as harmful as trying to integrate foreign energies into your personal identity.

The foundation for distinguishing past-life memories from ancestral contact is to develop a felt, body sense for the difference between the two. My default stance is to assume that any given stream of consciousness that (1) is not composed of memories from this incarnation and (2) reaches a level of intensity beyond simple daydreaming or imagination may be a case of contact with a distinct, other-than-me spirit. Often just pausing to ask "Is this an aspect of self or is this 'other'?" will help clarify the situation, as other beings will rarely wish to be perceived as merely an aspect of self. Any time you choose to devote attention to an ancestral spirit, consider asking your established guides whether you are dealing with a distinct spirit or with an aspect of yourself that is not yet integrated. Like living humans, other spirits may come into our lives for a period of time in order to help us integrate the things that they represent. In other words, even the ancestors or other helpful powers inevitably reflect some aspect of ourselves.

Integration Work with Family, Place, and Affinity Ancestors

The Buryat multiple-soul model of ami, suld, and suns souls roughly corresponds to ancestors of blood, place, and affinity or spirit. There are practices in the Buryat tradition for harmonizing the energy of these three souls in the body; if that cultural framework speaks to you, see the writings of Sarangerel Odigan. For others, how can you begin to harmonize your relationships with these different types of ancestors?

Depending on your life circumstance, these types of ancestors may not be particularly distinct to begin with. For example, my now deceased great-uncle Donald worked on a family farm in Bedford, Pennsylvania. Yes, ancestors of place in Bedford include the Shawnee and other Native peoples, and they also include three to five generations before Donald of Foors, Clarks, Samses, Bequeaths, and other blood ancestors that Donald and I share. Not only was there relatively high alignment between Donald's ancestors of blood and of place, but men and women along the Foor lineage have worked the land near Bedford as farmers since the late 1700s. And like many early immigrants from southwestern Germany who gave rise to Pennsylvania Dutch culture, Donald was a Lutheran. His ancestors of vocation and of spiritual lineage were congruent with ancestors of blood and place. Aside from the fact that, as a down-to-earth Lutheran, Donald might have found the ancestor topic a little too "out there," in his case practices to harmonize different types of ancestors would have been unnecessary and redundant.

Another example of harmonizing different types of blood ancestors is the unseen negotiation that takes place in committed relationships and parenting. We are each a convergence of many lineages, and intimate relationships are no exception. Even if you and your partner or partners share no children, ideally your respective ancestors harmonize for the well-being of the relationship. Children, of course, bring their own ancestral alchemy to the family. Parents raising adoptees or children from previous partners may benefit from working both with personal family ancestors and with the biological ancestors of the child. Having a simple communal altar to honor the different lineages can support integration and family harmony.

The following exercise can be used as a starting point for weaving together different strands of ancestor work. Make sure that you've completed exercise 11, "Harmonizing Your Four Primary Lineages," and exercise 14, "Ritual to Greet the Ancestors of Place." If necessary, take the following practice in pieces, completing one step at a time. Stay open to your dreams and remember to engage your creativity and intuition when approaching the ancestors.

❧

EXERCISE SIXTEEN
Harmonizing Ancestors
of Family, Place, and Affinity

INTENT: Introduce and gently harmonize ancestors of family, place, and affinity

WHAT YOU NEED: A ritual space with three basic altars or places of honoring, three cups or ritual vessels of fresh water, a fourth empty vessel larger than the others, and simple, natural offerings for each of the three types of ancestors

This exercise brings together, in a ritual sense, the different types of ancestors you've been working with. Be certain you have completed part 2 and the exercises in the previous section before proceeding, because this more advanced exercise builds upon previous work. As with any ritual, before you begin, consult your intuition and guidance to see if this is beneficial work for you at this time. You may get the message that it's fine to work with two of the three groupings of ancestors (e.g., *only* ancestors of family and of place, or *only* the ancestors of family and lineage). The exercise below describes how to harmonize all three types of ancestors, but modify it for just two of the three if needed. Trust your own rhythm; it's fine to proceed in stages.

1. **Establish a ritual space.** Set up a place for your ritual with three different places of honoring. You can keep this simple: for example, three different pieces of cloth as a base, three candles, and other offerings and symbols to honor these three different types of ancestors. Next, set out a ritual bowl or cup of clean water—one in each place of honoring—and a fourth empty cup near you. I suggest establishing the place of honoring for your family ancestors in the center, with the ancestors of place and of affinity to either side. The fourth empty vessel can sit closest to you, between you and the place of honoring for family ancestors.

2. **Open the ritual** with an overall invocation or prayer. Tune in to each grouping of ancestors, starting with your ancestors of family and/or blood.

- Ask your family ancestors to be present, and be sure you are tuning in only to those ancestors who are already well and bright in spirit. Make a simple offering of appreciation and respect, and notice if they have any messages for you at this time. After giving them an opportunity to speak, reconfirm that they wish to participate. If so, ask them to infuse the cup of water with their blessings. Sit patiently with them until this process feels complete.

- Shift your body and attention to the second place of honoring, and call your ancestors of affinity or spiritual lineage to be present. Again, be sure you are already in relationship with them on their own terms before doing this exercise. Present your offerings, and notice if they have messages for you at this time. After sharing a moment of listening from the heart, confirm that these ancestors also wish to participate. If you hear a yes, ask them to infuse the vessel of water with their blessings. Sit with them patiently until this process feels complete.

- Shift your body and attention to the third place of honoring, and invite the ancestors of place to be present. As above, make sure you are already in relationship with them, and only call upon those with whom you have already established relationship. Present your offerings, and reconfirm that they do in fact wish to participate. If you hear a yes, invite these ancestors to infuse the cup of water with their blessings. Again, sit patiently with them until this process feels complete.

3. **Return to your center,** to a neutral position, and notice the presence of these three groupings of ancestors, each distinct and present in the shared ritual space.

- When you are moved to do so, transfer the blessing-infused water from your family ancestors to the empty fourth vessel. Next, choose one of the other two vessels of blessed water (from either ancestors of place or affinity) and add this to the fourth vessel. After combining these two cups of water, hold these two groups of ancestors in your awareness with the intent that they will enjoy a proper introduction. You may be moved to speak aloud or to simply listen; in any event, allow space for this meeting to occur.

- When your family ancestors and the second grouping of ancestors feel settled and harmonized, proceed to include the third grouping. Once you have added their blessed water to the fourth vessel, hold all three groupings of ancestors in your awareness. Either aloud or with the silent voice of the heart, hold the intent that they will enjoy a proper introduction to one another. Allow time for this meeting to play out, and notice if they have any messages for you at this stage.

- Pick up the fourth vessel that now holds the combined blessings from all three groupings. Notice if there is anything further they wish to express or add to these blessings before you partake, and when the time is right, drink up. Obviously, don't feel that you need to finish everything if you now have a large vessel of water. If you are accustomed in your ritual practice to working with alcoholic spirits (e.g., gin, mead, wine), you may consider substituting shot glasses with these substances in place of the vessels of water. Just make sure the liquids lend themselves to being combined and are agreeable to the ancestors present.

4. **Sit in quiet reflection.** After taking in the combined blessing, spend some time in reflection. Notice the dynamics between your family and affinity ancestors. Hold them both in your awareness at the same time. Is there anything that these two groupings of ancestors want to communicate to you about their relationship? Do the same between your family ancestors and ancestors of place. Is there anything they want to convey? How does it feel to hold both of these groups in your awareness? Finally, hold all three in your awareness. Are there any areas of tension or disharmony from their side? Any surprising connections or natural alignments between them?

5. **Close the ritual by giving thanks** to all of your ancestors. Commit to honoring the diversity and the common humanity of each. They are different souls and lineages, but they can also be experienced as a complex and (more or less) harmonized energy, your personal interface with the larger spirit of humanity.

TWELVE
JOINING THE ANCESTORS

A final aspect of relating to the dead remains to be addressed: the transition from this life to the next. In this chapter you'll be invited to reflect on your own mortality and on ways in which you wish to be honored when you die. You'll learn about the role of the elements (fire, water, wind, and earth) in rituals to care for the body after death and in symbolism surrounding the afterlife. This chapter ends with practices for supporting at funerals, ways to navigate stages of the post-death journey, and suggestions for honoring the one-year anniversary of a loved one's passing.

Preparing for Death

When we are invited to reflect on our own death, it's tempting to imagine being surrounded by loved ones at the end of a long life, releasing ourself quietly from the body with very little pain. A few of us will actually enjoy some version of this fairy tale ending, the classic "good death." Personally, I am not convinced that doing inner work and living as a conscious and ethical human being has any particular bearing on the timing and manner of our exit from this world. To believe otherwise is to fuel the illusion that, unlike other people, you control the timing of your death and the workings of fate and destiny. But the evidence overwhelmingly suggests that even good and wholesome people sometimes die early in life and in ways that are violent, surprising, and agonizing. For many of us, death will arrive suddenly, with pain or fear, and in states that are anything but lucid. Death is not about what we deserve, and dying, at least in most cases, is not about punishment. Nevertheless, the following section assumes an optimal scenario of several relatively pain-free months in which to prepare for death.

Final Months

If you believe you are going to die within the next few months, before going skydiving or making a spiritual pilgrimage to faraway lands, consider first tending to your personal affairs and relationships. This includes caring for legal matters and financial assets as well as determining the fate of your personal possessions. All of these can be addressed relatively easily by creating a will; however, less than half of all Americans have actually taken this step. Those forced to handle a loved one's legal and financial complexities in tandem with a grieving process can attest to the benefits of proactively creating a last will and testament. When reflecting on the fate of personal possessions, can you think of any items that you would like to have buried or cremated with you? Are there any ritual items that need to be passed along to other practitioners of your tradition or require some type of special care? When my friend Sarangerel Odigan passed suddenly in 2006, I remember stories of the confusion and emotional turmoil surrounding the care of her consecrated tools and spirit bundles. A legal will that speaks to these concerns can often be created in a few hours using online resources. It can bring tremendous peace of mind to your family in the event of an sudden passing. It is also, at the very least, useful in getting current with your life.

Planning ahead will also enable you to have the last rites of your choosing. Do you know what you would like to be done with your body after death? If you die with your eyes open, would you like them to be closed for you? Would you like to donate your organs for medicine or your body to scientific research? If you are to be buried or cremated, do you first want your body washed or dressed a certain way? Would you like your loved ones to hold a vigil or any other honoring rituals in the days immediately after your death? Consider sharing your answers to these questions and others that feel important to you with someone you trust or putting a funeral plan in writing. This can be included in your will or in a "final arrangements" document intended to complement the will. The following section, "Funeral Rites and the Body after Death," may help clarify options.

Once practical affairs are in order, are there important completions that remain with the living? As discussed in chapters 8 and 9, leaving this world with unfinished business can function as a drag on our journey forward and can adversely affect living family and friends in need of their own closure. In pragmatic terms, emotional resolution helps us become ancestors. If you have a few lucid months or even a few lucid days before you die, consider meeting in person with key people in your life and communicating in some way with others who may benefit by hearing from you. When this is not possible, written correspondence is a great way to concretize important sentiments, even if someone else has to do the writing for you, or if you want the letters to be read only after your passing. Practices from many traditions encourage us to face and make peace with our death, to be ready to die at any time. This preparation absolutely includes staying as current as possible with people in our lives.

Skydiving aside, when you have tended to other completions, are there outstanding items on your "bucket list"—experiences that would make your soul sing? If so, why not do what's possible to make them a reality? Although a few months of life don't negate years of prior experience, the soul is also a dynamic creature capable of quick shifts and changes. When stepping through the threshold of death, the state of our heart and mind bears at least some impact on what happens next, and spending time doing things that enliven the soul can only help in the journey after. After reflecting on experiences you'd like to be a part of your final months, ask yourself if it's possible to fulfill any of these plans and visions now, even if you have no reason to believe you're currently dying.

Final Days

If you got to spend your final week pain-free and in whatever way you like, what would you include in your last days? Would you set an alarm or sleep in? Would you rather be at home, out in nature, or somewhere in public enjoying favorite places? How much would solitude and introspection be a part of your final days on Earth? Do you have a spiritual practice that you would turn to in a more focused way? If you don't already have such a practice but feel resonance with a certain tradition, you could request a practitioner of that tradition to accompany you or conduct a ceremony on your behalf. For example, a local minister could hold a prayer service at your home, a Buddhist teacher could share teachings on navigating death, or a practitioner of Lakota tradition may be available to offer a pipe (*chanunpa*) ceremony or even a purification lodge (*inipi*) to clear the way for your passing. Most spiritual teachers and communities respond well to requests for support in the dying process. This can be a comfort to the living family and to the dying, a source of support for the soul that is moving on to the next life, and of course a precious gift to those who offer this help.

Often the dying choose to spend at least part of the days before death seeking completion and spending quality time with loved ones. If relationships have been conflicted or distant, this can be a time to ask for forgiveness and to share sensitive information that felt too complicated to express before the finality of death. As my dying grandmother said to my mother, "Don't wait until you're dying to tell people how you feel about them." The fewer surprises (e.g., "I'm not your real father"; "You have a sister you've never met") to be expressed in your final days, the more you'll be able to enjoy the company of friends and family. Staying current from your side also makes more space for any emotional bombs, positive or challenging, that loved ones may share with you. Showing up for this potentially difficult side of saying goodbye will support a good death, a less tangled grieving process for the living, and a smoother transition to join the ancestors.

When final ceremonies and meetings with loved ones are complete, little stands between you and the next world. Can you remember when, before a big trip or life transition, you have projected your attention to the new reality, imagining what it will be like once you're there? Perhaps we do this as a comfort in times of change—sending part of ourselves ahead to greet us when we arrive. When you know you're about to die, it's natural to engage in this same type of anticipatory reflection. Caregivers and other loved ones who serve as companions to the dying often report dialogue between the ancestors and the one on the verge of death, as if the dead are present in the room.

The big question then arises: "What happens when you die?" Not for people in general, but for *you* in particular. Do you have a sense of what it's going to be like for *you* in the minutes, hours, and days after your body ceases to function? Will you eventually go somewhere other than here on Earth? To heaven, some other dimension, or rebirth? Maybe you will merge with the elements or nature in some way? Are there spirits or forces waiting to assist you with these next steps?

Those with strong beliefs about the coming reality will have an easier time imagining the path ahead. In this way believers are better equipped to approach the transition without fear, as they have the skeleton of belief on which to project the part of themselves that will travel ahead and scout the way. Those with a meditation practice or an instinctive appreciation for the unknown are also more likely to view the journey of the soul after death with interest rather than fear. Even if you have no set beliefs or spiritual practice, don't let fear postpone important reflections on death until the final hours. Try turning your attention to the next reality and summoning the spirit of courage and open-heartedness in your mind and heart. If you've done the practices in this book, consider asking your loving ancestors and spirit guides if they want to share anything with you about the dying process. If you do, be gentle with yourself and make it clear that you only wish to know as much as is helpful for you at this time. And remember that many who nearly or temporarily die, even avowed atheists, return to report experiences of expansive love, bliss, and happy reunion with ancestors.

Final Moments

In this version of the good death, let's imagine you wake up rested from a peaceful dream at three in the morning and know that you'll pass in a few hours with the sunrise. If your family and friends are sleeping in the next room, do you wake them, or do you prefer to spend your final hours in solitude? Are your loving ancestors present with you? If you have cultivated a positive relationship with them during life, they are likely to welcome you to their ranks at the time of your death. Are there other deities, spirits, or powers (including God) with whom you have a long-term relationship and wish to call upon? Let's assume that part of your final hours includes calling upon some type of support from the unseen worlds (e.g., ancestors, spirit guides, deities, God/dess) and that you are able to receive this support and to enjoy their guidance for what's to come.

Buddhist teachings on navigating the moment of death have always struck me as especially inclusive, useful, and encouraging. Physical death is seen as a time of great opportunity, partly because it is a threshold state, a time when one mode of consciousness ends and another begins. Imagine yourself, on a journey over many lifetimes, arriving at a rural train station on a clear moonless night, a transfer point from one line to the next. In the time it takes to exit one train and board the one waiting, the teachings encourage pausing on the platform to look up at the stars, to directly witness the temporarily more exposed nature of reality. The teachings suggest that, if we can seize the opportunity, this moment at or just after death can be a time of tremendous opening for the soul. To increase your chances of remembering to look up at just the right moment and see the stars, seek to enter the gateway of death with clarity and presence, even if you have no prior experience with Buddhist practice. This aligns with the general encouragement in Buddhist teachings to bring awareness to times of transition (e.g., entering and exiting sleep, undergoing anesthesia, starting and ending intensive meditation). What practices can help you enter the moment of death in the most present and aware state possible?

Remember that death in this world looks like birth and homecoming from the perspective of the otherworld and the ancestors. When we left the otherworld to step through the gateway of human birth, it meant saying goodbye to our companions in the unseen realms; it was a kind of death or loss for them and also for us. Likewise, death on Earth signals the birth of an ancestor. As one chapter in the long journey of the soul finishes, another begins.

Funeral Rites and the Body after Death

Human beings are not the only species to relate in intentional and ritualized ways to the bodies of ancestors. A fifty-thousand-year-old Neanderthal burial site in southeastern Spain shows that our now-extinct primate kin honored their dead in symbolically significant ways.[1] Elephants show interest in the bones of other elephants and may spend days in focused attention over remains of elephants or human beings. Other living primates—along with cetaceans, dogs, cats, and some birds—also relate to the bodies of deceased relatives in ways that resemble the human experience of grief. Even if you are not particularly religious, you likely have an instinctive preference about how others should relate to your remains. When presenting the material that follows, I make the assumption that death of the physical body begins a rite of passage that ends when the soul arrives at the ancestral realm, or perhaps at the slightly later stage of becoming established as a helpful ancestor.

The following section explores funerary customs in light of the four elements of fire, water, wind, and earth. As you read it, reflect on your current beliefs on the post-death journey. How do they inform your preference for how others will treat your body? By examining diverse ways to deal with the body in the days after death, I explore how the natural elements play an important role in many funerary practices and in symbolism surrounding the post-death journey.

Worldwide the two most common ways of handling deceased human bodies are interment and cremation; however, there are also well-established traditions of burial at sea, sky burial, mummification, and other forms of ritualized natural decomposition. Sometimes necessity trumps preference (e.g., insufficient fuel for a cremation fire, death while at sea, required burning to reduce disease transmission). Also, cultural status and protocol may dictate different post-death treatment of individuals, even ones from the same culture and faith. Other relevant factors can include health codes, a scarcity of burial space, and a preference for practices with reduced ecological impact.

Throughout this exploration, remember that the relationship between the living and the dead often contains an element of mirroring. This sensory, tactile experience of human incarnation (i.e., life on Earth) is in a dynamic reflection or call-and-response with the unseen, the spirit world, or heaven. Elders in Ifá/Òrìṣà tradition sometimes convey this mirroring within a larger unity as a calabash or gourd (*igbá*) composed of two halves: the material world or Earth (*ayé*) and the unseen or heaven (*òrun*). Physical birth and death are doorways between the worlds, and the land of the living and the dead are two halves of a coherent whole. Remember also that references to the realm of the dead, the spirit world, or heaven do not necessarily mean a literal place in any spatial direction but can also refer to the unseen. Heaven is not only in the sun and stars but pervades, overlaps, and intersects our lives on Earth, including these bodies. Burying our dead in the ground so that the departing souls pass through to the unseen mysteries in the Earth does not break the connection between the soul and the stars, but rather extends the realm of heaven beneath the cover of soil and vegetation.

Cremation and Death by Fire

Fire is a thermodynamic event or process expressed in light, heat, and chemical reactions whereby fuels are changed from one condition to another. Roughly one million Americans per year, close to three thousand individuals per day, begin their ancestral journey through the mediating power of fire. Almost 50 percent of the U.S. population now favors cremation. Major religious traditions that encourage this practice include Hinduism, Buddhism, Jainism, and Sikhism. Many worldwide indigenous traditions, as well as ancient Greek, Roman, and other European Pagan cultures, practiced or still practice cremation. Most Christian denominations also now accept it as an alternative to burial. The ashes and fragments of bone that remain after cremation may be buried, kept by relatives, or scattered in nature. For many people, spreading a loved one's ashes in meaningful places is one way to strengthen the ancestor's connection to specific elements and locations. If you choose to go this route, you will want to be sure to check legally, culturally, and spiritually before scattering ashes. Human inhabitants and other spirits of place may not welcome you introducing cremated remains to certain sacred locations or bodies of water. Furthermore, depending on local laws, the practice might be illegal.

Some individuals also die by means of fire. Death by fire may be voluntary (e.g., self-immolation) or, more commonly, accidental or involuntary (e.g., house fires, explosions, electrocutions, nuclear explosions, volcanic eruptions). Some medical conditions may be seen as the results of excess heat (e.g., fever, heat stroke, allergic reactions, some infectious diseases) or too little electrical or metabolic fire (e.g., heart failure, cessation of brain activity, hypothermia). The means of death may or may not be viewed as spiritually significant for the soul of the deceased, but in cases where a meaningful association is made with elemental fire, this can play a helpful role in the ancestralization process. For example, a friend shared that her three nieces died in a house fire. As part of her annual devotions, she lights a candle for each of her loved ones, visualizing their transformation into angelic light. From the fifteenth through the eighteenth centuries, largely in continental Europe, at least forty thousand women, men, and children were executed, often by being burned alive, for the alleged crime of witchcraft.

Modern Pagans sometimes reclaim this ancestral association with fire as a source of strength and connection with these persecuted ancestors.

Volcanoes are epicenters of deaths by elemental fire. The ancient Greeks viewed Sicily's highly active Mount Etna as the location of Hephaistos's smithy, and his Roman counterpart, Vulcan, was venerated at volcanically active sites throughout the empire. On August 24, 79 CE, only one day after the annual Vulcanalia festival to honor the deity of fire and volcanoes, Mount Vesuvius erupted near Pompeii in southern Italy, killing more than fifteen thousand people. Do the souls of those who die in volcanic eruptions retain links with elemental fire or the spirits of place? If so, can calling on these elemental powers aid in the transition of these souls to the ancestral realms?

Even if fire played no role in the means of death and the body was not cremated, you can still work with fire to elevate and ancestralize the dead. Four common themes linking fire and the ancestors include purification, release, transformation, and illumination. In Christianity and Islam, the afterlife for less fortunate souls, more popularly known as hell, is sometimes characterized as a blazing hot furnace of purification. Theologians and mystics differ on whether hell implies eternal damnation or a finite stage of purification after which the soul is released or elevated. European alchemy and metallurgy also affirm the power of fire to purify or refine base metals by burning away heavier elements.

Some psychics who claim to communicate with the souls of the recently deceased report that they may face a life review or reckoning with their life on Earth before fully joining the ancestors. If, in your desire to assist a deceased loved one, you have the impression that they are bearing witness to the consequences of their choices while on Earth, be hesitant to interfere. This reckoning may be important for their journey. From a distance you can pray that they be blessed with courage and humility in their process of atonement, and after a period of weeks or months you can check back in to see if they have made progress in their journey to the ancestral realms.

Hindu and Buddhist traditions often emphasize the power of crematory fire to sever unnecessary attachments to earthly life and support the soul's release from its most recent incarnation. Insofar as physical remains may function as a soul-level link to this dimension, cremation breaks down the body to ash much more quickly than the decomposition associated with burial. Fire ritually destroys the house of the body, leaving the soul with little choice but to face toward the reality of the next world. This ritual completion may be accompanied by sadness and loss, but it may also be met as relief and release, especially when life on Earth was characterized by suffering. The quality of release associated with fire can be most directly called upon in the time surrounding cremation. Before or, if possible, during the cremation process, consider holding individual or family prayer that your beloved dead release the attachments to this life that no longer serve them.

In addition, fire is by nature a process of transformation. This aspect can be invoked during cremation rituals, or simply by lighting a candle with the intent of encouraging the swift transformation from one state (incarnate life on Earth) to the next (becoming a discarnate ancestor). Describing the connection between fire and the ancestral realms, Malidoma Somé wrote, "The Dagara language uses the same word *di* (pronounced 'dee') to mean burn, consume, and eat. The connection, however, is not about destruction, but about transformation."[2] He characterizes inner fire as a force that bonds us to the ancestors and the otherworld, "a rope that connects us to the world we abandoned when we were born into a human body."[3] Ancestral associations with the sun, the stars, and celestial lights are another way in which fire expresses connectivity with the realm of the dead. Fire in this way is both the energy that transforms and a tangible expression of the ancestors themselves.

Whether as lightning, magma, flames, or star power, fire also illuminates. This illumination can be expressed in small ways, like the lighting of a lamp to help guide the soul of the deceased, or more brightly, like the blaze from a collective funeral pyre along the banks of Mother Ganges. The Hindu deity Agni (Sanskrit: *agni,* "fire"; Latin cognate: *ignis*; English: *ignite*) features heavily in the several-thousand-year-old scripture of the Rigveda and still plays an important role in many rites of passage, including cremation. You can call upon elemental fire as a messenger to help guide the soul to its next destination and to transmute the life force of the deceased into a condition of enlightenment and radiant connectivity. When you envision the world beyond this life, is there a quality of brightness and illumination? If so, consider calling upon that brightness in your prayers and devotions.

Sea Burials and Water-Related Death

Relatively few cultures prefer submersion in water as a means of ritual completion for the body after death. Some Pacific Island cultures traditionally return select individuals to the sea, although these practices have diminished in recent centuries. In the wetlands and bogs of northern Europe, naturally mummified bodies have been found dating from 9000 BC to the time of the Second World War. Many of these bog bodies appear to be from executions or sacrifices, while others are richly adorned with ritual offerings.

Although a sea burial is usually not the first choice, death while at sea may necessitate respectful disposal or acceptance of the loss of the deceased into aquatic environments. In light of this reality, most major world religions as well as modern navies have modified burial rites for settings at sea. Conditions during World War II called for sea burials of U.S. Navy personnel aboard aircraft carriers in the Pacific. In 2011 the United States arranged with Saudi Arabia for Osama bin Laden's last rites to be performed somewhere in the North Arabian Sea to prevent focus on a physical gravesite. His body was washed and Islamic protocol was observed for the last rites and sinking of the body.

Other types of water-related deaths include drowning, natural disasters (e.g., floods, tsunamis), and failure of human infrastructure (e.g., levee and dam failures). Medical conditions such as internal bleeding or swelling, dehydration, and other blood and circulatory complications may be understood as death by water. Homicide victims sometimes die by drowning or are disposed of in water to discourage recovery of the body. Does death by drowning or return of the physical remains to bodies of water imply a connection between the deceased and elemental water? At Teotihuacán and in later Aztec tradition, the god Tlaloc presides over storms, fertility, and water. He also receives those who die by drowning, by lightning, and from water-borne illness. Rather than being cremated, those in Tlaloc's care are traditionally buried with seeds planted in their faces and a digging stick for planting in their hands.

From Yorùbá-speaking West Africa, Ayo Salami wrote:

> In cases of drowning, divinations have to be performed to determine the type of burial to be done. Inquisitions have to be made to know if the corpse should be taken home or if the "deity of the river" would take it over. It has to be known if the spirit of the deceased had become part of the water. If he is confirmed to be part of the spiritual constituent of the river or lake, it is believed that taking the corpse home could spell misfortune for the immediate family. Therefore such bodies are buried beside the river.[4]

Why ritually address water-related deaths differently if not for an important connection between the deceased and the gods of water? How can work with elemental water support the deceased in becoming an ancestor?

Many cultures include both literal and symbolic water in funerary rituals. Recurring themes include cleansing, sacred grieving, journey to the ancestral realm, and connectivity through blood. As death is often messy, washing the body before the last rites is common both in Western medical practice and in many spiritual traditions. The symbolism surrounding this final washing can include clearing away of heavy or troubling energies, dissolving of attachments to this world, and absolution from past harms. If you ever have the honor of washing a deceased loved one as a part of their last rites, consider first infusing the water with prayers or other sacred medicines. Allow tradition and intuition to guide you about any plants to add to support your prayers (e.g., cedar, juniper, or bay laurel for purification). By holding a prayer for the deceased throughout the washing, you can help them prepare for the journey to come.

Tears shed for the dying are also offerings of water, a most intimate type of libation for the ancestors. Allowing grief and other emotions to be expressed in healthy ways encourages personal well-being and open-heartedness and provides tangible support for your beloved dead one to join with the ancestors. Knowing that their lives mattered, that they are loved and remembered, can help the deceased let go of this life and embrace their new form as ancestors. In addition to the salty offerings of your tears, you may offer your ancestors cool water, tea, coffee, spirits, or any other beverages that bring them happiness. Liquid offerings can be placed out or poured as libations at a family shrine, a grave, or any receptive place in nature. If you make libations of tears or other liquids, consider joining these offerings with spontaneous prayer, song, or other good words from the heart.

Many cultures express the journey of the dead as navigating a river by boat or crossing a large body of water to reach the realm of the ancestors. Early medieval Norse cultures cremated most of their dead but interred others, either in an actual ship with offerings or in stone and earth formations resembling ships. In ancient Egypt, both the Milky Way and the Nile were seen as important pathways for human souls, and elaborate funerary boats were interred near people of status to help them navigate the night sky and the ancestral waters. The Greek psychopomp Hermes sometimes leads wayward souls to the stewardship of Charon, ferryman of the river Acheron and gatekeeper to Hades. The souls of the dead must cross the water to enter or leave. As noted earlier, Martín Prechtel wrote of Maya tradition, "The Tzutujil believed that the dead rowed themselves to the other world in a 'canoe made of tears, with oars made of delicious old songs.' Our grief energized the soul of the deceased so it could arrive intact onto the Beach of Stars where the dead go to the other side of the ocean, the salty Grandmother Ocean who tossed and surged between us and the next world."[5] Further north, some Native California peoples speak of the human soul as going west toward the setting sun and ocean. Even in traditions such as Hinduism that cleanse the body with fire after death, ashes may be added to a body of water (e.g., the River Ganges) as ritual enactment of the journey from this life to the next along the waterways that join the worlds. What is the vessel by which the deceased navigate the waters between this world and the next? Who are the guides and gatekeepers along the way?

For poets, scientists, and shamans alike, blood is a direct and potent link with ancestral consciousness. Stem cells in our bones give rise to the blood in our veins, and both contain the genetic script of our biological ancestors. Decades before Watson and Crick discovered the molecular structure of DNA, German poet Rainer Maria Rilke opened his third "Duino Elegy," an extended exploration of ancestral influence, with: "It is one thing to sing the beloved. Another, alas, to invoke that hidden, guilty river-god of the blood."[6] In his book *The Tree of Enchantment*, Orion Foxwood, a teacher of European Paganism, wrote, "The first contact in this work is ancestral, there is no way around this. Contact with the Ancestor awakens your blood, which awakens your bones and flesh. The path to the wisdom of the ancestors is in your blood."[7] The following poem by Elise Dirlam Ching beautifully evokes the river of blood as a passage to and from the realm of the ancestors.

WHEN THE RAIN BEGINS

I say not to worry.
One year there was no harvest.
One day Earth ripped apart
like the gut of a sick deer.
One moment I looked at myself
in the eye of the Moon
and I was afraid:

Even she is being licked away
by the black mouth of Heaven
and next to her this life
is a small dry stick burning.

One year the Bear plunged among us mad
and tore many lives
before the arrow stopped his pain.
I cried for us and for the Bear.
One day Ocean came across the land to our doorways
took some of us to feed his creatures
sent the rest of us into the mountains
leaving new Gods among us.
One moment I looked down the chasm of the past
into the red river of my birth
and readied myself to leave
my children and their children.

I grow old.
Sun has clawed my face.
Earth bent my spine.
My eyes are clouded moons.
My ears are closed to song and terror.

Lay me in a plain canoe
without ceremony
and when the Moon is hidden
and the rain begins
give me to the River
to the whims of stones and currents
and a violence
that is natural and becoming.

ELISE DIRLAM CHING

Sky Burials and Death by Wind

Death symbolism surrounding wind, air, and sky often includes themes of purification, breath, transformation, and flight. In southeastern Turkey near the Syrian border, the site of Göbekli Tepe dates to about 10,000 BCE and is the oldest known human religious structure on Earth. This and other sites in the eastern Mediterranean region (e.g., Çatalhöyük, Jericho) show strong evidence for "sky burials," including elevated platforms and ritual attention to vultures as catalysts in the death process. In contemporary times the two most established lineages of sky burial are found in Zoroastrian tradition and Tibetan Buddhism. In Tibet, sky burials were practiced alongside cremation for at least eight hundred years before the Chinese occupiers outlawed it in the 1960s. A famous scene in the Martin Scorsese film *Kundun* depicts the current Dalai Lama's father being ritually dismembered and fed to vultures. In the 1980s the Chinese government loosened restrictions on sky burial, and the practice has resumed to some degree.

Why did these ancient ancestors prefer to offer their dead to the birds? The highest-flying birds on Earth, vultures can transform rotting flesh into usable energy in ways that few animals can. Their stomach acids are highly corrosive, and their featherless heads reflect their specialization in the work of cleaning corpses. The vultures currently eating the most human flesh on Earth live among the Parsis or Zoroastrians of northwest India. Sadly, nearly all nine species of Indian vulture are now in danger of extinction as a result of diclofenac poisoning, and there are now too few vultures to consume the corpses in a timely way at the traditional Zoroastrian *dakhmas, cheel ghar,* or "towers of silence." Imagine the impact of being forced to break from this tradition if your family had worked in partnership with hundreds of generations of vultures for the cleansing and care of your ancestors' bodies. In addition to vultures, ravens and crows are notorious for their love of human eyeballs and other bits that can be scavenged after battles or natural disasters. What is your intuitive sense of the effect on the deceased to have the corpse consumed by birds? Can birds who are scavengers or "death eaters" help neutralize and purify heavy energies in the life of the deceased? If it were culturally acceptable, affordable, and ecological, would you prefer a sky burial?

Even if birds don't clean your bones, we all stop breathing, and for many people, cessation of breathing is the primary means of death. Airborne pathogens, respiratory conditions, and accidental or intentional suffocation may be considered types of air or wind death. Larger-scale asphyxiation events include volcanic ash clouds, mining and submarine accidents, upwelling of submerged carbon dioxide (e.g., lakes in Cameroon and Congo), and deadly use of chemical weapons. Popular film and literature often show the soul departing with the last breath or after final words. In English the word *spirit* is derived from the Latin *spiritus,* which refers directly to the breath. In Jewish tradition the word *ruach* literally refers to the breath of living beings and also to the spirit and animating life force. In Ifá/Òrìṣà tradition Ọya, whose name in Yorùbá literally means "to tear" or "rip," speaks through natural disasters, wind, and storms. She is also intimately associated with the human ancestors and rituals of ancestralization. In her form as a goddess of wind, Ọya enters with the first breath and inhales back into her fullness the last breath of every human being. If you have been with someone during their final breath, what did you notice about the link between the breath and soul? Do you have any beliefs or customs surrounding your last breath?

As the most mutable and dynamic of all the elements, elemental wind is also associated with sudden and profound transformation. Storms and high winds convey this potency, as do the risks of aviation. Types of sudden death brought about by the powers of wind include flight accidents and fatalities during hurricanes, tornadoes, and storms. During World War II about four thousand Japanese pilots, along with many in the Allied forces, died in intentional suicide missions targeting American and British naval forces in the Pacific. Kamikaze pilots or "divine winds" (*kami:* "god/spirit/divinity" + *kaze:* "wind") were assured by the Japanese leadership that their souls would be welcomed after death at the Yasukuni Shrine, a Shinto temple famous for housing the *kami* or souls of those who die fighting for the emperor of Japan (see plate 17). Presumably at least some kamikaze pilots felt this alignment with the spirit of the wind and with the ancestral homeland at the moment of impact. Does death from the sky and belief that you are one with the spirit of the wind affect what follows after? Aside from the tragedy of an early death by war and the distortion of traditional Shinto values to bolster questionable imperialist goals, did taking on the mission of a kamikaze affect the ancestralization process of these men?

If any of your beloved dead lost their lives through elemental air, consider making prayers and offerings for the happiness and well-being of these ancestors to the forces who are wind and weather. If they were cremated and you carry some of their ashes, determine if it would strengthen your prayer to return a pinch of their body to the wind. Or more simply, align your prayers with the spirit of wind by dedicating a stick of incense or other ritual smoke to the ancestors' elevation.

The human soul has been likened to a bird perhaps more than to any other creature.[8] Mediators between Earth and heaven and expressions of freedom and flight, birds are also invoked to express the soul's release from the "cage" of the body after death. Ancient Egyptians believed that the *ba* (one of at least five souls that comprise human beings) plays a large role in our unique personality, and hieroglyphs depict the ba as a bird with a human head. In the Buryat Mongol tradition, the ami soul is understood to take flight after death and roost back in the upper world to await future incarnations. In his twelfth-century epic poem *The Conference of the Birds,* the famous Persian mystic Farid ad-Din Attar tells of the soul's longing to know God through the language of different birds.

Notice if specific birds appear during dreams or during waking life around the time when friends and family members are leaving this life. Stay open over time to associations between your beloved dead and family lineages with specific birds, as our winged relatives are common messengers for the ancestors in this world.

Burial and Death in the Earth

Although Neanderthals were known to have ritually buried some of their dead, the oldest definitive evidence of human burials dates to 100,000 to 130,000 years ago in what is now Israel.[9] Many indigenous ways of life, including some pre-Christian European traditions, still favor interment, and Islam, Christianity, and Judaism all encourage burial over cremation. Unlike in many other industrialized nations (e.g., England, Japan, Australia), the majority of the dead in the United States (about 60 percent) are buried rather than burned. Currently, in the early twenty-first century, about 150,000 human beings die every day on Earth (about fifty-five million per year). Although rates of cremation and burial vary widely from culture to culture, at least half of these recently deceased are placed into the cool dark body of Earth. For the approximately seventy-five thousand human bodies buried each day, the natural rate of decomposition varies depending on local soils and hydrology, type of container for the body (if any), and chemical treatment (if any) of the cadaver. Even embalmed bodies sealed in metal coffins and covered in concrete will likely be reduced to teeth, bone, and residual tissue within a year if not sooner. Cases of bodies preserved in coffins or other burial environments for decades or longer are the exception rather than the norm.

To a greater degree than cremation, sea burials, or being eaten by vultures, interment affirms a link between the deceased and the place of burial. On a purely physical level, teeth and bones almost always remain on location. Of the roughly thirty million human bodies buried every year, the vast majority will remain on-site until long after the flesh and bones have become landscape and the deceased have passed from living memory. Like stone, fragments of bone can endure for centuries and in some circumstances for thousands of years. Rituals to honor and commune with the ancestors at the burial site reinforce the association between those ancestral souls and their final resting place. If you have visited the bones of known ancestors, what was your sense of the connection between them and their place of burial? See "Home Is Where the Bones Are" (page 201) in chapter 10 on the connection between the bones and place.

Some ways of dying seem especially connected to elemental earth. Examples of "earth deaths" include avalanches, landslides, and earthquakes; building collapses; underground mining accidents; or any other type of fatality delivered by earth and stone. In California's Sierra foothills, the entrance to Moaning Caverns features an easy-to-overlook two-hundred-foot plunge to the floor of the main chamber. The first Europeans to explore these caves in the 1850s reported hundreds of human skeletons piled beneath the cave's opening, with one layer of bones likely more than ten thousand years old. Whether they were intentionally thrown into the cave or died by accident, we can ask whether the manner and location of death informed the experience of these souls after death. Do those ancestors whose remains were later moved deeper into the caves maintain any link with the caves? Another form of death, far more common than falling into giant caves, comes from exposure to heavy metals and other substances extracted from the Earth, which can be fatal, often over a period of years. What other means of death can you think of that might create a significant association between the deceased and elemental earth, metal, and stone?

Stories of the journey of the soul after death often parallel natural cycles (e.g., solar rhythms, water cycles, plant growth, migrating animals). Consider the symbolism surrounding earth burials through three basic stages of plant growth: planting the seed (body), germination in the unseen, and emergence of new growth. In the days after the breath ceases to animate the body, most people will be planted in the ground and ritually covered in earth. And when the living family throws fresh earth over the recently lowered coffin, the earthly front door of initiation closes behind the recently deceased and the expectation emerges that they will step into their next reality as an ancestor. In many cultures the souls of the recently departed journey into the Earth rather than to the stars or heavens. The otherworld and the realm of the ancestors may reside in the spirit dwellings in the Earth, so we place the bodies of our beloved dead into this living mystery, planting them as we would a seed.

To honor the first stage of burial, consider everything placed in the ground as an offering to the Earth Mother and to the sacredness that is this planet. These things include the body, the contents of the coffin (if one is used), and any other items buried with the deceased. "Green burials" are unfortunately still not widely available in the United States, but keeping burials as ecologically low-impact as possible respects the sanctity of the Earth and honors the well-being of the land.

If the body itself is the heart of the seed, everything buried with the body corresponds to the seed coat, fertilizer, and supportive ingredients for the next cycle of life. What prayers, offerings, or ritual items will help the deceased germinate in the darkness of earth as a bright and loving ancestor? If family and friends were willing to supply you with your "grave goods" of choice, what would you include? When participating in a burial, you could include seeds or grains infused with prayers for the recently deceased inside the coffin. The seeds/prayers can be seen as nourishment and momentum for the journey ahead; they also affirm the fertility or continuity of the soul and the eventual return to the surface and to daylight. You could also pray with seeds during the first month to a year after the passing of a loved one, store these prayers in a seed jar on your ancestor or family shrine, and return them to the Earth when the time is right.

Memorial trees and gardens are a great way to honor the ancestors and their affinity with the cycles of plants and the Earth. If it's not practical to plant a tree or dedicate a garden, consider including a new plant on your ancestor shrine or in your home. If cremation has been the choice, burial of the ashes can draw on symbolism and ritual surrounding both fire and earth. Biodegradable urns now allow for the planting of a tree fertilized by the ashes of cremated loved ones, an inspiring idea that, if popular, would give rise to memorial forests and groves wherever cremation is practiced.* Cremation remains can be offered at the base of living trees and gardens to affirm the reintegration of the body and soul into the larger flow of elemental energies and the Earth. Wood ash is also a great offering to make at the time of interment, as the potassium,

---

*See, for example, Gerard and Roger Moliné's Bios Urns at https://urnabios.com.

calcium carbonate, and other components of ash serve as fertilizer for new plant growth.

A second stage in burial symbolism begins when the initial funerary rites have been completed (usually within a week or two). This is often a time of relative quiet with respect to contact between the living and the dead. The cycle of time when new seedlings germinate in the Earth corresponds to the cool dark of night in the cycle of night and day. Philosopher, ecologist, and author David Abram notes, "For some indigenous cultures, it is precisely during this journey through the ground that the sun impregnates the earth with its fiery life, giving rise to myriad living things—human and nonhuman—that blossom forth on earth's surface."[10] Life as light and new growth is temporarily obscured from our perception as the sun disappears below the horizon and is planted in the Earth. Assuming that the soul of the deceased is now on its way to the ancestors, we mourn not only the loss of their physical presence but their temporary turn of attention away from the living.

Heartfelt grief and tears are excellent offerings in the months following a death, especially if combined with prayers and wishes for the happiness and successful transition of the loved one. Offering tears directly to the Earth serves to water the seed planted at burial and conveys love and remembrance to provide momentum for the soul's transformation into a bright and well ancestor. If possible, let your grief flow with supportive family and friends and in ways that communicate release and blessings for the dead. To honor the period of turning away between the living and deceased, consider directing any additional ritual offerings to the helpful deities and the already bright ancestors on behalf of the recently deceased person rather than to that person directly.

After being nurtured in the fertile darkness of the earth, the new sprout's first leaves reach toward the light of this world, the soul's activity becomes known to the living, and contact between the living and the newly established ancestor often resumes (or becomes possible). Some among the recently arrived ancestors may be more drawn to the realm of the living, while some may focus their attention more in the ancestral realm per se. As explored in the section on multiple souls in chapter 11, the soul, or souls, of the deceased may simultaneously become an established and helpful ancestor and take birth again among the living. This was apparent to me during several personal pilgrimages to Òdè Rẹ́mọ, Ògún State, Nigeria. In July 2013 the revered elder and patriarch Àràbà Adésànyà Awoyadé passed on to the realm of the ancestors at age ninety-nine. As is customary in Yorùbá culture, he was buried beneath his family residence, and during our group's first visit several weeks after his death, the earth over the Àràbà's grave was still fresh. The elders asked us at that time to refrain from invoking him as an ancestor so recently after his passing (i.e., do not disturb the recently planted seed). Shortly after our visit, we received news that the Àràbà's son and our host, Olúwo Fálolú Adésànyà Awoyadé, had welcomed a newborn son to the world. Divination confirmed this child, the late Àràbà's grandson, to be the reincarnation of the Àràbà, and he was given the name of Babátúndé (literally "Father returns"). During our second visit to Òdè Rẹ́mọ in February 2014, for those standing at the Àràbà's grave in praise while his son Olúwo Fálolú held his infant son (the reincarnated Àràbà), there was no contradiction between becoming an ancestor and being reborn on Earth. The Àràbà was ritually fed as a highly revered ancestor on the same day that diapers were changed for his living grandson and reincarnation, Babátúndé.

The light of this world may compel the ancestors to assist in affairs on Earth, or they may be more drawn by the light of the ancestral sun, the light of the otherworld. In either case, once established as ancestors, they are poised to reengage, to participate in the great unfolding of consciousness. The most important way to honor this third stage of the ancestralization process is to make a space in your life and heart for renewed relationship with the ancestor. For suggestions, see chapter 3, "Spontaneous Ancestral Contact," and the section below, "Ritual Tending in the First Year after Death." Once you sense that your beloved dead is well in spirit and has joined other vibrant lineage ancestors, it should be safe to interact with them directly.

⧄⧄

EXERCISE SEVENTEEN

Conscious Participation
in a Burial

INTENT: Participate as a spiritual ally during death rites leading to a burial

This exercise will provide basic suggestions for participation during a funeral and/or burial. The progression below is designed for participants who are at least one degree removed from the deceased (i.e., they are not among the primary mourners).

1. **Prepare for the ceremony.** Like other big changes, a death in the family can stir up heavy and difficult energies. Before you go to the funeral or burial, do what you need to do to energetically protect yourself. This may involve getting grounded in your body, calling your guides around you, and carrying or wearing some protective talisman. The goal is to be both protected and emotionally available.

2. **When you arrive,** don't feel that you have to tune in to the spirit of the one who has died. There's no need to reach for them or to do anything to help them become an ancestor. You are there to witness and support a natural process. Instead of trying to make something happen, you can hold a prayer that the bright and beloved ancestors of the one who has died be present to receive them in due time.

3. **Support others who are grieving.** Remember that grief provides momentum for the dead to transition. Allow your own grief to flow naturally, and when you feel well resourced, be available to support others. This may involve affirming, often without words, to those who are struggling to express their grief that their pain and tears are welcome. Those who are intensely grieving may benefit from a stabilizing presence and from knowing they're not alone. In this way, you can gently assist in regulating the flow of grieving, which in turn benefits the transitioning dead.

4. **At the place of burial,** you might acknowledge the guardian spirit of the cemetery and, more importantly, the Earth and land directly—giving

thanks to the Earth for receiving the dead. This can be done discreetly if needed and can shift the energy of the ceremony in a subtle way. You might offer flowers or another natural offering at the grave once the body has been lowered; trust what feels respectful.

5. **Before the ceremony or burial concludes**, include a prayer that the deceased release any unhelpful ties to his or her physical body. Picture the loving ancestors and any other helpful guides as being present to receive the spirit of the deceased. This is perhaps the most important part of this exercise—calling the loving ancestors and other helping powers to receive the dead. This does not mean that any particular thing will happen at the time of the funeral, because the timing of the transition is not up to the living; however, sincere wishes for the dead to be received do matter. The more who can hold this intent in a natural and humble way, the better.

6. **After the ceremony**, do a cleansing and self-care ritual for yourself and others. You might change out of the clothes you were in and pour yourself a cleansing bath with herbs or oils. Release yourself from the energies of the day and let your cleansing complete the ritual.

Remember to trust your instincts about honoring these sacred transitions. Death is messy, unpredictable, and often woven through with intense pain and emotion. Death is also highly personal. The symbols and exercise presented above are merely suggestions, catalysts to encourage love, creativity, and responsiveness in the face of the Mystery.

Ritual Tending in the First Year after Death

If you've lived through the death of a family member, you know that major losses take time for the mind and heart to metabolize. Immediately after a death, tending to your personal wellness is paramount, and a combination of tenacious self-care and reliance on friends and family can make all the difference. Also, there is no shame in welcoming help from psychotherapists, healers, priests, and other professionals. Excellent and often free resources in the form of books, audio recordings, movies, and community groups can also help you navigate the waters of profound grief. Make use of whatever helps you feel held and cared for, and remember that although we may never cease to miss our beloved dead, the months and years do tend to gradually soften the intensity of grief.

Although every religious tradition characterizes the post-death journey differently, consider a basic three-part progression found in many cultures: saying goodbye, turning away, and resuming contact. Each stage comes with certain encouragements and cautions, and understanding these can help you safely navigate the first year after a loved one's passing. As you read, reflect on your experiences of relating with deceased loved ones and on your beliefs about what awaits you after death.

Saying Goodbye

Most spiritual traditions acknowledge a window of time immediately following the death of the body when the soul is still around. This period usually lasts a few days to two weeks. Typically it includes the major funerary rites as well as ritual completions with the body. Whether it is a matter of throwing dirt over a coffin, witnessing a loved one's body enter a cremation oven, or simply being handed their ashes, making sure the body is no longer habitable often plays an important role in the process of saying goodbye. But what about the days preceding? This is traditionally a time *for both the living and the deceased* to say goodbye. Imagine you have just died. Why would you leave right before your closest family and friends are about to have a big send-off? Factor in the surprise, shock, or disorientation that many of the recently deceased experience, and you can see the challenge is not leaving too soon, but rather making sure to depart to the ancestral realms after the goodbyes are complete.

How can family and friends take into account basic teachings of ancestor reverence during this first stage? First remember that not all of the dead are well in spirit; therefore it may be important to maintain a boundary even after death. When an abusive or troubled relative dies, or in cases of sudden, tragic death, the recently deceased may be too consumed by their own confusion to graciously engage in heartfelt goodbyes. Even in cases when they do wish to engage with you, you may wish to maintain a boundary and navigate your emotional completions in other ways. That's your choice, and it's good to respect yourself and your limits. In this situation you can still pray for the well-being of the deceased and picture his or her elevated and loving ancestors bringing abundant support and opening the way for the next stages of the journey.

When you do feel good about engaging directly with the spirit of the recently deceased and they're available for this type of contact, allow yourself in the period shortly after a death to savor that quality time. Speak aloud to them, if living people in your immediate space won't think it too strange. Let your tears flow. Express whatever remains unsaid from this relative's time on Earth, and stay open to the mutual flow of forgiveness (see chapter 8 and exercise 8 for suggestions). Love them powerfully and completely, with the understanding that soon everything will be different. When funeral rites end and the ancestors are ready to accompany the deceased to their new status, let them go. If you are the one preparing to die, remember that after the goodbyes are complete with the living, the time will come to turn your attention to the next world and embrace the loving ancestors.

Turning Away

In many cultures, the ritual of burial or cremation marks the beginning of a period of time, often somewhere between a few weeks and a year, when the living turn attention away from the recently deceased. In many Buddhist lineages forty-nine days is an approximate time required for most souls to transition through the *bardos,* transitional states between worlds, before eventually settling into a new incarnation here on Earth, life as an ancestral spirit, or some other form. Especially after the death of a parent, Jewish tradition designates one year as a period of ritual mourning. It is the standard interval of time prescribed before unveiling the grave marker or monument. Speaking of the T'zutujil Maya perspective, Martín Prechtel writes, "After four hundred days of initiation into the next layer, these dead would graduate into the status of ancestors. In their new form they could help us here in this world."[11]

The famous post-death journey of Jesus of Nazareth, as presented in the New Testament, follows this ancient progression of the soul from this world to the next. After his body was planted in the cool darkness of the tomb, he arose to face the living. On the third day after his crucifixion, the Gospels report Jesus leaving the tomb and rising from the dead. Interpretations vary on the degree to which the resurrection was in the flesh or in a tangible spirit form, but in either case, most Christians believe that Jesus appeared to various disciples over the next forty days and then ascended to heaven. During this forty-day window, Jesus appeared to Mary Magdalene, saying, "Touch me not: for I am not yet ascended to my Father."[12] This passage gives the impression that after rising from the grave, Jesus was still between the worlds, that his new status was tenuous or transitional, and that he was saying his final goodbyes and speaking to his relatives and devotees before joining his companions in heaven.

Customs of temporary turning away acknowledge that prematurely calling the recent dead back to the world of the living risks disrupting their transformation. When family and friends choose to turn away from the deceased for a period, they are showing trust in the transformation. Unless you and the deceased share a specific tradition on how long to wait before contact resumes, consider allowing a full year to pass. Even if we don't try to call their attention back to this world, the dead may still choose to engage us through both dreams and waking encounters during this time of transition. If they do come to you, honor this contact. Try not to place demands on them or encourage them to stick around unless you're certain they have taken their place among the bright ancestors. If they indicate that they are suffering or have yet to join the bright ancestors, seek to understand what role, if any, you may play in helping them along. Ask for help if needed. Once the ancestors have clearly received them, resume the practice of giving space and respectfully turning away until they settle into their new status. If you are personally preparing for death, remember that when your goodbyes are complete, the journey to the ancestral realm will require love, courage, and trust in your own ability to navigate the great waters of this larger reality. Remember that you are not alone and that the well ancestors are cheering you on and waiting with great kindness to receive you.

Resuming Contact

At this third stage, the recent dead become sufficiently settled in the otherworld to safely reengage the living, or, from the perspective of the otherworld, the elder ancestors grant visitation privileges to newly established ancestors. These recent ancestral graduates may reach out spontaneously, or they may respond warmly when contacted through prayer, meditation, and ancestor ritual. If contact resumes and feels positive, make it a point to experience this ancestor in the context of the bright and loving lineage, to honor his or her new status as one of many. See if there are offerings he or she would enjoy, or if there are other ways of honoring the connection. Allow space for both continuity and change as the relationship finds a new equilibrium.

Just because the dead settle into their new status as ancestors doesn't mean that all living relatives will immediately have a potent dream of ancestral reconnection or will necessarily know when their beloved dead have truly arrived. This lack of contact can occur for numerous reasons, even when the dead are well in spirit, and is not necessarily a sign of trouble. The ancestors may be more focused on the otherworld than on earthly affairs. They may be respecting the sensibilities of the living and not wishing to impose. They may still be learning how to contact the living through dreams, synchronicities, and waking visions. The living may still be deep in their grieving in ways that make renewed contact more challenging. Also, living relatives may lack a framework for ongoing relationship with the ancestors and may not be particularly open to renewed contact.

The following exercise presents one way to honor the anniversary of the death of a loved one.

EXERCISE EIGHTEEN

Ritual for the First Anniversary of a Death

INTENT: Invite reconnection with a beloved ancestor one year after death
WHAT YOU NEED: A quiet space, offerings, and whatever helps you connect with your ancestors

This exercise will guide you in honoring the one-year anniversary of a loved one's death. It's also a way for you to assess if they are well in spirit, and, if not, to help you determine what role you may play in assisting. If your religious tradition informs you about how to resume contact, honor that guidance and simply apply whatever is helpful from the exercise.

Also keep in mind that the first anniversary of the death may pass *before* it's beneficial to reengage. Conversely, the ancestor in question may be deeply at peace well before a year has passed. This exercise assumes that you have not already been in regular contact before the year anniversary and that you are not yet sure about the health of this ancestor.

1. **Before confirming that you will proceed with the ritual**, set aside a time to engage in prayer, use your intuition, and ask your guides for support. Ask if the deceased is decisively well in spirit, or if he or she is still in transition. If needed, refer to exercise 4, "Attuning to Your Four Primary Bloodlines" (page 91), to learn how to safely inquire. If you conclude that this ancestor is already well in spirit, proceed to step 2.

    If you determine that this ancestor is not yet well in spirit, ask the guides what role, if any, they wish you to play in this process. Possible actions could include reaching out for support from an established practitioner; initiating a cycle of ancestral repair work, if the deceased in need is an ancestor (see chapters 5 through 9); making offerings to the bright and loving guides on behalf of the person; and simply holding a prayer for his or her happiness while giving more time and space. Trust what the guides tell you, and respect their assessment.

2. After confirming that the guides support reconnection, **settle the practical aspects of the ritual**. Trust your instincts and guidance on the following questions:

- Will you offer this ritual alone, or are there others you wish to invite? If so, consider first clearing the invitations with your guides.
- Where will you offer this honoring ritual? At the gravesite? At your ancestor altar? Somewhere peaceful in nature? Or simply in a quiet and conducive indoor space?
- What will you bring? This may include flowers, incense or sage, tobacco, candles, or some food and drink that your ancestor would enjoy.
- What will you need to care for yourself emotionally? Are you open to letting tears flow and speaking from the heart with your ancestors?

3. **Open ritual space** in whatever ways work for you. Call to your loving ancestors and other spirit helpers and guides. Present any offerings and allow for a moment of silence and listening. Reconfirm with the well ancestors that the loved one with whom you wish to reconnect is in fact well in spirit.

When you feel ready, **invite the guides to hold space for you to relate directly to the spirit of your beloved dead**. Start by listening to what your newly arrived ancestor wishes to convey and, when moved, speak aloud to him or her. Welcome tears from a spirit of reconnection. **Notice the elder ancestors and guides holding a space for whatever needs to happen.**

Either at this time or later, ask to better understand how this newly arrived ancestor experiences his or her lineage of beloved dead. Are there any offerings this one would enjoy from you? If you have them available, consider making a second round of offerings now as part of the reconnection ceremony. If it feels right, you can ask this one for a blessing for your life.

4. **Finish with the honoring and reconnection ritual** by thanking the ancestor and seeing him or her rejoining the larger community of well ancestors. Thank all of them, let them know you are done focusing on them at this time, and tend to any ritual completions. Reflect on your experience and consider making notes on any messages or requests.

   In the hours after ritual, notice what helps you integrate and feel grounded. If you need to make a further transition from the time in ritual space, consider changing out of the clothes you wore during the ritual. Many people also use water as a way to cleanse and reset after times of spirit contact (e.g., washing hands and face, cleansing bath with herbs or oils). Eating a full, healthy meal is great if you need to feel more grounded in your body. Stay open to ancestral contact in dreams after the ceremony.

5. **In the days and weeks after the ritual, reflect on what level of contact with this ancestor feels right for you.** Don't assume that just because you can engage directly, it means you *should* engage. Some people didn't interact a lot during life, so there's not a great deal of regular contact after death. That's fine, no problem. Other recent ancestors are excited about supporting our lives on Earth. In these cases, commune as often as is good for you. Let any contact during dreams also inform the connection and keep everything in a good way. If you're not sure how often you wish to call upon this ancestor, you may make an intention to hold an honoring ritual the following year.

APPENDIX

DISTINGUISHING TALKING WITH SPIRITS FROM PSYCHOSIS

As a doctor of psychology and licensed psychotherapist as well as a practitioner of Earth-honoring traditions, I am aware of the ways in which these two domains of practice occasionally fail to align. Modern psychology tends to be skeptical about, or even pathologize, individuals who claim to talk with the spirits of the dead. This is unfortunate, as most contact with the ancestors, whether real or imagined, does not have anything to do with psychosis. People in the midst of a psychotic process typically experience some kind of break with reality that impairs their ability to function. This change is almost always apparent to others close to the person.

When people do experience clinical psychosis (temporary or ongoing), they may claim to relate with the spirits of the dead, but it's not an unusually prevalent feature of psychosis. Stanford anthropologist Tanya Luhrmann's research on schizophrenic patients in the United States, Ghana, and India suggests that local culture strongly shapes how individuals feel about the voices they hear and that other cultures often have a greater willingness to engage with spirit contact. Western psychology discourages relating with so-called auditory hallucinations as actual spirits, for fear that this will reinforce delusions, but older cultural forms of treatment suggest that being willing to engage, especially with helpful voices, can feel supportive to those who already hear them.

More commonly, individuals spontaneously contacted by the ancestors may believe they are "going crazy" simply because they lack a framework for relating with spirits. These individuals often have no (other) symptoms of psychosis or of a break with reality; they merely have no way to explain what they are experiencing and therefore wonder if they are losing their mind. People in this circumstance can often benefit from validation, kindness, and support. Because not all of the dead are well in spirit, an individual who is unwell may be at greater risk for contact from the troubled dead. In these cases, traditional healers, priests, and spirit workers may be called upon to collaborate with psychotherapists and psychiatrists to clarify the nature of the contact and to reduce its intensity.

Clients who seek support from mental health professionals have the right to respect for their spiritual beliefs and experiences, including real or perceived contact with the ancestors. Most therapists will likely be curious and respectful, even if they may not be able to relate themselves. If this is not your experience, you can invite professionals to educate themselves on practices of ancestor reverence, or if needed, you can seek a different practitioner who is more sympathetic. From my experiences both as a client of psychotherapy and as a marriage and family therapist, I believe that much of the suffering mental health professionals seek to treat can be worked with as intergenerational patterns, family karma, or ancestral influence. Our loving ancestors are capable, available, and invested in good outcomes for family and personal healing, and increasing numbers of mental health professionals are open to or have trained to support clients through diverse types of spiritual experiences.

If you have a history of mental illness that includes psychosis and you become concerned that your symptoms are returning, or if people you trust are telling you that you are not relating to the ancestors in balanced ways, consider getting other opinions. If possible, seek guidance from a mental health professional who respects the possibility of spirit contact. Go slow until you get a clear handle on what's happening. Despite the challenges, relating to the ancestors should be a source of blessings, beauty, and healing in your life.

NOTES

Introduction

1. Fischer et al., "The Ancestor Effect," 11–16.
2. National Society of Genetic Counselors, "Your Genetic Health."
3. Luskin, *Forgive for Good*.
4. Kellerman, "Epigenetic Transmission of Holocaust Trauma."

One.
My Personal Journey with the Ancestors

1. The Church of Earth Healing, "The Church of Earth Healing."
2. See Blain, *Nine Worlds of Seid-Magic,* and Paxson, *Essential Asatru.*

Two.
Who Are the Ancestors?

1. Harvey, *Animism*, 125.
2. Huffington Post, "Spooky Number of Americans Believe in Ghosts."
3. Epega and Niemark, *The Sacred Ifa Oracle*, 194.
4. Earth Medicine Alliance, "Voices of the Earth: Malidoma Somé Interview, Part 3 of 6."
5. Ibid.
6. Hetherington and Reid, *The Climate Connection*, 64.
7. Mayell, "When Did 'Modern' Behavior Emerge in Humans?"

8. Highman et al., "The Earliest Evidence for Anatomically Modern Humans in Northwestern Europe."

9. United Nations, "World's Population Increasingly Urban with More than Half Living in Urban Areas."

Three.
Spontaneous Ancestral Contact

1. Jung, *Synchronicity.*

Five.
Family Research and Initiating Ancestral Healing

1. Moore, *Facing the Dragon.*

2. Abrahamian, *A History of Modern Iran.*

3. BBC News, "Bosnia War Dead Figure Announced."

4. BBC News, "Rwanda: How the Genocide Happened."

5. ABC News, "Up to 100,000 Killed in Sri Lanka's Civil War: UN."

Six. Meeting with Ancestral Guides

1. Prechtel, *The Unlikely Peace at Cuchamaquic,* 404–5.

2. 1 Kings 19:12.

3. Odigan, *Chosen by the Spirits,* 34–35.

4. Ibid., 34.

Seven.
Lineage Ancestors and the Collective Dead

1. Prechtel, *Long Life Honey in the Heart,* 7.

2. Translation by John Tarrant via personal teachings.

3. Sanh. 4:9 or Sanh. 37a.

4. Somé, *The Healing Wisdom of Africa,* 219.

5. Somé, *Of Water and the Spirit,* 57.

6. Earth Medicine Alliance, "Voices of the Earth: Adapting Ceremonies over Time and Ancestors."

Eight. Assisting the Remembered Dead

1. Luskin, *Forgive for Good.*
2. Horn, *Ancestral Lines Clearing,* 34. Used with permission from Maryphyllis Horn.
3. Odigan, *Chosen by the Spirits,* 75.
4. Somé, *The Healing Wisdom of Africa,* 133.
5. Odigan, *Chosen by the Spirits,* 91.
6. Somé, *The Healing Wisdom of Africa,* 196.
7. Prechtel, *Long Life Honey in the Heart,* 7–8.
8. Centers for Disease Control and Prevention, "National Center for Health Statistics FastStats: Deaths and Mortality."
9. Chief FAMA, *Sixteen Mythological Stories of Ifa,* 42–46.
10. Ingerman, *Soul Retrieval.*

Nine.
Integration and Work with Living Family

1. The Arabic translation is by Jihan Amer and Nevin Belbeisi; the Chinese translation is by Lydia Ridgway; the French translation is by Phillippe Levy; the Russian translation is by Julia Bernard; the Spanish translation is by Azucena Lemus.
2. Odigan, *Chosen by the Spirits,* 28, 40, 251.
3. Ibid., 28, 44–45.
4. Blain, *Nine Worlds of Seid-Magic,* 33.
5. Paxson, *Esssential Asatru,* 125.
6. Somé, *The Healing Wisdom of Africa,* 196.
7. Jung, *The Archetypes and the Collective Unconscious,* 188.
8. Somé, *The Healing Wisdom of Africa,* 195.

Ten. Ancestors and Place

1. Anderson, *Tending the Wild,* 363–64.
2. Sehee, "Green Burial."
3. National Highway Traffic Safety Administration, "Quick Facts 2014."
4. Centers for Disease Control and Prevention, "Suicide: Facts at a Glance 2015."

5. Centers for Disease Control and Prevention, "National Center for Health Statistics FastStats: Assault or Homicide."
6. Basso, *Wisdom Sits in Places*, 86.
7. Ibid., 91.
8. Odigan, *Riding Windhorses*, 173–77.
9. Herrera, "Spirits of Place."

Eleven.
Affinity Ancestors, Multiple Souls, and Reincarnation

1. Halifax, *The Fruitful Darkness*, 193.
2. Odigan, *Chosen by the Spirits*, 109.

Twelve. Joining the Ancestors

1. Viegas, "Did Neanderthals Believe in an Afterlife?"
2. Somé, *The Healing Wisdom of Africa*, 213.
3. Ibid., 209.
4. Salami, *Yoruba Theology and Tradition*, 208.
5. Prechtel, *Long Life Honey in the Heart*, 7.
6. Rilke, *Selected Poetry*, 163.
7. Foxwood, *Tree of Enchantment*, 84–85.
8. Cirlot, *A Dictionary of Symbols*, 26–28.
9. Pettitt, *The Palaeolithic Origins of Human Burial*, 59.
10. Abram, *The Spell of the Sensuous*, 221.
11. Prechtel, *Long Life Honey in the Heart*, 7.
12. John 20:17 (King James Version).

BIBLIOGRAPHY

ABC News. "Up to 100,000 Killed in Sri Lanka's Civil War: UN." Last modified May 20, 2009. www.abc.net.au/news/2009-05-20/up-to-100000-killed-in -sri-lankas-civil-war-un/1689524.

Abrahamian, Ervand. *A History of Modern Iran*. Cambridge, United Kingdom: Cambridge University Press, 2008.

Abram, David. *The Spell of the Sensuous: Perception and Language in a More-Than-Human World*. New York: Vintage, 1997.

Anderson, M. Kat. *Tending the Wild*. Berkeley, Calif.: University of California Press, 2005.

Basso, Keith. *Wisdom Sits in Places*. Albuquerque, N.Mex.: University of New Mexico Press, 1996.

BBC News. "Bosnia War Dead Figure Announced." Last modified June 21, 2007. http://news.bbc.co.uk/2/hi/europe/6228152.stm.

BBC News. "Rwanda: How the Genocide Happened." Last modified May 17, 2011. www.bbc.com/news/world-africa-13431486.

Blain, Jenny. *Nine Worlds of Seid-Magic*. London: Routledge, 2002.

Centers for Disease Control and Prevention. "National Center for Health Statistics FastStats: Assault or Homicide." Accessed March 7, 2016. www.cdc.gov /nchs/fastats/homicide.htm.

———. "National Center for Health Statistics FastStats: Deaths and Mortality." Accessed March 7, 2016. www.cdc.gov/nchs/fastats/deaths.htm.

———. "Suicide: Facts at a Glance 2015." Accessed March 7, 2016. www.cdc.gov /violenceprevention/pdf/suicide-datasheet-a.pdf.

Chief FAMA. *Sixteen Mythological Stories of Ifa*. San Bernadino, Calif.: Ilé Ọrúnmìla Communications, 1994.

Ching, Elise Dirlam. "When the Rain Begins." In Elise Dirlam Ching and Kaleo Ching, *Faces of Your Soul: Rituals in Art, Maskmaking, and Guided Imagery*. Berkeley, Calif.: North Atlantic, 2006.

The Church of Earth Healing. "The Church of Earth Healing." Accessed March 5, 2016. www.church-of-earth-healing.org.

Cirlot, J. E. *A Dictionary of Symbols*. 2nd ed. Translated by Jack Sage. Mineola, N.Y.: Dover, 2002 [1962].

Earth Medicine Alliance. "Voices of the Earth: Adapting Ceremonies over Time and Ancestors (Part 4/7)." Last modified April 19, 2011. www.youtube.com /watch?v=Wszu9aKXa1Q.

———. "Voices of the Earth: Malidoma Somé Interview, Part 3 of 6." Last modified February 17, 2013. www.youtube.com/watch?v=zGKf-tSAK4M &list=PLF03504E0C350F15B&index=3.

Epega, Afolabi A., and Philip John Niemark. *The Sacred Ifa Oracle*. San Francisco: HarperSanFrancisco, 1995.

Fischer, Peter, Anne Sauer, Claudia Vogrincic, and Silke Weisweiler. "The Ancestor Effect: Thinking about Our Genetic Origin Enhances Intellectual Performance." *European Journal of Social Psychology* 41, no. 1 (2011): 11–16.

Foxwood, Orion. *Tree of Enchantment: Ancient Wisdom and Magic Practices of the Faery Tradition*. San Francisco: Red Wheel/Weiser, 2008.

Halifax, Joan. *The Fruitful Darkness*. New York: HarperCollins, 1993.

Harvey, Graham. *Animism: Respecting the Living World*. New York: Columbia University Press, 2005.

Herrera, Catherine. "Spirits of Place." Presentation at the Annual Conference of Earth Medicine Alliance, San Francisco, October 22–23, 2011.

Hetherington, Renée, and Robert G. B. Reid. *The Climate Connection: Climate Change and Modern Human Evolution*. Cambridge, United Kingdom: Cambridge University Press, 2010.

Highman, Tom, Tim Compton, Chris Stringer, Roger Jacobi, Beth Shapiro, Erik Trinkaus, Barry Chandler, Flora Gröning, Chris Collins, Simon Hillson, Paul O'Higgins, Charles FitzGerald, and Michael Fagan. "The Earliest Evidence for Anatomically Modern Humans in Northwestern Europe." *Nature* 479 (2011): 521–24.

Horn, Maryphyllis. *Ancestral Lines Clearing*. Self-published, 1996.

Huffington Post. "Spooky Number of Americans Believe in Ghosts." Last updated February 8, 2013. www.huffingtonpost.com/2013/02/02 /real-ghosts-americans-poll_n_2049485.html.

Ingerman, Sandra. *Soul Retrieval: Following Your Soul's Journey Home.* New York: HarperOne, 1994.

Jung, C. G. *The Archetypes and the Collective Unconscious.* Translated by R. F. C. Hull. Princeton, N.J.: Princeton University Press, 1968.

———. *Synchronicity: An Acausal Connecting Principle.* Translated by R. F. C. Hull. Princeton, N.J.: Princeton University Press, 1973.

Kellermann, Natan P. F. "Epigenetic Transmission of Holocaust Trauma: Can Nightmares Be Inherited?" *Israel Journal of Psychiatry and Related Sciences* 50, no. 1 (2013): 33.

Luskin, Frederic. *Forgive for Good: A Proven Prescription for Health and Happiness.* New York: HarperCollins, 2002.

Mayell, Hillary. "When Did 'Modern' Behavior Emerge in Humans?" National Geographic News, February 20, 2003. http://news.nationalgeographic.com /news/2003/02/0220_030220_humanorigins2.html.

Moore, Robert L. *Facing the Dragon: Confronting Personal and Spiritual Grandiosity.* Wilmette, Ill.: Chiron, 2003.

National Highway Traffic Safety Administration. "Quick Facts 2014." Accessed March 7, 2016. http://www-nrd.nhtsa.dot.gov/Pubs/812234.pdf.

National Society of Genetic Counselors. "Your Genetic Health: Patient Information." Accessed March 5, 2016. http://nsgc.org/p/cm/ld/fid=51.

Odigan, Sarangerel. *Chosen by the Spirits: Following Your Shamanic Calling.* Rochester, Vt.: Destiny Books, 2001.

———. *Riding Windhorses: A Journey into the Heart of Mongolian Shamanism.* Rochester, Vt.: Destiny Books, 2000.

Paxson, Diana. *Esssential Asatru.* New York: Citadel Press, 2006.

Pettitt, Paul. *The Palaeolithic Origins of Human Burial.* New York: Routledge, 2011.

Prechtel, Martín. *Long Life Honey in the Heart.* Berkeley, Calif.: North Atlantic Books, 1999.

———. *The Unlikely Peace at Cuchamaquic.* Berkeley, Calif.: North Atlantic Books, 2011.

Rilke, Rainer Maria. *The Selected Poetry of Rainer Maria Rilke.* Translated and edited by Stephen Mitchell. New York: Vintage, 1989.

Salami, Ayo. *Yoruba Theology and Tradition: The Man and the Society.* Self-published, 2008.

Sehee, Joe. "Green Burial: It's Only Natural." *Property and Environmental Research Center Report* 25, no. 4 (2007). Accessed March 7, 2016. www.perc.org/articles/green-burial-its-only-natural.

Somé, Malidoma. *The Healing Wisdom of Africa*. New York: Jeremy P. Tarcher/ Putnam, 1998.

———. *Of Water and the Spirit*. New York: Jeremy P. Tarcher/Putnam, 1994.

United Nations. "World's Population Increasingly Urban with More Than Half Living in Urban Areas." July 10, 2014, www.un.org/en/development/desa /news/population/world-urbanization-prospects-2014.html.

Viegas, Jennifer. "Did Neanderthals Believe in an Afterlife?" Discovery News, April 20, 2011. http://news.discovery.com/history/archaeology/neanderthal -burial-ground-afterlife-110420.htm.

INDEX